ISBN:0-9661677-1-6

Attention: This guide is available at quantity discounts for education, resale, fundraising, sales and promotional uses.
Please contact:
Seabrook Scott Trading Company, 1512 West Chester Pike, #174
West Chester, PA 19382
(610) 722-0919.
E-mail: Seabrooksantique@Juno.com

Seabrook's Mid-Atlantic Antique Shop Guide

The comprehensive directory to the antique shops of the Mid-Atlantic.

Covering: 3600 shops in Pennsylvania, New Jersey, Delaware, Maryland & Washington, D.C.

2ND Edition

A publication of Seabrook Scott Trading Company
West Chester, Pennsylvania

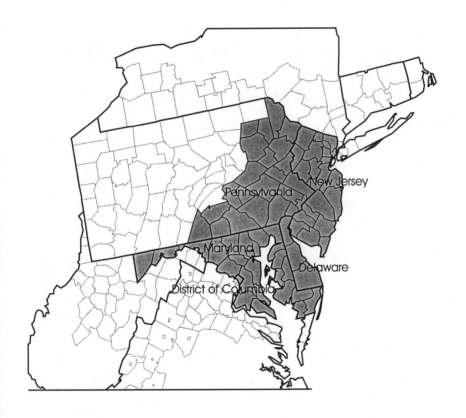

Seabrook's Coverage Area

Table of Contents

9

Introduction

Dear Readers:

Welcome to the *2nd edition of Seabrook's Mid-Atlantic Antique Shop Guide* (formerly *Seabrook's Antique Shop Guide*). This year you will notice two important changes. One, the coverage area has been expanded, from the original coverage area of Southeastern Pennsylvania, New Jersey and Delaware, to include the additional areas of Eastern Pennsylvania, Maryland and Washington D.C. Two, where possible, we have provided a basic description of most shops. This should assist the collector who is searching for specific items.

Seabrook's goal is to provide comprehensive coverage of all antique shops in order for you, the collector, dealer or designer, to find the things you need to create warm, comfortable, interesting and exciting living spaces. To that end we present you with over 3600 antique shops, antique co-ops and malls, antiquarian booksellers, auction houses, flea markets and thrift shops in the Mid-Atlantic Region.

And I would also like to share some reader feedback. A young couple contacted us after finding *Seabrook's* in a local bookstore. They mentioned their previous interest in antiques but their lack of knowledge regarding how to begin or where to go. Now they needed furniture for their new home and had to begin in earnest. Their collecting adventure included everything from thrift shops, to auction houses to all varieties of antique shops. Several days later they drove home with a "truckload of furniture." They splurged on some things, integrated their old belongings and found less expensive older and used pieces. They said they learned a lot about: averaging their costs, where and how to splurge, furniture periods & construction and a bit of history too. They now have a wish list for future pieces and they are still collecting. (Quite a number of experienced dealers were guided by *Seabrook's* to the same result as the aforementioned new homeowners.)

From one dealer, collecting is about crawling around in people's attics. He said, "Sometimes I find mouse droppings and 30 year old Christmas tinsel and sometimes I find something extremely rare, simply beautiful, incredibly odd or amusingly bizarre." Someone else told us we helped her finish her 1950's kitchen. I met someone who collects rug beaters, she "just likes them."

The preceeding feedback illustrates the many motivations for novice and experienced collectors. In the first instance it was about filling a need. Often people begin collecting by perusing thrift shops out of a basic need to fill space. As collectors develop and refine their styles and increase their knowledge, collecting later becomes about: wanting to own a piece of history, the thrill of the chase, finding the perfect item for the perfect space, changing furniture arrangements to fit changing needs and lifestyles. Necessity, passion, sentimentality, history lesson, recycling, sheer beauty, appreciation for or interest in a certain period or style. Whatever the reason, collecting often results in beautiful, unique and warm living spaces.

Collective dealer and consumer feedback also presented us with 5 major pieces of advice:

1. Buy what you like.
2. Create a wish list. A wish list helps you prioritize your needs and wants, helps you when planning your interiors, provides focus, guidance (financial and emotional) and perspective (you may may fall in love with something out of your price range but may be able to find a less expensive version or plan an annual splurge.)
3. Look at everything carefully.
4. Measure your spaces and measure the pieces you are interested in.
5. The nature of the antiques business dictates varied and or seasonal hours. Therefore, it is highly recommended that you call several shops to prior to planning day or weekend visits.

Whatever the motivation of the collector, the collecting process is about picking through thrift shops, the thrill of the auction bidding process, quietly viewing fine antiques in a gallery setting, or drawing inspiration from tastefully decorated boutique-style shops. You will find precisely this mix of shop styles as you investigate each area. Also, as you peruse each section, we are confident that you will be surprised to notice many previously undiscovered shops and unknown and new "hot spots".

We appreciate all feedback, positive or negative, and look forward to hearing from you. Contact us at (610) 722-0919, fax (610) 722-0440 or E-mail: Seabrooksantique@Juno.com.

Happy Hunting.

Helene C. Jesnig
Editor

How to Use this Guide

Seabrook's Mid-Atlantic Antique Shop Guide is arranged geographically and alphabetically and is composed of 6 main sections: Eastern and Southeastern Pennsylvania, New Jersey, Delaware, Maryland & Washington D.C. The book is then divided into county subsections containing the towns (listed alphabetically) within each county and the antique dealers in each town (also listed alphabetically) under each town heading. This format provides a "snapshot" of the shops in each geographic area, enabling the traveler, local or out of town, to view the shops in each area and choose their destinations (and convenient stops along the way).

Our goal is to provide the reader with the most complete, comprehensive and factual information. Because of this commitment to quality, quantity and integrity, the shops in this directory were thoroughly researched. We do provide brief descriptions of most shops. In order to keep the book concise and portable we present the descriptions in an abbreviated format. Please see the abbreviations list.

If you are traveling, we recommend that you scan the table of contents for the town of your destination to find its county. This will present the other towns in the area. Then plan your trip accordingly. If you are looking for a specific town and you do not know the county, simply skim the state section in the table of contents.

Abbreviations

Please note: in order to be concise and remain portable we present the shops descriptions in an abbreviated format. Most of the abbreviations are fairly easy to interpret.

Am-*American*
Antiq-*Antique*
Appt-*Appointment*
Bedrm-*Bedroom*
Belg-*Belgian*
Chin or Chnse (as space allows)-
   Chinese
Col-*Colonial*
Coll-*Collectibles*
Cont-*Continental*
Dec-*Decorative Accessories*
Deco-*Art Deco*
Dep-*Depression*
Diningrm-*Dining Room*
Dlr-*Dealer*
Emp-*Empire*
Eng-*English*
Euro-*European*
Fed-*Federal*
Furn-*Furniture*
Fr-*French*
Garden-*Garden accessories*
Gen line-*General line. This means that this shop will sell a wide variety of just about anything at any given time. Often these shops do not specialize in any specific item, style or period.*
Germ-*German*
It-*Italian*
Jpnse-*Japanese*
Lg-*Large*
Mahog-*Mahogany*
Mem-*Memorabilia*
Occ-*Occupied*
OR-*Oriental*
Orig-*Original*

OP-*Out-of-Print*
Porc-*Porcelain*
Prims-*Primitives*
Repro-*Reproduction*
Russe-*Russian*
Salv-*Salvage*
Sculp-*Sculpture*
Spec-*Specialty*
Sterling-*Sterling Silver*
Silv-*Silver*
Usd-*Used*
Vic-*Victorian*
Vint-*Vintage*

Pennsylvania Counties

SOUTHEASTERN PENNSYLVANIA

Bucks County
Chester County
Delaware County
Montgomery County
Philadelphia County

BUCKS COUNTY

Andalusia

Blooming Glen

Bristol

Buckingham

Chalfont

Doylestown

Dublin

Forest Grove

Fountainville

Furlong

Gardenville

Holicong

Hulmeville

Ivyland

Lahaska

Langhorne

Levittown

Mechanicsville

Milford Square

New Britain

New Hope

Newtown

Perkasie

Penns Park

Pineville

Pipersville

Plumsteadville

Point Pleasant

Quakertown

Riegelsville

Rushland

Sellersville

Solebury

Southampton

Springtown

Telford

Trevose

Trumbauersville

Tullytown

Warrington

Washington Crossing

Wrightstown

Yardley

BUCKS COUNTY

Andalusia

Mathias Antiques
863 Bristol Pike
(215) 639-5111

Blooming Glen

Myers Antiques
712 Blooming Glen Rd.
(215) 257-7615
Early 20th c. oak
refinished furn.

Roger S. Wright Furniture
911 S. Perkasie Rd.
(215) 257-5700
Repro Colonial furn & custom work in the Col style.

Bristol

Another Time Antiques
307 Mill St.
(215) 788-3131
General line. Spec:
Victorian & lamps.

The Place
5 Pond St.
(215) 785-1494
Victrolas, Edison machines,
music boxes, records &
related items.

Buckingham

Brown Brothers Auction
Rt. 413
(215) 794-7630
Call for auction dates & times.

Bianco Gallery
3921 Rt. 202
(215) 348-4235
Art.

Edna's Antique Shop
General Greene Inn
Rt. 263 & Rt. 413
(215) 794-7261
Spec: architecturals, hardware
to doors.

Rice's Market
6326 Greenhill Rd.
(215) 297-5993
30 acre flea market,
Tues & Sat 6:30 am.

Chalfont

Bucks County
   Antique Gallery
8 Skyline Dr.
Chalfont, PA
(215) 997-3227
Consignment shop, mostly furniture.

Green Tomatoes Craft
   & Antique Mall
4275 County Line Rd.
(215) 997-3280
Multi-dealer co-op.

Doylestown

Best of France
   at Chestnut Grove
Rt. 202
(215) 345-4253
Fr furn & statuary.

C.R. Notoris
   Antique Clocks
11 W. Court St.
(215) 230-7180
Clocks & coins.

Doylestown Antique Center
W. State St.
(215) 345-9277
Vic mahogany & walnut
furn & dec.

Dragon's Den of Antiques
135 S. Main St.
(215) 345-8666
General line,
Early 19th c. -1950s.

Edison Furniture Store
1880 Easton Rd.
(215) 348-5841
Gen line, 20,000 sq. ft.

Interior Classics
812 N. Easton Rd.
(215) 489-8585
Multi-dealer co-op.

Nejad Gallery Fine
   Oriental Rugs
Main & State Sts.
(215) 348-1255
Oriental rugs.

Renaissance Furnishings
635 N. Main St.
(215) 348-3455
Gen line, new, vint & antiq.

Robertson & Thornton
4092 Rt. 202
(215)794-3109

The Frog Pond
70 W. State St.
(215) 348-3425
General line.

The Orchard Hill Collection
4445 Lois Lane
(215) 230-7771
Importers,Dutch Colonial
furn. By appt. warehouse.

Dublin

Emele's Antiques
443 Rt. 313
(215) 249-9123
Spec: country, Vic oak furn.
Stonewre,art pottry & lamps.

Hodge Podge Antiques
232 Rt. 313
(215) 249-9482

Kramer's Rainbow Rooms
104 Middle Rd. (Off 313)
(215) 249-1916
Dep era glass, china & pottery.

Forest Grove

Tomlinson's Antiques
1823 Forest Grove Rd.
(215) 794-2991
Gen line, primitves.
Spec: tools.

Fountainville

Ridge Farm Antiques
Rt. 313
(Part of the Ann Bailey
Complex)
(215) 348-1321
General line.

Furlong

Artefact
790 Edison Furlong Rd.
& Rt. 263
(215) 794-8790
Architecturals & garden
appointments.

Cash Cow Antiques
790 Edison Furlong Rd.
(215) 837-0126
Architecturals & garden.

Gardenville

Durham Cabinet Shop
Rt. 413
(215) 766-7104
Country furn, clocks,
pottery & quilts.

Holicong

Route 202 Market
Rt. 202
(215) 794-3405
Multi-dealer co-op.

Hulmeville

Hidden Creek Antiques
#3 Main St. & Trenton Rd.
(215) 750-7399

Miller Topia Designers
518 Washington Ave.
(215) 757-3004
Importers, Euro furn.
By appt. only.

The Old Mill Flea Market
Trenton & Hulmeville Rds.
(215) 757-1777
Indoor year round flea market.

Ivyland

Susan Golashovsky
180 Jacksonville Rd.
(215) 441-8060
18th & 19th c. Am & Eng
furn & dec. By Appt.

The Cat & The Penguin
363 Almshouse Rd.
(215) 357-7879
Am country furn, dec &
silver . By appt.

Lahaska

Alba Limited
5979 Rt. 202
(215) 794-8228
General line.

Antique Addicts Attic
Rt. 202
(215) 794-2152
Multi-dealer shop.

Charlie's Girl
1448 Street Rd.
(215) 794-8974
Repro lighting.

Cottage Farms Antiques
Rt. 202
(215) 794-0840

Darby-Barrett Antiques
Rt. 202
(215) 794-8277
19th & early 20th c. Am
paintings. Objets d'art.

Grady's Antiques
6123 Rt. 202
(215) 794-5532

Knobs 'n Knockers
Peddler's Village
(215) 794-8045
Repro hardware, cupolas
& weathervanes.

Lahaska Antique Courte
Rt. 202
(215) 794-7884
Multi-dealer co-op.

Lloyd & Lee
6236 Lower York Rd.
(215) 862-1900

Oaklawn Metalcraft
& Antiques
Rt. 202
(215) 794-7387
Antiq & repro lighting,
hardware & toools.

Le Cabinet Scientifique
5806 Rt. 202
(215) 794-7333
Spec: Scientific
insturments.

Langhorne

Cottage Crafters
Langhorne Square
Shopping Center (Rt. 1)
(610) 366-9222
Multi-dealer co-op.

Levittown

Nana's Attic
1037 Oxford Valley Rd.
(215) 946-7746
General line.

Mechanicsville

Hamilton Hyre's
Buck House Antiques
3336 Durham Rd. (Rt. 413)
(215) 794-8054

Milford Square

Milford Antiques
& Used Furniture
Rt. 663 on Milford Sq. Pike
(215) 536-9115

New Britain

Consignment Galleries
470 Towne Center (Rt.202)
(215) 348-5244
General line.

Y-Know Shop
New Galena Rd. & Rt. 313
(215) 249-9120

New Hope

A'brial's Antiques
Rt. 202
(215) 794-2887

A Stage in Time
16 W. Bridge St.
(215) 862-6120
19th c. & 20th c. furn
& ligthing. Spec: Mission.

Brancusi & Sulei
40 W. Bridge St.
(215) 862-3427
Jewelry, porc, silver, art
& figurines.

Bridge Street Old Books
129 W. Bridge St.
(215) 862-0615

Christopher House
12 W. Mechanic St.
(215) 862-2722
Gen line. 18th c. lamps &
17th c. Paintings.

Clock Trader
6106 Lower York Rd. (Rt. 202)
(215) 794-3163

Cockamamie's
9A Bridge St.
(215) 862-5454

Crown & Eagle Antiques
Route 202
(215) 794-7972
Spec: Native Am Indian
artifacts.

David Mancuso
Rt. 202 &
Upper Mountain Rd.
(215) 862-5828

Don Robert's Antiques
38 W. Ferry St.
(215) 862-2702
18th & 19th c. Eng & Am
furn& art. Chinse export porc.

Ferry Hill
15 W. Ferry St.
(215) 862-5335
Staffordshire china, trunks
& coll.

Gardner's Antiques
6148 Lower York Rd.
(215) 794-8616/794-7759
Importers, Fr furn & dec.

Hall & Winter
429 York Rd.
(215) 862-0831
18th & early 19th c.
Am & Eng furn & dec.
Spec: dining rm furn.

Hobensack & Keller
57 Bridge St.
(215) 862-2406
Gen line. Spec: OR rugs
& garden appointments.

Ingham Springs
  Antique Center
Rt. 202
(215) 862-2145
18th & 19th c. Am,
Eng & Cont furn, dec &
clocks. 18th and 19th c. Art.

Katy Kane Antiques Inc.
34 W. Ferry St.
(215) 862-5873
Antq. clothing & linen

Lyons Antiques
6220 Lower York Rd.
(215) 862-0160
18th & 19th c. Euro Gothic
& Rennaissance style furn,
bronzes &garden .

Merndale Antiques
429 York Rd. (Rt.202)
(215 862-2886
Country furn, beds,
kitchenware & primitives.

Old Hope Antiques
Rt. 202
(215) 862-5055
Folk art & 18th & 19th c.
painted furn.

Oriental Gallery
6444 Rt. 202
(215) 862-0366
Orientals: furn, art,
carvings, sculp & china.

Queripel Antiques
93 W. Bridge St.
(215) 862-5830
By Appointment.

Raymond James & Co.
6319 Lower York Rd.
At Ingham Springs
(215) 862-9751
18th & 19th c. furn, art & dec.

Ronley at Limeport
2780 River Rd.
(215) 862-2427
18th & early 19th c. furn & dec.

Sally Goodman's Antiques
21 West Ferry St.
(215) 862-5754
Staffordshire, Faience,
prints, furn & dec. Spec:
copper,brass & treen.

The Pink House Antiques
Bridge St. (Rt. 179)
(215) 862-5947
18th c. Fr, Eng & Chinse
porc. Prints & 18th c. Fr furn.

Trappings
6444 Lower York Rd.
(215) 862-0981

Newtown

Hanging Lamp Antiques
140 N. State St.
(215) 968-2015
Furn, glass, copper, iron,
brass & jewelry,1800-1920.

BUCKS COUNTY, PA

Miller & Company
15 S. State St.
(215) 968-8880
2,000 sq. ft. of American
& European furniture;
fine art & accessories.
Specializing in formal
& country dining rooms.
Closed Monday.

Temora Farm Antiques
372 Swamp Rd.
(215) 860-2742
18th c. & early 19th c.
furn & dec.

Perkasie

The Treasure Trove
6 S. 7th St.
(215) 257-3564
Jewelry, vint clothing &
linens, furn , smalls & dec.

Penns Park

Red Sleigh Antiques
2310 Second Pike (Rt. 232)
(215) 598-3017
Country & Vic furn & dec.

Pineville

Midge's Barn Antiques
740 Rt. 413
(215) 598-3304
Country furn. Wrought &
cast iron furn & wicker.

Pipersville

Nadia's Trash or Treasure
Easton Rd. (Rt. 611)
10 miles N. of Doylestown
(215) 766-7827
General line,Vic-1950s.

Plumsteadville

Tess Sands
5912 Rte. 611
(215) 766-9593
General line, antiq & repro.

Point Pleasant

1807 House
4962 River Rd. (Rt. 322)
(215) 297-0599
Indian artifacts. Country
furn. 18th & 19th c. smalls.

River Run Antiques
166 River Rd.(Rt. 32)
(215) 297-5303
Specializing in antique
toys, games and holiday
items. Hours: Saturday,
Sunday & Monday
11:00-5:00.

Time and Tide
56 Byram Rd.
(215) 297-5854
Country Fr furn, hardware,
clocks & statues.

Quakertown

Curio Corner
E. Broad St. &
Hellerstown Ave.
(215) 536-4547
Multi-dealer co-op.

Dunngeon Antiques
215 W. Broad St.
(215) 538-9355
General line.

Grandpa's Treasures
137 E. Broad St.
(215) 536-5066

Quaker Antique Mall
70 Tollgate Rd.
(215) 538-9445
10,000 sq. ft. Includes:
antiques, collectibles,
jewelry, ephemera,
Civil War memorabilia,
furniture, crafts &
American girl items.

Quakertown Heirlooms
141 E. Broad St. &
Hellertown Rd.
(215) 536-9088
Multi-dealer co-op.

Trolley House Emporium
108-114 E. Broad St.
(215) 538-7733
General line. Spec: lighting,
fashions & textiles.

Riegelsville

Allen's Antiques
666 Easton Rd. (Rt. 611)
(610) 749-0337
General line, Spec:
19th c. furn.

Rushland

Old Maps & Prints
987 Penns Park Rd.
(215) 598-3662
Prints:botanicals,birds,
Audobons, engravings &
maps 1700-19th c.

Sellersville

Bittersweet Shoppe
202 N. Main St.
(215) 257-0944

Buck's Trading Post
930 Old Bethlehem Pk.
(215) 453-0623

Solebury

Lehmann's 202 Shoppes
6154 Lower York Rd. (Rt. 202)
(215) 794-7724
Multi-dealer shop.

Whitley Studio
Laurel Rd.
(215) 297-8452

Southampton

Auctions by Stephenson's
1005 Industrial Blvd.
(215) 322-6182
Call for auction dates & times.

Springtown

Long Spring Antiques
2789 Slifer Valley Rd. &
  Hickory Lane
(610) 346-7659
Am Indian artifacts, jewelry
& weaponry. By appt. only.

Telford

Byron Hecker Cabinetmaker
260 Telford Pike
(215) 721-1566

Koffel's Curiosity Shop
26 Madison Ave.
(215) 723-9365

Telford Exchange
527-B S. Main St.
(215) 723-9870

Trevose

The Brownsville Antique
  Centre
1918 Brownsville Rd.
(215) 364-8846

Trumbauersville

Trumbauersville Antiques
  & Music
19 E. Broad St.
(215) 536-6305

Tullytown

Wilhemina's Antiques
369 Main St.
(215) 945-8606
Spec: linens, glass & china,
mid 1800s-mid 1900s.

Warrington

First Penn Precious Metals
  & G & G Antiques
25 N. Easton Road (Rt. 611)
(215) 674-5910
Gen line Spec: jewelry, fine
& costume.

Upstairs Downstairs
215 Pebble Ridge Rd.
(215) 343-6605

Washington Crossing

Hanging Lamp Antiques
1077 River Rd.
(215) 493-0563

Wrightstown

Bucks County Art
  & Antiques Co.
532 Durham Rd. (Rt. 413)
(215) 345-1885

Nostalgic Nook
591 Durham Rd. (Rt. 413)
Carousel Village
(215) 598-8837
General line. Spec:
china, glass.

Trading Post Antiques
532 Durham Rd. (Rt. 413)
(215) 579-1020
Multi-dealer co-op.

Yardley

Antiques in Yardley
6 S. Main St.
(215) 493-0137
Country prims, glass,
Staffordshire, furn & dec.
18th c.-1920s.

C. L. Prickett
930 Stoney Hill Rd.
(off I-95 & Rt.332)
(215) 493-4284

CHESTER COUNTY

Avondale
Berwyn
Birchrunville
Chadds Ford
Chester Springs
Coatesville
Devon
Downingtown
Exton
Frazer
Glenmoore
Kemblesville
Kennett Square
Kimberton
Knauertown
Lionville

Ludwigs Corner
Malvern
Marshallton
Mendenhall
Oxford
Paoli
Parkesburg
Phoenixville
Spring City
Strafford
Thorndale
Toughkenamon
Unionville
Valley Forge
West Chester
West Grove

CHESTER COUNTY

Purveyors of Fine 18th Century Reproduction Furniture

15 Waterloo Avenue, Berwyn, Pennsylvania 19312

Carmen DiGiovanni
Proprietor

(610) 640-0470
Fax (610) 640-0477

Avondale

Antiques & Images
Gap-Newport Pike
(610) 268-0226
Multi-dealer co-op.

Berwyn

Anything & Everything Shop
36 Waterloo Ave.
(610) 647-8186

Carolyn Platt Antiques
724 Lancaster Ave.
(610) 644-0100
Furn, dec & rugs.

Circa Antiques
712 Lancaster Ave.
(610) 651-8151
18th,19th & 20th c. furn &
dec.

Deja vu Antiques
11 Waterloo Ave.
(610) 296-2737
Country furn, dec,
& folk art.

Eldred Wheeler
15 Waterloo Ave.
(610) 640-0470
A charming shop in a re-
stored bldg, offering
reproductions of 18th c.
furniture which range
from Windsor chairs &
simple tea tables to bon-
net-top secretaries &
highboys and accessories.
Each item is handcrafted
& hand finished using the
woods, methods & tech-
niques common to the
period. E-mail:
Berwyndsgn@aol.com

Hidden River Antiques
19 Waterloo Ave.
(610) 408-8759

Main Line Clock
Restorations
626 Lancaster Ave.
(610) 644-8608
Specializing in the
Repair, Maintenance,

Restoration and Sales
of Fine Clocks. Hours:
Mon-Fri 10-6, Sat 10-3.

McCoy Antiques & Interiors
722 W. Lancaster Ave.
(610) 640-0433
Furn & dec.

Old Forest Antiques
680 Lancaster Ave.
(610) 725-0700
Gen line.

Pennsylvania Art
Conservatory
636 Lancaster Ave.
(610) 644-4300
Late 19th c.-mid 20th c. oils.
Conserve,repair & restore.

Queen's Anne's Lace
722 Lancaster Ave.
(610) 647-6441

St. Jude Thrift Shop
Berwyn Ave.
(610) 644-8509
Thrift shop.

Surrey Consignment Shop
16 Waterloo Rd.
(610) 647-8632
Consignment shop.

Birchrunville

Richard Wright Antiques
Hollow & Flowing
 Springs Rds.
(610) 827-7442

Chadds Ford

Aaron Goebel's Antiques
261 S. Rt. 202
(610) 459-8555
Architecturals & furn.

Alleman & Company
880 Baltimore Pike
(610) 388-8491
New & antiq furn.

Antique Reflections
Village Shoppes at
 Chadds Ford
170 Fairville Rd.
(610) 388-0645
Period furn.

Barbara & Co, Inc.
516 Kennett Pike
Village of Fairville
(610) 388-8445

Brandywine River
878 Baltimore Pk.
(610) 388-2000
Multi-dealer co-op.

Candlelight Antiques
1110 Smithbridge Rd.
(610) 358-6053

Diane's Antiques
Rt. 1
(610) 388-3956

Frances Lantz
Rt. 202 & State Line Rd.
(610) 459-4080

John F. Joyce
1611 Baltimore Pike
(610) 388-7075

Olde Ridge Village
Rt. 202 & Ridge Rd.
(610) 565-2834
Multi dealer co-op.

P-R Antiques & Furniture
3911 Pyle Rd.
(610) 459-7890
General line.

Paul Maynard Antiques
536 Kennett Pike (Rt. 53)
Village of Fairville
(610) 388-6521

Pennsbury-Chadds Ford
Antique Mall
Rt. 1
(610) 388-6546/388-1620
Multi-dealer co-op.

Pitt's Antiques
95 Baltimore Pk.
(610) 558-8950

Rogers H. Hopkins
Old Baltimore Pk.
(610) 388-7160

Spring House
101 Baltimore Pike
(610) 388-7075

Stockard's Attic
Rt. 1 & Rt. 100
(610) 388-9588

**The Stencil Shoppe
Olde Ridge
Village Shoppes
Rt. 202 & Ridge Rd.
(610) 479-8362
"The leader in Stencils &
Supplies." Over 1200
Stencils. Classes, Gifts,
Faux Finish Supplies**

and more! Other convenient locations:
The Stencil Shoppe
Talleyville Towne Shoppes
(302) 479-0759
The Stencil Shop
Fairfax Shopping Center
(302) 498-5888.

The Village Peddlar
161B-Baltimore Pk.
(610) 388-2828
Country & prim furn & pottery. Quilts, fabrics & lighting.

**The Wooden Knob
Rt. 1 & 100
(610) 891-9422
A fine selection of American antiques & fine older
furniture as well as a
beautiful line of gift ware
& colorful floral arrange-**

ments. Custom decorating services available for
window treatments,
upholstery, pillows &
more. Open Daily 10-5,
Sunday 12-4 Closed
Tuesday.

Chester Springs

Centuries Ltd. Antiques
At the Rising Sun Tavern
1251 Conestoga Rd.
(610) 827-3054

Chester Springs Antiques
1733 Conestoga Rd.
(610) 827-2229

Gatherings
Shops at Pickering Mill
Rt. 113 & Yellow Springs Rd.
(610) 827-1870

Coatesville

Chet Ramsay Antiques
2460 Strasburg Rd.
(610) 384-0514
Specializing in sales and
complete and total restor-
ation of antique music
boxes and phonographs.

Windle's Log Cabin
Gum Tree Rd.
(610) 857-3416
Country antiques & prims.

Devon

Joseph & Peter Antiques
Devon Design Center
111 E. Lancaster Ave.
(610) 254-0600
18th & 19th c. Am, Eng
& Cont furn & dec.

Downingtown

Collector's Corner
31 E. Lancaster Ave.
(610) 269-9196
Gen line.

Frantiques
527 W. Lancaster Ave.
(610) 269-4307

Gary Pennington
5031 Horseshoe Pike (Rt. 322)
(610) 873-6966
General line.

Hodge Podge Shoppe
Rt. 322 W. (Horseshoe Pike)
(610) 269-7735
General line.

Nesting Feathers
30 W. Lancaster Ave.
(610) 269-4155

Oak Emporium Antiques
147 E. Lancaster Ave.
(610) 269-3632

Philip H. Bradley Co.
1101 E. Lancaster Ave.
(E. Lincoln Hwy.)
(610) 269-0427

Pook & Pook, Inc.
113 & Bus. Rt. 30
(610) 269-4040
By appt.

Exton

Ball & Ball
436 W. Lincoln Hwy.
(610) 363-7330
Repro & antiq hardware,
lighting, furn & fireplace.

John W. Bunker & Son
431 E. Lincoln Hwy.
(Business Rt. 30)
(610) 363-7436
18th & 19th c. Antiques
& Accessories. Furniture
restoration & refinishing.
Custom made furniture.

Frazer

Frazer Antiques
351 Lancaster Ave.
(610) 651-8299
Multi-dealer co-op.

Stevens Antiques
627 Lancaster Ave.
(610) 644-8282
American, English &
Continental furniture
with appropriate lighting
and accessories. Nice
things in a comfortable,
unpretentious setting.
Open Daily 9-5. Closed
Wed & Sun.

Glenmoore

Ludwig's Corner House
Rt. 110 N. of Rt. 401
(610) 458-5066
Gen line.

Kemblesville

Harold S. Hill & Son Inc.
Rt. 896
(610) 274-8525
Call for auction dates & times.

Kennett Square

Antiquus
120 W. State St.
(610) 444-9892

Clifton Mill Shoppes
162 Olde Kennett Rd.
(610) 444-5234

Fancy Branches
11 S. Union
(610) 444-5063
Vic furn,glass,china & lamps.

Longwood Garrett
864 E. Baltimore Pike (Rt. 1)
(610) 444-5257

McLimans
940 W. Cypress St.
(610) 444-3876
13,000 sq. ft. of antiques
& fine pre-owned furni-
ture. All periods & all
styles. One of the largest
inventories in the tri-state
area. Buy & sell.
"McLiman's is filled with
fabulous deals."

Philadelphia Magazine.
Closed Monday &
Tuesday.

Nancy Pitt's Antiques
116 W. Stae St.
(610) 444-7808
Country furn & dec.

Nesting Feathers
109 S. Broad St.
(610) 444-7181

Perennials Thrift Shop
19 New Garden Town Sq.
350 Scarlett Rd.
(610) 444-1438
Thrift Shop.

The Moon Dial
101 E. Locust Ln.
(Off Rt. 82N.)
(610) 444-2995
Clocks, choronometers
& watches. Restorers.

Thomas Macaluso Used
& Rare Books
130 S. Union St. (Rt. 82)
(610) 444-1063
25,000 Usd, OP & rare
books, maps & prints.

Kimberton

Corner Cupboard Antiques
Kimberton Rd.
(610) 933-9700
Am furn & dec.

Kimber Hall
Hares Hill Rd.
Kimberton, PA
(610) 933-8100

**Thorums
Prizer Rd.
(610) 933-3121
"Thorum's Antiques &
Good Used Furniture is a
must stop."** The inventory
is ever changing thanks to
their customers who are
from all walks of life and
include; antique dealers,
decorators & homeown-
ers. The 5,000 sq. ft.
building overflows w/
19th & 20th c. furniture,
antiques & collectibles in
every style. Be sure to
look up, down & side-

ways. Courteous service
& fair prices. 8 mi. W. of
Valley Forge. 30 mins
from the Mainline, Phila
& West Chester. Easily
accessible from the PA
Turnpike & Rts: 23, 100,
202, 113, 401 & 724. Open
every Thurs & Fri-
10:00am-8:00pm. Open
the first & last Sat of
each month, 8:00am-
10:00pm.

Knauertown

H. D. Wilder
Rt. 23
(610) 469-9774

Lionville

The Hawley House
95 E. Welsh Pool Rd.
(610) 594-9790

Ludwigs Corner

The Eagle Lantern
Corner Rt.s 100 & 401
Ludwig Village Shops
(610) 458-8964
18th c. style repro lighting.

Malvern

Capriola's Architectural
Antiques & Salvage
218 Warren Ave.
(610) 647-3380
A large & constantly
changing inventory of
stained glass windows,
wall units, doors, church
pews, columns, mantles,
light fixtures, iron rail-
ings, statuary & antique
artifacts. Mon-Sat 10-5,
Sun-call.

Conestoga Antiques
Conestoga Rd.
(610) 647-6627

Hobby Horse
Sugartown Rd.
(610) 644-2386
Furn crafted from antiq
wood salvage.

Kendall Chew
& John Formicola
690 Sugartown Rd.
(610) 647-3339
19th & 20th c. oil &
watercolor paintings.

Cobblestone Crossing
307 E. King St.
(610) 695-9290
Multi-dealer shop.

**KING STREET TRADERS
& GALLERY**
ANTIQUES & FINE ART

16 EAST KING STREET IN
HISTORIC MALVERN, PA
(610) 296-8818
CLOSED SUNDAYS

**King Street Traders
& Gallery
16 E. King St.
(610) 296-8818**
Offering 18th & 19th cen-
tury fine art and antiques
as well as high quality
accessories and estate
jewelry for the discrim-
inating collector.
Closed Sunday.

Lee Bowman Antiques
103 E. King St.
(610) 644-4838

Nesting Feathers
218 E. King St.
(610) 408-9377
Multi-dealer co-op

Pickering Place
1 W. King
(610) 993-0601

**Portobello Road
138 E. King St.
(610) 647-7690**
Unique & decorative 18th
& 19th century furniture,
silver, orientalia, porcelain, paintings, textiles
and accessories. Open:
Tues-Sat 10:00-4:30 and

by appt.

The Cranberry Cellar
148 E. King St.
(610) 647-7763
Multi-dealer shop.

The Olde General Store
2447 Yellow Springs Rd.
(610) 647-8968/644-1734

Van Tassel & Baumann
690 Sugartown Rd.
(610) 647-3339
18th & early 19th c. furn.
Delval schoolgrl needlewrk.

**White Orchid Antiques
134 King St.
(610) 725-0474
Antiques & decorative
appointments including:
glass, porcelain, art,
lighting and furniture
in an intimate gallery
setting. Items bought
and sold. Entire estates
purchased.**

Marshallton

The Blacksmith Shop
1340 W. Strasburg Rd.
(Rt. 162)
(610) 696-2469
Antiq lamp bases, small
furn & Blacksmith tools.

TUES.-SAT.
10:00 - 4:30
and by appointment
(610) 647-7690

18TH & 19TH CENTURY EUROPEAN
ANTIQUES & ACCESSORIES
138 E. King Street • Malvern, PA

Rita Balee
Marsha McKerr

Primitives ☆ **Unique Smalls** ☆ **Candles** ☆

The Muxin Room

Purveyor of Colonial Wares
Olde and New For the Home

Furniture ◆ Gifts ◆ Antiques ◆ Accessories

Wednesday, Thursday, Friday, & Saturday
10am to 5 pm
(610) 932-2991
2700 Baltimore Pike, Oxford, Pa.
Directions: From Rt 1 Bypass take Exit 10
through Oxford Pass Acme on Left.

☆ **Angels** ☆ **Country Furnishings** ☆ **Wreaths** ☆

Mendenhall

Antique Reflections
170 Fairville, Rd.
(610) 388-0645

J & L West Antiques
Rt. 52 & Fairville Rd.
(610) 388-2014

Sally Borton Antiques
534 Kenntt Pike (Rt. 52)
Village of Fairville
(610) 388-7687

William Hutchinson
330 Kennett Pike (Rt. 52)
(610) 388-0195/388-2010
Books, prints & art.

Oxford

Antiques at Ramsgate
Lower Hopewell Rd.
(610) 932-5052
Gen line. Spec: country
store & advertising.

Shank's Barn
12700 Limestone Rd.
(610) 932-9212

Sullivan's Antiques
Lyons-Bonesmill Rd.
(Oxford Rd.)
(610) 932-9454
Furn, Dep glass, cap guns,
prints & Limoges.

**The Muxin Room
2700 Baltimore Pike
(610) 932-2991
Purveyors of Colonial
Wares, Olde & New, for
the home. Angels, country
furnishings, wreaths, Folk
Art, herbs, Primitives,
unique smalls, candles,
lighting, textiles & tin.
Directions: from Rt. 1
Bypass take Exit 10
through Oxford, Pass
Acme on left. Open Wed,
Thurs, Fri & Sat.
10:00am-5:00pm.**

Paoli

**Paoli Antiques
4 E. Lancster Ave.
(610) 640-3332
(610) 348-4545
Buy & sell Oriental rugs**

**and antique furniture.
Appraisals & estate sales.
Also see us at Clocktower-
Stoudtburg Village in
Adamstown, PA.**

Richard Herzog
44 N. Valley Rd.
(610) 695-9770
18th & 19th c. repro furn.

Parkesburg

Cackleberry Farm
5003 Rt. 30
(717) 442-8805
Multi-dealer co-op.

Pheasant Run Antiques
4824 W. Lincoln Hwy.
(717) 442-4090

The Paxson House
337 Rt. 30
(610) 857-5750

Phoenixville

Bridge Street Fine Arts
& Antiques
234 Bridge St.
(610) 917-9898
Gen line. Spec: Art
pottery & Art glass.

Eye of the Phoenix
222 Bridge St.
(610) 917-8444

Old Picket Fence
Nutt & Mason Rd.s.
(610) 917-9992
Country furn & garden
accents.

Phoenixville Antiques
237 Bridge St.
(610) 933-8477
Gen line. Spec: mem,
prims & art smalls.

Scioli's Used Furniture
235 Bridge St.
(610) 935-0118
General line, new, usd
& antiq.

The Copper Rooster
847 Valley Forge Rd.
(610) 917-9965

The Shop Around The Corner
26 S. Main St.
(610) 983-4477

Tomes of Glory
The Shop of Korner Shops
843-847 Valley Forge Rd.
(610) 935-9510
Usd., rare & OP books. Spec:
Military & Civil War.

Spring City

Rich Moyer's
Bonnie Brae Auction Co.
2 Bonnie Brae Rd.
(610) 948-8050
Call for auction dates & times.

Strafford

Interiors
Spread Eagle Village
503 W. Lancaster Ave.
(610) 989-9665
Eng prints & smalls.

Wilson's Main Line
329 E. Conestoga Rd.
(610) 687-5500
Importers, Am, Eng, & Cont
& OR furn, art & coll.

Thorndale

Eric Chandlee Wilson
16 Bondsville Rd, (Rt. 340)
(610) 383-5597
Clock restoration, sales &
appraisals.

Toughkenamon

New Garden Stable Shops
New Garden Rd.
(610) 268-0428
Multi-dealer co-op.

Unionville

The Merry-Go-Round Room
Rt. 82
(610) 347-0482

Valley Forge

Mullen Antiques
Rt. 23 & Pawlings Rd.
(610) 933-2324

West Chester

Ann Powers Antiques
& Artworks
1497 Wilmington Pike
(610) 459-4662
Furn, art, glass, china,
OR items & jewelry.

Antiquities
134 N High St.
(610) 429-5678
All Victorian.

Baldwin's Book Barn
865 Lenape Rd.
(610) 696-0816
Usd, rare, OP books
& older prints.

County Seat Antiques
41 W. Gay St.
N.E. Corner,
Church & Gay Sts.
(610) 696-0584

David K. Ely Antiques
20 Ellis Lane
(610) 696-4593
Country furniture.

Dilworthtown Country Store
275 Brintons Bridge Rd.
(610) 399-0560
Country & formal repro.

H. L. Chalfant Antiques
1352 Paoli Pike
(610) 696-1862
17th, 18th & early19th c.
Am furn & dec.

Herbert Schiffer Antiques
1469 Morstein Rd.
(610) 696-1521
18th & 19th c. Am &
Eng furn. Chinse porc.

Herman Woolfrey Antiques
1433 S. Whitford Rd.
(610) 363-2073
By appointment.

J. Palma Antiques
1144 Old Wilmington Pk.
(610) 399-1210
18th & 19th c. furn & dec.

Laurean Antiques
128 E. Gay St.
(610) 918-0087
Fr furn, smalls & dec.

Monroe Coldren Antiques
723 E. Virginia Ave.
(610) 692-5651
Am hardware &
architecturals.

Newsome, Thomas
& Morris Antiques
106 W. Market St.
(610) 344-0657

Old Mill Antiques
20 N. Ellis La.
(610) 696-4593
Country furniture.

Olivier Fleury, Inc.
708 Oakborne Rd.
(610) 692-0445
18th & 19th c. Provincial
Parisian furn & dec.

Partner's Used Furniture
125 W. Market St.
(610) 431-6639
New & usd. furn.

Polito Antiques
820 Sconneltown Rd.
(610) 696-4860

RM Worth Antiques Inc.
1388 Old Wilmington Pike
(610) 399-1780
18th & 19th c. Am furn,
painting & dec arts.

The Bring and Buy Shop
E. Gay & Gay St. Plaza
(610) 696-2576
Consignment shop.

The Cartophile
934 Brindle Lane
(610) 692-7697
Maps, atlases & early Am
& West travel. By appt.
& mail order.

William H. Bunch Gallery
11 N. Brandywine St.
(610) 696-1530
Call for auction dates & times.

Women's Exchange
10 S. Church St.
(610) 696-3058
Consigment shop.

West Grove

Barbara Hood's
Country Store
378 Hoods Lane
(610) 869-8437

DELAWARE COUNTY

Ardmore
Aston
Booths Corner
Chester Heights
Drexel Hill
Folsom
Glen Mills
Glenolden
Gradyville
Haverford
Havertown
Holmes
Lansdowne
Media
Newtown Square
Prospect Park
Ridley Park
Swarthmore
Upland
Upper Darby
Villanova
Wayne

DELAWARE COUNTY

Ardmore

Daniel Wilson
24 E. Lancaster Ave.
(610) 645-9533

En Garde Antiques &
Collectibles
2-4 Lancaster Ave.
(610) 645-5785
Gen line.

Harry's Treasures &
Collectibles
22 E. Lancaster Ave.
(610) 642-4775
Gen line.

Interior Works
28 Rittenhouse Place
(610) 658-0155
Decoratives.

Porter's Book Store
24 Ardmore Ave.
(610) 896-8913
Usd, rare & OP books.

Aston

Martins Auction
142 Rt. 322
(610) 497-7745
Call for auction dates & times.

The Barn
404 Chester Pike
(610) 485-7400
Gen line.

Booths Corner

Robert Briggs Auction
1315 Naamans Creek Rd.
(610) 566-3138/485-0412
Call for auction dates & times.

Booth's Corner Farmers
Market
1362 Naaman's Creek Rd.
(610) 485-0775
Two dealers.

R.L. Beck
1104 Naamans Creek Rd.
(610) 459-3476
Reproduction furniture.

Chester Heights

Wilson's Auctioneers
& Appraisals
342-344 Valleybrook Rd.
(610) 565-1616
Call for auction dates & times.

Drexel Hill

**Ardmart Antique Village
State Rd & Lansdowne Ave.
(610) 789-6622
(40 dealers)
Over 13,000 sq. ft. 40
dealers specializing in
quality antiques, collectibles, toys, clocks, advertising, paper, ephemera,
Art Nouveau, books,
Victoriana, Orientalia,
jewelry, glass, china,
linens, silver, paintings,
Primitives, antique & better used furniture, base-**

ball memorabilia &
much more!
Open Friday 11-8,
Saturday & Sunday 11-6.

Clock Services
2255 Garrett Rd.
(610) 284-2600
Antiq & new clocks.

Fields Antique Jewelers
Lansdowne & Windsor Aves.
(610) 853-2740
Jewelry, fine and costume,
watches & smalls.

Springhouse Antiques
4213 Woodland Ave.
(610) 623-8898
A large inventory of Victorian, Country, Period
furniture, upholstered &
fine furniture. Accessories
& collectibles including,
fine china, silver, pottery,
kitchen and country
primitives, Depression
glass & much more.
Wed. & Thurs. 12:-5,
Fri. & Sat. 12-6.

Folsom

A Little of This
& A Little of That
Rt. 301 & Macdade Blvd.
(610) 534-4545

Glen Mills

Candlelight Antiques
1110 Smithbridge Rd.
(610) 358-6053
Gen line, country antiques.

Elizabeth L. Matlat
134 Wilmington Pike/Rt. 202
Brandywine Summit Center
(610) 358-0359
Gen line.

Pratt & Company
128 Glen Mills Rd.
(610) 558-3404
Gen line. Antiq & handmade
repros.

Glenolden

Uniques & Antiques
In Rt. 452 Business Center
(610) 485-7400
Call for auction dates & times.

Gradyville

Den of Antiquity
Rt. 352 & Gradyville Rd.
(610) 459-2836
Gen line. Spec: antiq
x-mas ornaments & mem.

Haverford

Chelsea House Ltd
45 Haverford Station Rd.
(610) 896-5554
18th & 19th c. Eng, Cont
& Am furn & dec.

French Corner Antiques
16 Haverford Station Rd.
(610) 642-6867
Importers furn & dec,
18th c.-1930's.

James S. Jaffe Rare Books
367 W. Lancaster Ave.
(610) 649-4221
Rare & 1st ed. books.

McClees Galleries
343 W. Lancaster Ave.
(610) 642-1661
Turn of cent Am & Euro
oils & watercolors.

The Mock Fox
15 Haverford Station Rd.
(610) 642-4990

Havertown

Tamerlane Books
516 Kathmere Rd.
(610) 449-4400
Books, maps, prints &
ephemera.

Holmes

Rita's Relics
215 Holmes Rd.
(610) 534-7070
Gen line. Spec:
coins & stamps.

Lansdowne

Ann's Antiques & Curios
213 W. Baltimore Pike
(610) 623-3179
Gen line.

**Before Our Time Antiques
54 W. Marshall Rd.
(1 mile from Ardmart
Antiques Mall, Drexel Hill)
(610) 259-6370
Tues-Sat 11-6.
Buy, sell or browse in this
friendly neighborhood
shop where service is
never a thing of the past.
A bit of something for
everyone-furn, china,
glass, silver & jewelry,
all at affordable prices.
Dealers always welcome.**

Good Old Days Antiques
201 E. Plumstead Ave.
(610) 622-2688
Gen line.

Lansdowne Auction Galleries
11 S. Lansdowne Ave.
(610) 622-6836/622-6936
Call for auction dates & times.

Media

Antique Exchange
23 W. State St.
(610) 891-9992
Gen line.

Atelier
36 W. State St.
(610) 566-6909
General line.

Remember When
21 W. State St.
(610) 566-7411
General line.

Rhodes Affordable Place
200 W. Baltimore Pike
(610) 566-4436
General line.

The Fitzgerald Group
220 W. Baltimore Ave.
(610) 566-0703
China, glass, silver, costume
jewelry & small furn.

Newtown Square

The Consign &
Design Gallery
3716 West Chester Pike
(610) 359-8889
Consignment shop.

Tymes Remembered
15 Alban's Circle
(610) 353-9677
Vic & Country furn,
glass & linens.

Prospect Park

Old Odd & Otherwise
1038 Lincoln Ave.
(610) 583-5525
Glass, china & furn.

Old Odd & Otherwise
1040 Lincoln Ave.
(610) 583-5525
Weapons.

Tri State Antiques
1100 Lincoln Ave.
(610) 237-0746
Euro Vic porc & furn.

Ridley Park

The Barn
440 Chester Pike
(610) 521-9473
General line.

Swarthmore

Cantona & Milbourn
7A S. Chester Rd.
(610) 541-0338

Cricket Way LTD
102 Park Ave
(610) 604-0225

Upland

Serendipity Shop - CCMC
One Medical Center Blvd.
(610) 872-2428
Thrift & consignment shop.

Upper Darby

Delaware Valley Thrift
& Antiques
809 Garrrett Rd.
(610) 352-9430

Henry A. Gerlach
414 S. State Rd.
(610) 449-7600
Clocks, jewelry & art.

Park Avenue Shop
26 Park Ave. & S. Cedar Ln.
(610) 446-4699

Villanova

Elinor Gordon
Villanova, PA
(610) 525-0981
17th & 18th c. Chinese
export porc. By appt.

Wayne

Consignment Galleries
163 W. Lancaster Ave.
(610) 687-2959

Lifestyle Treasures
405 W. Wayne Ave.
(610) 688-5909
Gen line. Sat, 10:00-12:00
or by appt.

Neighborhood League Shop
191 Lancaster Ave.
Wayne, PA
(610) 688-0113
Consignment shop.

Painted Past
201 E. Lancaster Ave.
(610) 293-7420
Handmade & custom furn
from salvage.

Scallywag Antiques
308 W. Lancaster Ave.
(610) 688-8212
Country Eng pine.
Fr furn & dec.

The Antique Collection
161 Lancaster Ave.
(610) 902-0600
Multi-dealer shop.

The Pembroke Shop
167 W. Lancaster Ave.
(610) 688-8185

MONTGOMERY COUNTY

Ambler
Bala Cynwyd
Blue Bell
Bryn Mawr
Collegeville
Colmar
Conshohocken
Creamery
East Greenville
Flourtown
Fort Washington
Glenside
Green Lane
Harleysville
Hartford
Hatboro
Hatfield
Huntingdon Valley
Jeffersonville
Jenkintown

King of Prussia
Kulpsville
Lafayette Hill
Lansdale
Montgomeryville
Narberth
Norristown
North Wales
Palm
Pennsburg
Plymouth Meeting
Pottstown
Roslyn
Schwenksville
Skippack
Souderton
Sumneytown
Worcester
Wynnewood
Zieglersville

MONTGOMERY COUNTY

Ambler

F.J. Carey III
555 Lewis Ln.
(215) 643-4664
Am formal furn, 1740-1840.
Chinese Export Porc.

Ross G. Gerhart
55 N. Main St.
(215) 646-0474
General line.

Bala Cynwyd

General Eclectic
159 Bala Ave.
(610) 667-6677
Jewelry & pottery
& glass.

Pieces of Tyme
323 Montgomery Ave.
(610) 664-2050
Smalls, dec & sports mem.

Blue Bell

Troll House Antiques
910 Valley Rd.
215-646-3166/800-470-4842
18th c-Arts & Crafts furn.
Dec, silver & pewter.

Copper Cricket Antiques
990 Dekalb Pike
Rte. 202 at Rte. 73
(610) 239-5939
Multi-dealer shop selling:
antiques, decorative arts,
collectibles & jewelry.
Offer consignment. Offer
interior design service.
Buy one piece or entire
estates.

Bryn Mawr

American Ordinance
Preservation Association
311 Millbank Rd.
(610) 519-9610
Military items. By appt.

Bryn Mawr Hospital
Thrift Shop
County Line Rd.
Thrift shop.

Bryn Mawr Antique Mart
844 County Line Rd.
(610) 525-8922
Gen line. By appt.

Greentree Gallery
825 W. Lancaster Ave.
(610) 526-1841
19th & 20th c. furn, pottery,
glass, paintings & silver.

Sandy De Maio
860 W. Lancaster Ave.
(610) 525-1717
Jewelry, Vic, Edwardian,
Art Deco. Coll.

Susan Vitale Antiques
835 W. Lancaster Ave.
(610) 527-5653
Gen line: 19th c. Eng,
Cont & OR furn & dec.

Collegeville

The Bejamin Cox
House Herbary
310 Black Rock Rd.
In the Village of Oaks
(610) 933-5036

The Power House
45 1st Ave. (Off 29)
(610) 489-7388
Multi-dealer. Sun only.

Trappe Antiques
1639 W. Main St.
(Rt. 422)
(610) 489-0714
Early Am & Euro furn.

Colmar

Barbie J's Antiques
842 Bethlehem Pike
(215) 822-7624
Country furn, pottery & dec.

Conshohocken

Nelly's Place
14 E 5th Ave.
(610) 825-7971
Smalls.

Garden Accents
4 Union Hill Rd.
West Conshohocken
(610) 825-5525

Creamery

Jerry's Antiques
& Used Furniture
Rt. 113
(610) 409-9479
General Line.

East Greenville

Nanna's Nook & Cranny
239 Main St.
Main Street Plaza
(215) 679-8686
New & usd (early 1900s)
furn, paper & vint clothing.

**Zionsville II Antique
  Mall
649 Gravel Pk.
(Rt. 29 S.)
East Greenville, PA
(215) 541-9187
Over 100 vendors in
10,000 sq. ft. filled with
antiques & collectibles.
South of Allentown,
North of Philadelphia &
Northeast of Adamstown.**

Flourtown

Bob's Antiques
  & Used Furniture
1505 Bethlehem Pk.
(215) 233-9007
Furn, 1930-40s
Mahogany & Cherry.

The Treasure Hunter
1614 Bethlehem Pk.
(215) 233-4026
Jewelry, oils, rings, watches, &
cameras

Fort Washington

Dolores & Irvin
  Boyd Antiques
509 Bethlehem Pk.
(215) 646-7614
18th & 19th c. furn.

Michael J. Whitman
427 Bethlehem Pk.
(215) 646-8639
Spec: Am, Eng & Euro
metalware.

The Green Tureen
431 Bethlehem Pk.
(215) 628-3792

Glenside

Kirland & Kirkland
237 Keswick Ave.
(215) 576-7771
General line.

Ludwig's Scattered
  Treasures
221 W. Glenside Ave.
(215) 887-0512
Gen line. Spec: vint linens.

Pinky Lil' Hammer
235 Keswick Ave.
(215) 884-6722
General line.

Sadie's Early Birds
16 E. Glenside Ave.
(215) 572-1116
Consignment shop.

Yesterday & Today
4 Roberts Block
Glenside Train Station
(215) 572-6926
Vint clothing, jewelry
  & glass,1900—1940's.

Green Lane

Colonial House Antiques
Corner Rts. 29 & 63
(215) 234-4113
General line.

Harleysville

Old Mill Antiques
279 Maple Ave.
(215) 256-9957

Hartford

Phil's Used Furniture
  & Antiques
Routes 29 & 100
(215) 679-8625

Hatboro

Joys & Toys
53 S. York Rd.
(215) 675-2880
Toys & dolls.

The Old Country Attic
Old York Rd.
(215) 441-4232
Gen line.

Hatfield

Alderfer Auction Co.
501 Fairgrounds Rd.
(215) 393-3000
Call for auction dates & times.

Huntingdon Valley

Interior Consignment
Justa Farm Shopping Center
1966 County Line Rd.
(215) 396-8000
General line: pre-owned furn
& dec.

Valley Antiques
2511 Huntingdon Pk.
(215) 947-7858
General line.

Jeffersonville

Stephen Arena Antiques
2118 W. Main St.
(610) 631-9100

Jenkintown

Anthony's Curiosity Shop
805 Greenwood Ave.
(215) 885-2992

Breslin Consignment
719 West Ave.
(215) 884-5444
Consignment shop.

Jeffrey Ceasar Antiques
214 Old York Rd.
(215) 572-6040
Antiq. lighting & Vic dec.

Palinurus Books
101 Greenwood Ave.
(215) 884-2297
Science, medical &
economics books, pre1840.

King Of Prussia

Weigh Back When Antiques
251 S. Henderson Rd.
(610) 992-1692
Furn, jewlry art, glass, china,
Spec: antique scales.

Kulpsville

Kulpsville Antiques
1375 Forty Foot Rd.
(215) 361-7910
Multi-dealer co-op.

Lafayette Hill

The Resettlers Marketplace
651 Germantown Pike
(610) 828-9633/828-9637

Lansdale

Furniture by Choyce
7 N. Mitchell St.
(215) 855-3377
Furniture.

Montgomeryville

The General Hancock
    Antique Center
735 Bethlehem Pk.
(215) 361-7404
Multi-dealer co-op.

Narberth

Ruth Blum Antiques
227 Haverford Ave.
(610) 660-8030
Jewelry, silver, porc & dec.

Norristown

Debbie's Thrift
522 Marshall St.
(610) 272-5005
Gen line, new, usd & antiq.

Felber Ornamental
    Plastering Corp.
1000 W. Washington St.
(610) 275-4713
Period architectural details.

Larry's Thrift Shop
406 W. Marshall St.
(610) 279-6387
General line.

The Shops at Logan Square
Rts. 202 & Johnson Hwy.
(610) 275-3500
Three antiq shops.

North Wales

Sweet Repeats
115 S. Main St.
(215) 661-8800
Furn, jewelry & vintage
costumes.

Palm

The Barnyard at
    Summer Brook Farm
Rt. 29
Palm, PA
(215) 679-0773

Pennsburg

Geryville Country Store
1830 Geryville Pk.
(215) 541-0881

Plymouth Meeting

Cold Point PA Antiques
2501 Butler Pike
(610) 825-3342

Plymouth Meeting Gallery
(610) 825-9068
Am Impressionist paintings
& Bucks County School.

MONTGOMERY COUNTY, PA

Pottstown

Half Crown Farm
1226 Warwick Furnace Rd.
(610) 469-6649/469-9296
18th & 19th c. PA country
& semi-formal furn. & dec.

Oletowne Jewelers
211 High St,
(610) 323-7900
Jewelry.

Shaner's Antiques
403 N. Charlotte St.
(610) 326-0165
Gen line. Spec:
children's items.

Thomas R. Galloway
326 N. Charlotte St.
(610) 718-1292

Used To Be
100 W. Schuylkill Rd.
(610) 326-8773

Roslyn

Heirloom Jewel Company
1186 Easton Rd.
(215) 886-3886

Schwenksville

Need to Be Remembered
96 Main St.
(610) 287-7813
Gen line.

Skippack

Douglas Antiques
3907 Skippack Pike
(610) 584-6102

From The Past
4039 Skippack Pk.
(610) 584-5842
Jewelry.

Kay's Antiques
3859 Skippack Pk.
(610) 584-1196
General line.

Remains to be
Seen Antiques
4006 Skippack Pk.
(610) 584-5770
Country antiques bought,
sold & enthusiastically
discussed. Wed through
Sun, 12-6.

Seasons of Skippack
Rt. 73 & Store Rd.
(610) 584-6799

Snyder Antiques
4006 Skippack Pk.
(610) 584-6454
General line.

Thorpe Antiques
4027 Skippack Pk.
(610) 584-1177

Souderton

Ye Olde Cowpath Antiques
59 Cowpath Rd. (Rt. 463)
(215) 723-5768
Oak & primitive furn.

Sumneytown

Sumneytown School House
Sumneytown Pike
(215) 234-8707

Worcester

Allen Antiques
3004 Skippack Pk.
(610) 584-5559
General line.

Wynnewood

Alexander Horn & Co.
33 E. Wynnewood Rd.
(610) 896-7494
Clocks & watches.

Zieglersville

Antiques & More
6 Big Rd.
(610) 287-8266

PHILADELPHIA COUNTY

Chestnut Hill
Manayunk
Philadelphia

PHILADELPHIA COUNTY

Chestnut Hill

Antiques at the
  Secret Garden
12-14 E. Hartwell Ln.
(215) 247-8550
Multi-dealer market.

Antique Lighting
6350 Germantown Ave.
(215) 438-6350

Bird In Hand
8419 Germantown Ave.
(215) 248-2473 11/23
Silverplate, china, glass,
crystal, pictures & lamps.

Blum's Chestnut Hill
43-45 E. Chestnut Hill Ave.
(215) 242-8877

Chandlee & Bewick
7811 Germantown Ave.
(215) 242-0375

Diane Bryman Orientals
8038 Gernmantown Ave.
(215) 242-4100
Persian & Euro carpets

Dobbins Oriental Rug
8219 Germantown Ave.
(215) 247-2227
Oriental rugs, new, usd,
Semi-antiq & antiq.

Garden Gate Antiques
8139 Germantown Ave.
(215) 248-5190
Multi-dealer markets

Helen L. Jones French
  Country Antiques
8436 Germantown Ave.
(215) 247-4944
Fr country furn & Pottery,
early 1800's.

Hobe Atelier
7918 Germantown Ave.
(215) 247-5733
Am. art pottery.

Porch Cellar
7928-30 Germantown Ave.
(215) 247-1952
Multi-dealer shop.

P.S. Consignments
8705 Germantown Ave.
(215) 248-5230
50's -60's Modern furn, art &
dec.

Smalls Antiques Market
7932-34 Germantown Ave.
(215) 247-1953
Multi-dealer shop.

The Antique Gallery
8523 Germantown Ave.
(215) 248-1700

The Leather Bucket
84 Bethlehem Pike
1st fl. Rear
(215) 242-1140
18th & 19th c. Eng & Am
furn & silver, porc & art.

The Philadelphia Print Shop
8441 Germantown Ave.
(215) 242-4750
Prints & maps.

The Post Light
51 E. Bethelehem Pike
(215) 242-3810
Lighting fixtures. By appt.

Manyunk

Antique Lighthouse
4400 Dexter St.
(215) 483-8221
Restored lighting. By appt.

Antique Marketplace
3797 Main St.
(215) 482-4499
Multi-dealer co-op, over 100 dlrs.

Bob Berman Antiques
4456 Main St.
(215) 482-8667

Ida's Treasures
4388 Main St.
(215) 482-7060
Am & Euro art pottery.
Eng Chintz & Majolica.

**Manyunk Antique Shops
  & Belle Maison
Main & Leverington Ave.
(215) 482-9004
Belle Maison:
Vintage & European
linens for the bed, bath &
table. Antiques, home furnishings, architectural
finds & garden treasures
with a French flavor.
(215) 482-6222.
Manyunk Antique Shops:
Quality antiquities, furniture, lighting, artwork,
jewelry, pottery, porc-
elain, hardware, garden
& architectural artifacts,
books, toys and the unique.
Friendly dealers, friendly
prices. Ample free parking
(215) 482-9004**

**Philadelphia Antique Center
126 Leverington Ave.
(One block above Main)
(215) 487-3467
10,000 sq. ft. of antiques
& collectibles. Shipments
arriving from England &
France every 7-8 weeks.
French Deco & Nouveau,**

Mission, Black Collectibles, Architectural antiques, Prints, Paintings, Lighting & Victorian Furniture. Offer: Design service, shipping, packing & framing. Wed-Fri 11-5, Sat & Sun 11-6.

Sandy De Maio
4359 Main St.
(215) 508-0200
Jewelry, Vic, Edwardian & Art Deco. Coll.

Two By Four
3791 Main St.
(215) 482-9494
General line. Spec: smalls.

Philadelphia

Aida's Antiques
615 S. 6th St.
(215) 922-7077
Multi-dealer shop.

Alan's Antiques
413 S. 20th St.
(215) 545-6464
Pottery, porc, jewlry, lamps. Vic -70's.

Albert Maranca Antiques
1100 Pine St.
(215) 925-8909
19th c. Fr Cont furn & sculpture.

Alfred Bullard
1604 Pine St.
(215) 735-1870

Anastacia's Antiques
617 Bainbridge St.
(215) 928-9111
Vic & early 20th c. furn, lighting, smalls & jewelry.

Anthony Stuempfig Antiques
2213 St. James St.
(215) 561-7191
Am Classical Revival & Empire furn, 1805 -1835.

Antiques & Interiors
1010 Pine St.
(215) 925-8600

Antique Design
1102 Pine St.
Restored stained glass.
Euro Art Deco furn.

Antique Fair Inc.
2218 Market St.
(215) 563-3682

Antique Showcase
of Philadelphia
1625 Pine St.
(215) 545-0860
18th & 19th c. Euro furn dec, clocks & lighting.

Antiquarian's Delight
Antique Market
615 S. 6th St.
(215) 592-0256
Multi-dealer market.

Architectural Antiques Exchange
715 N. 2nd St.
(215) 922-3669
Architectural Salvge: mantels, doors, stained glass, bars & back bars.

Bainbridge Collectables
514 Bainbridge St.
(215) 922-7761
Multi-dealer shop.

Ballyhoo
160 N. Third St.
(215) 627-1700
Men's & women's vint. clothing, 1930-1970s.

Barry S. Slosberg Inc.
2501 E. Ontario St.
(215) 425-7030
Call for auction dates & times.

Bauman Rare Books
1215 Locust St.
(215) 546-6466

Belle Epoque Antiques
1029 Pine St.
(215) 351-5383
Art Deco & Nouveau porc, ceramics & furn.

Berman Gallery
136 N. Second St.
(215) 733-0707
20th c. Mission.

Bob's Old Attic
6916 Torresdale Ave.
(215) 624-6382
Gen line.

Bobby J. Antiques
7th & Bainbridge Sts.
(215) 922-7009
Gen line.

Calderwood Gallery
1427 Walnut St.
(215) 568-7475

Carriage House Antiques
516 Kater St.
(215) 625-0705
Country & Vic furn.

Charles Neri
313 South St.
(215) 923-6669
Am furn & lighting, 1820-1920.

Crossroads
2135 S. 61st St.
(215) 726-1368

Dante's Furniture Refinishing
1631 Meadow St.
(215) 744-7345
Custom furn, all styles; antiq-
modern.

David David Gallery
260 S. 18th St.
(215) 735-2922

DeHoogh Gallery
1624 Pine St.
(215) 735-7722
Am, Chinse, Japnse, Pre-
colombian art objects.

Dorety's
900 South St.
(215) 625-2728
Architecturals & furn.

Eberhardt's Antiques
2010 Walnut St.
(215) 568-1877
Porc, china & Orientalia.

Elena's Discoveries
509 S. 6th St.
(215) 925-0566
Smalls & coll, 1890-1960.

Estate Antique & Oriental
Rug Gallery
1034 Pine St.
(215) 922-5714
Euro furn, rugs & dec.

Findings
246 Race St.
(215) 923-0988
Furn & prims. Spec: Tribal Art.

First Loyalty Antiques
1036 Pine St.
(215) 922-5594
Furn, silver & jewelry, Vic,
& Art Nouveau & Deco.

Francis J Purcell Inc.
251 N. 3rd St.
(215) 574-0700
18th c. fireplace mantels.
18th c. Am, Eng & Russian
furn, clocks & dec.

Freeman/ Fine Arts
of Philadelphia
1808 Chestnut St.
(215) 563-9275
Call for auction dates & times.

G.B. Schaeffer Antiques
1014 Pine St.
(215) 923-2263

Gargoyles Limited
512 South 3rd St.
(215) 629-1700
Props, old & new.

Graham Arader III
1308 Walnut St.
(215) 735-8811
Artwork.

Hotel Furniture Liquidations
5301 Tacony St. Bldg. 44
(215) 744-4645
Old hotel furn.

I. Brewster & Co.
1628 Walnut St.
(215) 731-9200

Jack McGlinn Antiques
5314 Germantown Ave.
(215) 438-3766
Gen line.

Jansen Antiques
1042 Pine St.
(215) 922-5594
Furn, silver & jewelry.

Jeffrey Lee Biber
1030 Pine St.
(215) 574-3633
Cont & Am sterling, mantel
clocks, lamps & bronzes.

Jules Clock Shop
216 Market St.
(215) 922-3418

Kohn & Kohn Antiques
1112 Pine St.
(215) 923-0432

Liao Oriental Antiques
607-09 Bainbridge St.
(215) 574-9410
Chinse & Japnse art, furn & textiles.

M. Finkel & Daughter
10th & Pine Sts.
(215) 627-7797

Maggie's Drawers
706 S. 4th St.
(215) 923-5003

Mario's Antique Shop
1020 Pine St.
(215) 922-0230

Marshall Gold Leaf & Art
Conservation Studios
610-341-0909/800-340-9475
Consortium, restoration &
conservation of dec arts.

Material Culture
4700 Wissahickon Ave.
(215) 849-8030
Furn, art, rugs, artifacts
& architecturals from
many cultures.

Maude's Curiosity Shop
6665 Germantown Ave.
(215) 438-1189

Metro Antiques
257 S. 20th St.
(215) 545-3555
Gen line. Tribal to
contemporary.

Mode Moderne
159 N. 3rd St.
(215) 627-0299
20th c. designer furn
& dec.

Moderne Gallery
111 N. 3rd St.
(215) 923-8536
20th c. dec arts, Fr Art Deco.

Newman Galleries
1625 Walnut St.
(215) 563-1779
Art.

Niederkorn Antique Silver
2005 Locust St.
Philadelphia, PA
(215) 567-2606
Jensen, Spratly & Tiffany.

**Olde City Antiques
& Collectables
33 S. 2nd St.
(215) 413-1944
Consignment house located
in an old furniture ware-
house. Four floors packed
with smalls to furniture;
antique, old and new.
Buy, sell & trade.**

Old City Mission
162 N. Third St.
(215) 413-1944
Am Arts & Crafts: furn,
pottery, metal, lighting
& textiles.

Pennyfeathers
1312 South St.
(215) 772-1945
Men's and women's vint clothing, 1800-1970s.

Phila. Estate Liquidators
501 Fairmount Ave.
215- 925-8690/609-541-4270

Philadelphia Trading Post
4021 Market St.
(215) 386-9855
Gen line,new, usd.& antiq.

Portobello Antiques
9 W. Highland Ave.
(215) 247-0181
China,crystal, vint linens &
sterling.

Reese's Antiques
930 Pine St.
(215) 922-0796
17th-20th c. furn, art, brass,
copper & porc.

Scarlett's Closet
261 S. 17th St.
(215) 546-4020

Schwarz Gallery
1806 Chestnut St.
(215) 563-4887
Art.

Sorger & Schwartz Antiques
1108 Pine St.
(215) 627-5259
19th c. furn, art & dec:

South Street Antiques
Market
615 South 6th St.
(215) 592-0256
Multi-dealer shop.

South Street Jewelry
Exchange
648 S. St.
(215) 925-9600
Rare coins, jewelry &
watches.

Southwood House
1732 Pine St.
(215) 545-4076

**The Classic Lighting
Emporium
62 N. 2nd St.
(215) 625-9552
Over 1 million pieces in
stock. The Emporium
maintains the largest
selection of lighting in the
U.S. Chandeliers, floor
lamps, shades, wall
sconces, prisms, outdoor
lights, globes, table lamps
and original parts. Full
restoration services avail.**

The Den of Antiquities
16 3rd St.
(215) 592-8969
1890 - 1960 furn, coll
& oddities.

The Treasure Hunter
1614 Bethlehem Pike
(215) 233-4026

Thompson Antiques
16th & Pine St.
(215) 545-1639

Thrift for AIDS
629-33 South St.
(215) 592-9014
Thrift shop.

Urban Artifacts
4700 Wissahickon Ave.
(215) 844-8330
1850-1920 Am & Fr furn
& fireplace mantels

Ursula Hobson
1600 Spruce St.
(215) 546-7889
17th-19th c. art &
restoration.

Via Bicycle
606 South 9th St.
(215) 627-3370
Vint bicycles & related
items.

Washington Square Gallery
221 Chestnut St.
(215) 923-8873
By appointment only.

Watson 20th Century
307 Arch St.
(215) 923-2565
Smalls.

Yesteryear
6526 Rising Sun Ave.
(215) 342-9570 12/4
Gen line.

EASTERN PENNSYLVANIA

Adams County
Berks County
Carbon County
Cumberland County
Dauphin County
Franklin County
Lackawanna County
Lancaster County
Lebanon County
Lehigh County
Luzerne County
Monroe County
Northampton County
Pike County
Schuylkill County
Wayne County
Wyoming County
York County

ADAMS COUNTY

Abbottstown

East Berlin

Fairfield

Gettysburg

Littlestown

McKnightstown

New Oxford

York Springs

ADAMS COUNTY

Abbotstown

Cooper's Antiques
7013 York Rd.
(717) 624-7412
General line.

Lyn Kay Shoppe
6789 York Rd.
(717) 624-8805
Prims, toys & children's things.

Patricia Clegg Antiques
183 E. King St.
(717) 259-9480
Country furn, decoys, baskets, textiles & gameboards.

Wallace's Antiques
320 W. King St.
(717) 259-7021
Gen lin. Spec: primitives.

East Berlin

Corner Cupboard Treasures
132 W. King St.
(717) 259-0967
General line.

J. Blyler Hoffman Antiques
412 West King St.
(717) 259-7676
Painted furn.

Lion & The Lamb
530 W. King St.
(717) 259-7676
Late 18th c.-early 19th c.
Country prim PA furn, folk art & textiles.

Red Dog Antiques
426 W. King St.
(717) 259-7443
General line.

Fairfield

Fairfield Antique Gallery
110 E. Main St.
(717) 642-6629
Multi-dealer co-op.

Wooden Horse
2886 Waynesboro Pk.
(717) 794-2717
Gen line.

Gettysburg

Abe's Antiques
238 Baltimore St.
(717) 337-2121
Gen line. Spec: Lincoln & Civil war related items.

Antique Center of Gettysburg
7 Lincoln Sq.
(717) 337-3669
Multi-dealer co-op.

Di's Jewelry
12 Baltimore St.
(717) 334-0969

Farnsworth House Inn
401 Baltimore St.
(717) 334-8838
Militaria.

Fields of Glory
55 York St.
(717) 337-2837
Civil War: photos, rifles, cannnblls, diaries & swords.

G. Craig Caba Antiques
206 York Rd.
(717) 732-3204
18th & 19th c. Am furn & dec. Appt. suggested.

Hartlaub's Antiques
1924 York Rd.
(717) 334-3988
Majolica, glass, graniteware & 19th c.prim furn.

Hope Springs Antiques
2540 Mummasburg Rd.
(717) 677-4857
Stoneware, quilts, hearth & kitchen, lighting & furn.

Knorrwood Antiques
140 York Rd.
(717) 334-4759
Furn, redware & ironstone.

Maggie's Another
  Place & Time
52 Chambersburg St.
(717) 334-0325

Mel's Gettysburg Antiques
103 Carlisle Rear
(717) 334-9387
Multi-dealer mall.

Mil-g Farm Antiques
Rt. 116
(5 mi. W. of G-burg)
(717) 642-5507
Furn & gen line.

Sword & Saber
2159 Baltimore Pk.
(717) 344-0205
Civil War items.

The Horse Soldier
777 Baltimore St.
(717) 334-0347
Everything related to the Civil War.

The Union Drummer
34 York St.
(717) 334-2350
Civil War artifacts.

Time Travelers Antiques
312 Baltimore St.
(717) 337-0011
19th c. furn, quilts, textiles,
smalls & Civil War.

TT&G's Antiques
2031 York Rd.
(717) 334-0361

Littlestown

Betty & Jack's Antiques
31 W. King St.
(717) 359-4809
Period & PA state furn & dec.

King & Queen's Antiques
1 S. Queen St.
(717) 359-7953
Furn & restored trunks.

Kooney's Barn
1295 Frederick Pk.
(717) 359-7411
Rustic furn, pottery, dolls &
Americana.

Kowalczyk's Old
Furniture
9 Monarch St.
(717) 359-4907

Little's Antique Shop
129 W. King St.
(717) 359-5730
General line.

Ma's General Store
5227 Baltimore Pk. (Rt. 97)
(717) 359-7831
Hoosiers, cupboards & coll.

Second Chance &
Yesterday's Stuff
4895 Baltimore Pk.
(717) 359-4038
Gen line, 1800s-present.

Two Taverns Antiques
7 Two Taverns Rd.
(717) 359-8252

McKnightstown

Farcry Farm Antiques
Rt. 30 to Fairview Fruit
Rd. to Hilltown Rd.
(717) 677-8191
Americana, old guns &
Civil War artifacts.

New Oxford

Adam's Apple Antiques
3 Lincold Way W.
(717) 624-3480
N.E. period furn & dec.
Stained glass & garden.

America's Past Antiques
114 Lincoln Way E.
(717) 624-7830
Smalls, spinning wheels
& Indian artifacts.

Authentic American Lighting
4335 York Rd.
(717) 624-7125
Period lighting & restoration.

B & E Junction
2 Lincoln Way E.
(717) 624-4372
Electric trains.

Barry L. Click Antiques
145 New Chester Rd.
(717) 624-3185
Country & farm furn, clocks,
hardware & relics.

Betty & Gene's Antiques
110 Lincoln Way W.
(717) 624-4437
Glass, china & furn.

Center Square Antiques
16 Center Square
(717) 624-3444
Restord lighting,1850-1900's.
Furn, Architecturals & cash
registers.

Charlie's Place
4335 York Rd.
(717) 624-7039
Collectible toys.

Collector's Choice Gallery
330 Golden Lane
(717) 624-3440
Multi-dealer co-op.

Conewago Creek Forks
1255 Oxford Rd.
(2 mi. N of New Oxford)
(717) 624-4786

Evelyn Jones Antiques
343 Lincoln Way W.
(717) 624-7872

Fountain View
Antiques N Things
10 Center Square
(717) 624-9394
Glass & china.

Golden Lane Antique
Gallery
11 N. Water St.
(717) 624-3800
Two quality controlled
galleries. Featuring over
150 dealers offering 18th ,
19th & early 20th century
antiques. Over 60,000 sq.
ft. Open daily 10:00-5:00.

Hart's Country Antiques
2 Carlisle St.
(717) 624-7842
Prims, furn, stoneware, toys &
smalls.

Hartland Antiques
111 Lincoln Hwy. E.
(717 624-9686

Henry's Hideaway
335A Lincoln Way W.
(717) 624-8809
Lamps, scales, glass, china,
clocks, brass & Victrolas.

Kehr's Corner Cupboard
20 Lincoln Way E.
(717) 624-3054
Furn, pine & oak.
Copper accessories.

Lau's Antiques
112 Lincoln Way E.
(717) 624-4972
Multi-dealer co-op.

Lawrence's Antiques
411 Lincoln Way W.
(717) 259-1050
Rough & finished furn.

New Oxford Antique Center
333 Lincoln Way W.
(717) 624-7787
Multi-dealer co-op.

Olde Stone House Antiques
100 Lincoln Hwy. E.
(717) 624-1500
Decoys & hunting &
fishing specialties.

Oxford Barn
330 Lincoln Way W.
(717) 624-4160
Pottery, furn & prims.

Oxford Hall Irish Too
106 Lincoln Way W.
(717) 624-2337
**Offering the best of Irish
treasures: clothing, food,
music & gift items. Feat-
uring "The Celtic Collection" antiquities; 5 buildings full. Dealers wel-
come.**

R & S Antiques
109 Lincoln Way E.
(717) 677-7162
Spec: oak. 200 pieces in stock
at all times.

Remember When Shop
4 Lincoln Way W.
(717) 624-2426
Gen line.

Rife's Antiques
4415 York Rd.
(717) 624-2546
Oak & Walnut furn.

Sarah's Antiques
109 Carlisle St.
(717) 624-9664

Storm's Antiques
1030 Kohler Mill Rd.
1.8 mi. from Rt. 30
(717) 624-8112
Oak furn.

York Springs

Bernie's What-Nots
7129 Carlisle Pike
(717) 528-4271
General line.

BERKS COUNTY

Barto
Bethel
Boyertown
Douglassville
Fleetwood
Hereford
Kutztown
Leesport
Maxatawney
Morgantown
Oley
Pikeville
Reading
Shartlesville
Sinking Spring

BERKS COUNTY

Barto

Lake Leggio Antiques
424 Niantic Rd.
(610) 845-0051
General line.

Bethel

Garden Gate
8495 Lancaster Ave.
(717) 933-8366

Boyertown

Boyertown Antiques
1283 Weisstown Rd.
(610) 367-2452
Early Am Grandfather
clocks & furniture.

Castle Hall Antiques
5 E. Philadelphia Ave.
Boyertown, PA
(610) 367-6506
Country to formal furn & dec.

**Greshville Antiques
1041 Reading Rd.
(610) 367-0076
18th c. American tallcase
clocks, Victorian grand-
father clocks, Period &
Centennial furniture-
Country to formal. 19th
& 20th c. American &
European art, featuring
Pa. Paintings & Berks
County Artists such as
Ben Austrian, C.H.
Shearer, J.H. Raser.
Open: Tuesday through
Saturday 10-4:00 or
by appt.**

Partners In Time
3 E. Boyertown Ave.
(610) 367-6145

The Bashful Barn
1 E. Philadelphia Ave.
(610) 367-2631

The Twin Turrets Inn
11 E. Philadelphia Ave.
(610) 367-45113
Vic bed & breakfast furn &
paintings

Douglassville

Stepp's Antiques
1528 Weavertown Road
(610) 582-5918
Am Country Furn.

**Merritt's Antiques Inc.
1860 Weavertown Rd.
(610) 689-9541
Over 55,000 sq. ft. of**

antiques, reproductions, clocks and clock repair supplies. www.merritts.com Buy and sell. Top dollar paid immediately.

Fleetwood

Antique Complex
of Fleetwood
Rt. 222
(610) 994-0707
General line.

Hereford

Corinna'a
Old Rt 100 & 29
(215) 679-8802
Country furn & coll.

Phil's Used Furniture
& Antiques
Rts. 29 & 100
(215) 679-8625
Weekends only.

Kutztown

Baver's Antiques
232 W. Main St.
(610) 683-5045
Lighting, 1920 - 1940

Greenwich Mills
1097 Krumsville Rd.
(610) 683-7866
Primitive furn & Pennsylvaniana.

Kutztown Art Glass Gallery
230 Noble St.
(610) 683-5714
Art glass, stained glass,Vic
& Art Nouveau style.

Louise's Old Things
163 W. Main St.
(610) 683-8370
Flow Blue & Blue Willow,
1700 - present. Childrens dishware

Renninger's Antiques
Noble St.
(610) 683-6848
Multi-dealer co-op.

Leesport

Leesport Antique Mart
162 Center Ave. (Rt. 61)
(610) 926-2019
Multi-dealer co-op.

Maxatawny

Antiques Etc.
15878 Kutztown Rd.
(610) 683-8834
Primitives, art objects
& small furn.

Yesterday's Memories
Antiques
1587 Kutztown Rd.
(610) 683-5657
Primitives & oak furn.

Morgantown

**The Mill Property
Rt. 23
W. Main St.
Main (610) 286-8854
Lower level (610) 286-7711
90 dealers. 10,000 sq. ft.
containing a mix of primitives, kitchenwares, tools,
postcards, textiles, pottery, furniture, china, silver & garden. Open 7
days, 10:00-5:30.**

Morgantown's Antique
Connection
238 W. Main St. (Rt. 23)
(610) 286-4785
Multi-dealer co-op.

Treasure Hill Antiques
W. Main St. (Rt. 23)
Morgantown, PA
(610) 286-7119
Multi-dealer co-op.

Wrights Auction
Rts. 10 & 23
Morgantown, PA
(610) 286-0555
Call for auction dates & times.

Oley

Covered Bridge
2693A W. Philadelphia Pk.
(610) 689-4882
General line.

Oley Valley Auction Co.
Rt. 73 & Oley Rd.
(610) 987-9080
Call for auction dates & times.

Oley Valley Reproductions
6321 Oley Turnpike Rd.
(610) 689-5885
Am period formal &
country reproductions.

Pikeville

Houseman Auction
Hill Church Rd.
(610) 987-6826
Call for auction dates & times.

Pikeville Antiques
Oysterdale Rd.
(610) 987-6635
Primitive furn & Colonial dec.

Reading

Green Hills Auction Center
1540 New Holland Rd.
(610) 775-2000
Call for auction dates & times.

Memories
622 Penn Ave.
West Reading, PA
(610) 374-4480
Vint clothing & jewelry.

Ocasio New, Used
& Antique Furniture
312 N. 9th St.
(610) 375-7896
General line.

Pennypacker-Andrews
  Auction Centre
1530 New Holland Rd.
(Rt. 222)
(610) 777-6121
Call for auction dates & times.
Auctions held in Goglersville.

Ray's Antiques
401 N. 5th St.
(610) 373-2907

Sylvia Christy Antiques
1008 Penn St.
(610) 478-0599
General line. Spec: jewlry,
esp.1890-1930.

The Christy Collection
1015 Penn St.
(610) 375-4060
Spec: Political & historical
mem.

Weaver Antique Mall
3730 Lancaster Pike (Rt. 222)
(610) 777-8535
Multi-dealer co-op.

White's Store Front
304 N. 5th St.
(610) 374-8128

Shartlesville

Antique Treasures
Roadside Dr.
(610) 488-1545

Heritage Quilts
  & Antiques
3rd & Main Sts.
(610) 488-0808
General line, country &
primitive. Spec: quilts.

Sinking Spring

Alternative Furnishings
3728 Lancaster Pike.
(610) 796-2990
Spec: garden accents.

Zerbes' Auction Center
138 Wheatfield Rd.
(610) 678-6685
Call for auction dates & times.

CARBON COUNTY

Albrightsville
Jim Thorpe

CARBON COUNTY

Albrightsville

Acorn Antiques
Rt. 903 & Old Stage Rd.
(570) 722-3001
Gen line & auction sales.

Jim Thorpe

Anne's Early Attic
23 Broadway
(570) 325-2299
General line.

Bear Mountain Trading
Route 903 & Church Rd.
(570) 325-4848

Bernard Dreher Antiques
932 Center Ave.
(570) 325-4141

Bits-N-Pieces
Route 903
(570) 325-8887
Gen line. Spec: oak furn.

TSS Antiques
14 Race St.
(570) 325-4776
General line

CUMBERLAND COUNTY

Camp Hill

Carlisle

Enola

Lemoyne

Mechanicsburg

New Cumberland

Shiremanstown

CUMBERLAND COUNTY

Camp Hill

Cordier Antiques
2424 Market St.
(717) 731-8662
Gen line. Spec: late 19th c.-
early 20th c. art.

Ivy House Ltd.
215 E. Main St.
(717) 737-5504

Lindstrom's Furniture
& Antiques
2161 Market St.
(717) 731-9503
Fine furniture, antiques,
accessories & restor-
ations. Buying & selling
antiques.
Open: Monday-Friday
10:00am-5:00pm.
www.webpa.com/lindstroms
E-mail: ktique@aol.com

Rose Marie's Antiques
2136 Market St.
(717) 763-8998

Carlisle

A Niche In Time
640 Belvidere St.
(717) 249-7243
Oil & watercolor paintings.
Prints.

Albion Point Antiques
At Carlisle Plaza Mall
E. High St & York R.d
Multi-dealer mall.

Antique Quilt Source
385 Springview Rd.,
Dept. SAG
(717) 245-2054
Am antiq quilts. Mail order
only.

Antiques On Hanover Street
17 N. Hanover St.
(717) 249-6285
Vic furn, formal mahogany.
Clocks, china, silver.

Busy Hands Country Shop
1953 Holly Pike
(717) 486-8879

Changing Hands
134 S. Hanover St.
(717) 241-0091
General line.

Country Heritage
24 N. Hanover St.
(717) 249-2600

Cover to Cover Books
138 N. Hanover St.
(717) 258-1114
Vint & coll books.

Downtown Antiques
152 N. Hanover St.
(717) 249-0395
Prim & late Vic furn & dec.

H & R Jewelry & Antiques
33 N. Hanover St.
(717) 258-4024

Hillcrest Antiques
31 E. Slate Hill Rd.
(717) 249-1987
European furn & dec.

Hubble's Antique Mall
2547 Ritner Hwy. (Rt. 11)
(717) 241-4332

K Street Antique Mall
1500 N. Pitt St.
(717) 241-4456
Multi-dealer co-op.

Lindstrom's Furniture
Restoration
1172 Newville Rd.
(717) 243-5115
Furn & dec: antiq & custom.
Restorations: caning, weav-
ing, veneer &carving.

Maggee's Barn
2341 Spring Rd.
Rt. 34 N.
(717) 249-3761
Furn & trunks.

Linden Hall Antiques
211 Old Stonehouse Rd.
717-249-1978
General line.

Lutz's Antique Trading Post
1233 Ritner Hwy. (Rt. 11)
(717) 241-0440
Uniques, furn, advertising
& coll.

Northgate Antique Mall
726 N. Hanover St.
(717) 243-9744
Multi-dealer co-op.

Old Country Barn Antiques
1554 Holly Pike
(717) 245-9303
Multi-dealer co-op.

Olde Bellaire Antiques
1 W. High St.
(717) 249-5726

Old Stone Tavern
2408 Walnut Bottom Rd.
(Village of Mooredale)
(717) 243-6304
Early furn, prims & dec.

Rowe's Antiques
2505 Ritner Hwy.
(717) 249-2677
Furniture.

Sandra of Pennrose
152 W. High St.
(717) 243-0198

Victoria & Albert
138 S. Pitt St.
(717) 245-9386
Vic: clocks, lamps, prints,
sterling & small furn.

Village Antiques
3331 Spring Rd.
(717) 249-6517
furn & smalls.

Enola

We Dabble
73 2nd St.
(717) 732-7680
Gen line.

Lemoyne

Classic Firearms
875 Market St.
(717) 731-0991

Foxden Antiques
1001 Market St.
(717) 761-2888
Furn, 1820-1920. Clocks,
porc, jewlry, silver & glass.

Barb's Antiques
701 Ohio Ave.
(717) 762-5123

Style Unlimited
656 State St.
(717) 763-4815

The Consignment Gallery
834 Market St.
(717) 730-9494
General line.

Mechanicsburg

Alexander's Antiques
6620 Carlisle Pike
(717) 766-5165
Smalls, cut glass, china
& wooden prims.

Country Gifts 'n Such
5145 E. Trindle Rd.
(717) 697-3555
General line.

Restoration Clinic
5222 E. Trindle Rd.
(717) 691-8881
Restored, antiq & vint furn.

Dave & Annie Brown
24 Hogestown Rd.
(717) 444-0039

Gallery Tricia & Maron
301 E. Main & Walnut Sts.
(717) 691-0263
Art, crystal & porc. Prim &
formal furn

Town's Antiques
4928 Simpson Ferry Rd.
(717) 761-7709
Restorations.

The Taylor House
4700 Old Gettysburg Rd.
(717) 761-1169
Multi-dealer co-op.

Touch of Gold
1151 Allendale Rd.
(717) 697-6937
Smalls & furn. Griswold
& Autumn Leaf.

New Cumberland

Checkered Past
1316 4th St.
(717) 774-7180
Vint clothing, 1920s-70s.

Honeycomb Shop
204 Limekiln Rd.
(717) 774-2683

Lamps n' Stuff
207 4th St.
(717) 774-4193
Lamps.

Roat's Collectibles
400 Granite Quarry Rd.
(717) 624-3440
Fostoria, Fenton & coll.

Shiremanstown

Collectors World
6 W. Main St.
(717) 763-8288

DAUPHIN COUNTY

Grantville
Halifax
Harrisburg
Hershey
Hummelstown
Middletown
Millersburg

DAUPHIN COUNTY

Grantville

Black Sheep
282 Bow Creek Rd.
(717) 469-1011
Multi-dealer co-op.

The Barn at Kelley Court
108 Kelley Court Rd.
(717) 469-0574
Multi-dealer co-op.

Halifax

Idle Bird Antiques
  & Jewelry
Route 225
(717) 896-3028

Harrisburg

Fissel & Company
1302 N. 3rd St.
(717) 238-3207
Vint & antiq furn,
1860-1940.

Snell's Collectors Corner
5581 Lancaster St.
(717) 564-0676

Test of Time
6295 Allentown Blvd.
(717) 652-8311
Multi-dealer co-op.

Hershey

Canal Collectibles
22 W. Canal St.
(717) 566-6940

Cocoa Curio
  Historical Militaria
546 W. Chocolate Ave. #A
(717) 533-1167
Military items, all wars,
all countries.

Ziegler's Antique Mall
825 Cocoa Ave
Corner Rts. 322 & 743
(717) 533-7990
Multi-dealer co-op.

Hummelstown

Hershey House
289 Hershey Rd
(717) 566-6042
Furn & smalls.

Olde Factory Antiques
139 S. Hanover St.
(717) 566-5685
Multi-dealer co-op.

Middletown

Beeb's The Past Recycled
417 Vine St.
(717) 944-7765

Days Gone By
2365 S. Geyers Church Rd.
(717) 944-4934
Prims, advertising, toys,
kitchen & farm related.

Freight Station Auction
Catherine & Wilson Sts.
(717) 944-6537
Call for auction dates & times.

Millersburg

Consignments Unlimited
231 Walnut St.
(717) 692-5458
Consignment shop.

Past Perfect
269 Market St.
(717) 692-4500
(800) 405-7060
General line.

Side Porch Antiques
354 Union St.
(717) 692-5459
Primitives.

FRANKLIN COUNTY

Chambersburg

Fayetteville

Fort Loudon

Green Castle

Mercersburg

Waynesboro

FRANKLIN COUNTY

Chambersburg

Gateway Gallery
643 Kriner Rd. (Exit 5 of I-81)
(717) 263-6512
Call for auction dates & times.

Open Hearth Antique Market
1495 Lincoln Way E.
(717) 261-1107
Multi-dealer co-op.

Fayetteville

Fayetteville Antique Market
3653 Lincoln Way E.
(717) 352-8485
Multi-dealer co-op.

Trader Todd's
3653 Lincoln Way E.
(717) 352-9411

Fort Loudon

M & M Antiques
& Flea Market
13324 Main St.
(717) 369-3997
Vic & oak furn.

Mountain Side Olde Stuff
3639 Lakeview Dr.
(717) 369-4488
Furn, glass & coll.

Greencastle

Greencastle Antique Mall
345 S. Washington St. Rear
(717) 597-3552
Multi-dealer co-op.

Myers' Classics
40 N. Washington St.
(717) 597-1609
General line.

Seekers Point
 Antique Center
I-80 Exit 3 & Pa Rt. 16
(717) 597-5400
Multi-dealer co-op.

Mercersburg

McCulloh's Antiques
Rt. 16
(1/2 mi. W. of Mercersburg)
(717) 328-9063
General line.

Waynesboro

Andy Antiques
32 E. Main St.
(717) 762-6595

LACKAWANNA COUNTY

Carbondale
Clarks Summit
Dalton
Dickson City
Dunmoore
Fleetville
Olyphant
Scranton
Taylor
Throop

LACKAWANNA COUNTY

Carbondale

Brierwood Antiques
251 Dundaff St.
(570) 282-4733

Ronald's Yesterday's &
Today's Antiques
40 N. Main St.
(570) 282-6034
Antiq & usd furn. Photos &
paper.

Clarks Summit

Carriage Barn Antiques
1550 Fairview Rd.
(570) 587-5405
Refinished furn & unusual dec
items.

Heritage House Shoppes
402 N. State St.
(570) 586-8575
Primitives.

R E Taylor's Cabinet
1311 Justus Blvd.
(570) 586-7270
Furn & Dep glass.

Dalton

Antiques & Uniques
200 Main St.
(570) 563-3056
Multi-dealer & artist co-op.

Pine Hill Antiques
Route 438
(570) 563-1709

Dickson City

Steve's Antiques
& Used Furnishings
721 Main St.
(570) 383-1656
20th c. usd furn.

Dunmore

Weinman's Antiques
202 E. Drinker St.
(570) 343-7065
Furn, costume jewlry & unusual items.

Fleetville

Appletree Antiques
Rt. 407
(1 mi. S of Fleetville)
(570) 945-9395
Pre-1900 country & period
furn w/ orig surface paint.

Country Corner Antiques
Rts. 107 & 407
(570) 945-3889
Furniture.

Cutler & Co. Antiques
Route 407
(570) 945-3747
Furn & dec.

Town 'n' Lake Auction
Route 107
(570) 945-5295
Call for auction dates & times.

Olyphant

Spirit Hill Antiques
RR1
(570) 563-0221

Scranton

ABC Antiques
268 N. Main Ave.
(570) 562-1662

ABC Antiques
1148 Philo St.
(570) 346-7842

Alma's Antiques
921 S. Webster Ave.
(570) 344-5945
General line.

Jones Treasure Chest
1712 Lafayette St.
(570) 344-6111
General line.

Jones' Antiques
1539 Dickson Ave.
(570) 347-2688
Furn, glass & china.

N B Levy's Jewelers
120 Wyoming Ave.
(570) 344-6187
Jewelry.

Originally Yours
1614 Luzerne St.
(570) 341-7600
Toys & dolls.

RIC & Art's Collectables
2436 N. Main Av.
(570) 347-2201
Furn, china, glass & linens.

Wildflower Antiques
700 A E. Market St.
(570) 341-0511
Furn, jewelry,
paintings & glass.

Taylor

Paradise Antiques
  & Used Furnishings
268 N. Main St.
(570) 451-3968

Ranger Grady's Toys
225 S. Main St.
(570) 562-0477
Vint toys, 1950-present.

Throop

Muto's Antiques
310 George St.
(570) 489-2933

LANCASTER COUNTY

Adamstown	Little Britain
Bainbridge	Manheim
Bart	Marietta
Bird In Hand	Middletown
Blue Ball	Millersville
Brickerville	Montville
Christiana	Mount Joy
Clay	Myerstown
Columbia	Neffsville
Denver	New Holland
Drumore	Paradise
East Earl	Quarryville
Elizabethtown	Reamstown
Ephrata	Reinholds
Gap	Ronks
Goodville	Schaefferstown
Lancaster	Soudersburg
Leola	Strasburg
Lititz	Willow Street

Adamstown Antique Mall

Route 272 N. of PA Tpk. Exit 21
Adamstown, PA 19501
Pottery, Glass, Paintings, Books
Advertising, Linens, Furniture & Military
Hours: Mon.-Thurs.-Fri. 10-5   717-484-0464
Sat.-Sun. 9-5, Closed Tues.-Wed.   Fax 717-484-4644

Adamstown

**Adamstown Antique Mall
Rt. 272
(717) 484-0464
5,000 square feet, 50 dealers offering: pottery, glass, paintings, books, advertising, linens, furniture & military items.
Hours: Sat & Sun 10-5, Daily 9-5, Closed Tues & Wed.**

Apple Works Antique Mall
Rt. 272
(717) 484-4404
Multi-dealer co-op.

Clock Tower Antiques
Behind Stoudtburg\Black Angus
(717) 484-2757
Multi-dealer co-op.

General Heath's Antiques
Rt. 272 & Calico Rd.
(717) 484-1300
Multi-dealer co-op.

Heritage I Antique Center
Rt. 272
(717) 484-4646
Multi-dealer co-op.

Heritage II Antique Center
Rt. 272
(717) 336-0888
Multi-dealer co-op.

Meade Antiques
Rt. 272
(717) 484-0669

Olde Smith Farm
Rt. 272
(717) 484-2611

Olley Valley Architectural
Rt. 272
(717) 35-3585
Architectural antiques & Vic furn.

Renningers Antique Market
Rt. 272
(717) 336-2177
Multi-dealer co-op.

Shupp's Grove
Rt. 897
(717) 484-4115
Outdoors only.

South Pointe Antiques
Rt. 272 & Denver Rd.
(717) 484-1026
Multi-dealer co-op.

Stoudtburg/ Black Angus
Rt. 272
(717) 484-4385
Multi-dealer co-op.

**Tex Johnson Antiques
40 Willow St.
(717) 484-4005
Furniture, porcelain, copper, fabrics, vintage clothing, silver, brass, prints. All pre-1900. Primitive to country to formal.**

The Country French
Collection
Rt. 272
(717) 484-0200
Country Fr furn.

The Ladies Shop
Rt. 272
(717) 484-1219

Bainbridge

Old Blacksmith Shop
15 S. 2nd St.
(717) 426-3842
19th c. Eng pine furn.

Bart

Oak Furniture & Antiques
Rt. 896
(717) 786-7852

Bird In Hand

Farmhouse Antiques
519 Beechdale Rd.
(717) 656-4854

Helen G. Warren
6878 Old Philadelphia Pk.
(717) 392-4233

Blue Ball

Carson's Country Stew
Rt. 322 & Grist Mill Rd.
(717) 354-7343
Painted furn, Folk art, prims &
smalls.

Brickerville

The 1857 Barn Antiques
Corner Rts. 501 & 322
(717) 626-5115
Multi-dealer co-op.

Nailor Antiques
Rt. 322
(717) 626-9508

Rice Antiques
Rt. 322
(1/4 mi. E. of Rt. 501)
(717) 627-3780
Early 19th thru 20th c. furn,
tall clocks & music boxes.

Christiana

Irion-Furnituremakers
1 S. Bridge St.
(610) 593-2153
Custom 18th c. furn.

Clay

Good's Collectibles
2460 W. Main St.
(717) 738-2033
Prims, furn, tin, iron &
unusual farm pieces.

Columbia

Angela House Antiques
401 Chesnut St.
(717) 684-4111
China, glass, Vic furn &
vint jewelry.

C.A. Herr Antiques
25-29 North 3rd St.
(717) 684-7850
Multi-dealer co-op.

Hobday's
3rd & Poplar St.
(717) 684-1888/684-7233
Fine art. Repro & antiq
furn.

Partners Antique Center
403 N. Third St.
(717) 684-5364
Two floors of antiques &
collectibles. Something
for everyone; serious col-
lector or novice. Open 7
days, 10-5. Ample free
parking & easy access.

Restorations Etc.
125 Bank Ave.
(717) 684-5454
Country furn, pre-1900.

Olde Carriage House Shoppe

A Quaint Country Gift Shop in the Village of Clay
2425 West Main Street, Ephrata, PA 17522 Ph. (717)733-1111
Sherrie L. Miller, Proprietor

The First National Bank
  Museum & Nora's Antiques
(717) 684-8864
Antique & art gallery.

Denver

Adams Antiques
2400 N. Reading Rd. (Rt. 272)
(717) 335-0001
Multi-dealer co-op.

Adamstown Antique Gallery
Rt. 272 (South)
(717) 335-3435
Multi-dealer co-op.

Antiques Showcase
  at the Blackhorse
2222 N. Reading
(717) 335-3300
Multi-dealer co-op.

Barr's Auction & Antiques
2152 N. Reading Rd.
(717) 336-2861
Euro, Dep & oak furn.
Glass & postcards.

**Covered Bridge Antiques
  & Collectibles
Rt. 272 (2-1/2 mi. S. of PA
trnpk., Exit 21)
(717) 336-4480
40 dealer co-op shop.**

**Wonderful mix of every-
thing from smalls to furniture. Open every day
from 9-5.**

Denver Fine Arts Gallery
Reading Rd. (Rt. 272)
(717) 484-4811
Fine art. Sunday or by
appt.

Lancaster County Antique Center
2255 N. Reading Rd. (Rt. 272)
(717) 336-2701
Multi-dealer co-op.

Drumore

Jockey Lot Antiques
  & Flea Market
1130 Lancaster Pk.
(717) 284-4984/284-4965
Multi-dealer co-op &
Flea market.

East Earl

Brossman's Valley Shoppe
462 Weaverland Valley
(717) 445-5771
18th & 19th c. country
& period furn & dec.

Elizabethtown

Furnace Hill
1 Centre Square
(717) 361-0400

Quilted Nest
386 Mt. Gretna Rd.
(717) 367-8434
Smalls, linens, small furn.

Ephrata

Grandma's Attic
1862 W. Main St.
(717) 733-7158
Painted furn, vint wicker &
braided & hooked rugs.

Mother Tucker's Antiques
566 N. Reading Rd.
(717) 738-1297
Multi-dealer co-op.

**Olde Carriage House
  Shop
2425 W. Main St.
(717) 733-1111
A quaint country gift
shop in the Village of
Clay. Offering: primitives
& country painted furn-
iture, crocks, jars, old
tin & new lighting.**

Summerhouse Antiques
1156 W. Main St.
(717) 733-6572/733-8989
By appointment only.

The Potting Shed
148 E. Farmersville Rd.
(717) 354-8484
Porch & garden pieces.

Gap

Don & Annie's Antique Row
Rt. 30
(between rts. 41 & 772)
(717) 442-3026
Furn, prims, coll & iron items.

N & N Sales
835 Rt. 41
(717) 442-4668

Rich Man, Poor Man
Rt. 30 (East)
(Next to Brass Eagle restaurant)
NO Phone

Goodville

School House Antiques
Main St. (Rt.23)
(717) 445-7384
Furn, stoneware, country
furn & Folk Art.

Lancaster

American Period Lighting
3004 Columbia Ave.
(717) 392-5649
Traditional & period lighting.

Carlos' Buy & Sell
339 W. Orange St.
(717) 299-0785
General line.

Estate Liquidations
1001 Lititz Ave.
(717) 399-8156
Gen line. By appt.

Fleckenstein's Gifts
738 Columbia Ave.
(717) 397-2585
Pottery, porc, pocket watches,
paintings & glassware.

Levi H. Hersey
2194 Old Philadelphia Pike
(717) 397-5794

Madison on Marietta
2435 Marietta Ave.
(717) 393-0990

Moongate Antiques
27 N. Prince St.
Lancaster, PA
(717) 393-9910
**The best & largest sel-
ection of Chinese antiques.
Offering: furniture, porcelain, pictures, scrolls,
cloisonne, lamps, wood
carvings & painted tiles.
Closed Sunday &
Monday.**

Olde Towne Interiors
224 W. Orange St.
(717) 394-6482

Pandora's Antiques
2014 Old Philadelphia Pk.
(717) 299-5305

Robert H. Linton
147 Bender Mill Rd.
(717) 872-4331
Handcrafted reproductions.

Steinmetz Coins & Currency
350 Centerville Rd.
717-299-1211/800-334-3903

The Book Haven
146 N. Prince St.
(717) 393-0920
Usd & rare books. Upstairs
gallery: ephemera.

The Buy & Sell Store
107 W. King St.
(717) 397-5542

The Stock Swap
1761-A Columbia Ave.
(717) 399-3638
Consignment shop.

Violet's Antiques
Hager Archade Bldg.
(717) 293-5710

Willcox Gallery
117 E. Chestnut St.
(717) 295-5414

Zap & Company
320 N. Queen St.
(717) 397-7405

Leola

Antiques & Uniques
110 W. Main St.
(717) 656-6978

Meadowbrook Farmers Market
W. Main St.
(717) 656-2226
Flea market Fri & Sat only,
year round.

Lititz

A Colorful Past
33 E. Main St.
(717) 627-7278
Stained glass, furn & coll.

Charlotte Heck Antiques
35 E. Main St.
(717) 627-0303
Consignment shop.

E.M. Murry Associates
23 N. Water St.
(717) 626-2636
Call for auction dates & times.

Eckman's Curiousity
  Warehouse
5 Juniper Lane
(717) 627-4978

Garthoeffner Gallery
122 E. Main St.
(717) 627-7998

H.B. Hardican Antiques
34 E. Main St.
(717) 627-460311/13
Quilts, textiles & country
smalls.

Heritage Map Museum
55 N. Water St.
(717) 626-5002
Maps, books, globes
& celestials.

Sue's Back Porch
6 Zum Anker Alley
(717) 625-2110
Prims & one-of-a-kind
twig furn.

Sylvan Brandt
653 Main St.
(717) 626-4520
18th & 19th c. building
materials.

The Workshop
945 Disston View Rd.
(717) 626-6031
Coll & prims.

Little Britain

Joy's Antiques
400 Nottingham Rd. (Rt. 272)
(717) 529-2693

Manheim

Conestoga Auction Company
768 Graystone Rd.
(717) 898-7284
Call for auction dates & times.

Exit 20 Antiques
3091 Lebanon Road
(Rt. 72 N.)
(717) 665-5008
Multi-dealer shop.

Gerald E. Noll
1047 S. Colebrook Rd.
(717) 898-8677

Manheim Country Store
   Antiques & Museum
60 N. Main St.
(717) 664-0022
Country store advertising &
furniture.

Stone Barn Antiques
Chiquies Rd.
(717) 898-1895

Marietta

Marietta Mobil Antiques
271 W. Market St.
(717) 426-2390

Perry House
30 E State St.
(717) 426-4560

Reminisce
1095 River Rd.
(717) 426-3000
General line.

Middletown

Days Gone By
Intersection Geyers
Church Rd. & Rt. 442
(717) 944-4934
Prims, smalls, motorcycle
mem & advertising.

Millersville

Birk's Antiques & Things
20 Sun Lane
(717) 872-4706/872-8959
Country & prim furn. Glass
& china.

Rock-A-Bye
138 W. Frederick St.
(717) 872-5990
General line.

Montville

Getz Antiques
2 E. Main St.
(717) 285-4301
Country furn & coll.

Mount Joy

Angelina'a Antique Shop
1195 W. Main St.
(717) 653-0505

White Horses Antiques
973 W. Main St
(Rt. 230)
(717) 653-6338
Multi-dealer co-op.

Myerstown

Union Canal Antique Mall
Rt. 422 (West)
(717) 866-7635

Neffsville

Dorothy Forster Antiques
2778 Lititz Pike (Rt. 501)
(717) 354-9153
Period & country furn.
China, tin, tools & prints.

Richard Hilton
2650 Lilitz Pike
(717) 569-6901

New Holland

Frederick & Sons
Fine Art
285 W. Main St.
717-354-8674/610-948-2254
Restorer of carousel horses.

School House Farm
Rt. 322
(717) 354-9153
Country furn & dec.

Witmer Quilt Shop
1070 W. Main St.
(717) 656-9526
New & antiq quilts.

Paradise

Brackbill's Country Antiques
3187 Lincoln Hwy. E. (Rt. 30)
(717) 687-6719
General line.

Ferree House
290 Old Leacock Rd.
(717) 768-7208
Small furn, stoneware,
redware, glass & dec.

H & H Auctions\Micklemine's
1904 Mine Rd.
(610) 593-5550
Call for auction dates & times.

JP Collectibles & Flea Market
Rt. 30 E.
(717) 442-8892

Lichty's Clock Shop
10 Cherry Hill Rd.
(717) 687-9243
Wall & mantel clocks.

Mary & Eds Upholstery
& Antique Shop
Rt. 30
(717) 687-8990

Paradise Primitives
3040 Lincoln Hwy. E.
(717) 687-9288
Multi-dealer co-op.

Paradise Village Antiques
3044 Lincoln Hwy. (East)
(717) 687-8089
Multi-dealer co-op.

Quarryville

Erma's Flower Shop
State St.
(717) 786-2512

Jayne's Antiques
27 E. State St.
(717) 786-8028
Glass, pottery, jewelry, furn &
coll.

Reamstown

The Doll Express, Inc.
Rt. 272
(717) 336-2414

Reinholds

Oley Valley Country Store
2684 N. Reading Rd.
(717) 484-2191

Ronks

Antique Barn
Rt. 30
(717) 687-7088

Dutch Barn Antiques
3272 W. Newport Rd.
(717) 768-3067
Spec: Lancaster county
farm antiques.

JA-Bar Enterprises
2812 Lincoln Hwy.
(717) 393-0098

Miller's Country Collectibles
215 Hartman Bridge Rd.
(717) 687-0490

**The Antique Market-
Place
2856 Lincoln Hwy East
(717) 687-6345
A warm & friendly 35
dealer cooperative under
the same management
since 1981. Quality
antiques & some col-
lectibles makes this a
regular stop for collec-
tors, browsers & dealers.**

Schaefferstown

Antiques on the Square
Main & Market Sts.
(717) 949-2819
Multi-dealer co-op.

Outlander Antiques
309 E. Main St.
(717) 949-2383

Soudersburg

**MR. 3L
(Leonard L. Lasko)
Rt. 30 East
(7 mi. E. of Lancaster)
(717) 687-6165
Unique large collectors'
Center. America's best
known dealer of collect-
ibles. Always buying,
selling & trading.**

Strasburg

Beechtree Antiques
1249 Penn Grant Rd.
(717) 687-6881
Am country furn, coll & prints.

Country Antiques
2855 Lincoln Hwy.
(717) 687-7088

Frey's Antiques
209 W. Main St.
(717) 687-6722
Furn, stoneware, china & glass.

Iron Star Antiques
53 W. Main St.
(717) 687-8027
By appointment.

Spring Hollow Antiques
121 Mt. Pleasant Rd.
Near Strasburg
(717) 687-6171
Gen line. Americana & textiles.

**Strasburg Antique
Market
At Rts. 741 & 896
(717) 687-5624
Quality Antiques in a re-
stored Tobacco Ware-
house. Over 40 dealers.
Open six days 10am to
5pm, Closed Tuesdays.**

Sugarbush Antiques
832 May Post Office Rd.
(717) 687-7179

Sweet Liberty Antique Center
1325 Village Rd.
(717) 687-9782

William Wood & Son
    Old Mill Emporium
215 Georgetown Rd.
(717) 687-6978

Willow Street

Aichele's Refinishing
366 Baumgardner Rd.
(717) 464-5244

Tomorrow's Treasures
2850 Willow St. Pk.
(717) 464-8675
Multi-dealer co-op.

LEBANON COUNTY

Annville

Campbelltown

Lebanon

Mount Gretna

Myerstown

Palmyra

LEBANON COUNTY

Annville

Antique Depot
1251 E. Main St.
717-867-4400/800-903-4077
Multi-dealer co-op &
flea market.

Campbelltown

Meadow View Antiques
RR 322 (Horseshoe Pk.)
1/2 mile E. of Campbelltown
(717) 838-9443
Multi-dealer co-op.

Silver Swan
1-1/2 miles S. on
Rt. 117 from 322
(717) 838-5292
Clocks, porc, china
& glass.

Lebanon

Dick's Antique Shop
518 East Cumberland St.
(717) 272-3991

Ginder's Wood Shop
& Antiques
1021 Cumberland St.
(717) 274-9797
Furn, brass, cast iron
& glass.

Kleinfelter Antiques
705 N. 3rd Ave. Rear
(717) 274-5067
Furn & smalls. By appt.

Kleinfelter Auction
105 N. Chapel St.
(717) 272-7078
Call for auction dates & times.

Tom's Gold & Silver Shop
23 S. 8th St.
(717) 273-1464

Mount Gretna

Ezell Auction Company
112 2nd St.
(717) 964-3780
Call for auction dates & times.

Myerstown

Union Canal Antique Mall
400 W. Lincoln Ave.
(Rt. 422)
(717) 866-8766
Multi-dealer co-op.

Palmyra

Tavern Treasures
601-1/2 Main St.
(717) 838-8703

LEHIGH COUNTY

Allentown
Bethlehem
Coopersburg
Emmaus
Fogelsville
Fullerton
New Smithville
New Tripoli
Slatington
Schnecksville
Whitehall
Zionsville

LEHIGH COUNTY

Allentown

Abe Ark Antiques
13th & Union
(610) 770-1454
General line.

Another Story
100 N. 9th St.
(610) 435-4433
Usd, rare & OP books,
1800's-1998.

Apple & Eve Antiques
2073 Walbert St.
(610) 821-9400
General line.

B & B Antiques
12 N. 7th St.
(610) 820-9588
General line.

Burick's Antiques
880 N. Graham St.
(610) 432-8966

Camelot Gallery
1518 Walnut St.
(610) 433-7744
Furn, prints, glass,china
silver & ephemera.

Cottage Crafters
Tighlman Shopping Center
4636 Broadway St.
(610) 366-9222
Multi-dealer co-op.

Duvall's Antiques
43 N. 9th St.
(610) 821-4878
By appt. only.

Estate Sales Inc.
Hamilton Blvd.
 & Minesite Rd.
(610) 366-8337

Golden Eagle Antiques
1425 Gordon St.
(610) 432-1223
Gen line. Curios,
prims & coll. By appt.

K D Smith Auctions
S. 12th & Vultee St.
(610) 797-1770
Call for auction dates & times.

Allentown Antiques
27 N. 10th St.
(610) 439-1117
Furn & smalls.

Little House Antiques
2705 S. Old Pike Ave.
(610) 791-2802

Lutz & Moyer
936 Allen St.
(610) 820-9924

Merchants Square Mall
S. 12th & Vultee St.
(610) 797-7743
Multi-dealer co-op.

Old Dreams
25 N. 10th St.
(610) 433-5077
Antiq & repro furn.

Pete's Used Furniture
 & Antiques
231 N. 7th St.
(610) 433-4481
Antiques & anything
from A to Z.

Toonerville Junction
 Antiques
522 Maple St.
(610) 435-8697
Antiques for men.

Bethlehem

Appleton's
2825 Cross Creek Rd.
(610) 866-9838
Hand-built 18th c. repro.

C & D Coin & Gun
125 E. Broad St.
(610) 865-4355

Opportunities Knock Twice
Third St.
(610) 866-8663

Splendid Choices
Rt. 378 & Walter Ave.
(610) 691-8311

Valley Antiques
731 W. Broad St.
(610) 865-3880
General line.

Wadsworth & Co.
107 E. Third St.
(610) 866-1577
19th c. furn.

Yesterday's Ltd.
2311 Center St.
(610) 691-8889
By appt. only.

Coopersburg

Liberty Metal Finishing
113 John Alley
(610) 282-1719
Antiq brass & copper items.

Emmaus

Lawsons Antiques
5386 Chestnut St.
(610) 966-4375
Spec: china, esp. Shelley.

Twin Jugs
4033 Chestnut St.
(610) 967-4010
General line.

Wotrings Auction Center
3320 Church St. (Rt. 873)
(610) 767-8610
Call for auction dates & times.

Fogelsville

Fogelsville Auction Center
Nursery St.
(610) 395-9643
Call for auction dates & times.

Schnecksville

Tom Hall Auctions
4644 Rt. 309 N.
(610) 799-0808
Call for auction dates & times.

Fullerton

Old Dairy Antique Village
105 Franklin St.
(610) 264-7626
Multi-dealer co-op.

Whitehall

Nejad Gallery Oriental Rugs
2350 MacArthur Rd.
(610) 776-0660
OR rugs.

New Smithville

Country Spice
3894 Blacksmith Rd.
(610) 285-6945
Oak & country furn.
Architecturals.

New Tripoli

W. S. Phillips
4555 Golden Key Rd.
(610) 285-6290
Tools & primitives.

Slatington

Charlotte's Web
1044 Main St.
(610) 760-8787
Gen line. Spec: pottery
& country store.

D. L . Stevens Antiques
560 Main St.
(610) 760-0685
Vic & country furn, glass,
frames & silver.

Lutz Moyer Antiques
200 Willow Ave.
(610) 760-1919
Furniture.

Zionsville

Zionsville Antique Mall
7567 Chestnut St.
(Rt. 100)
(610) 965-3292
The Lehigh Valley's
largest antique mall with
over 200 dealers in
30,000+ sq. ft. offering
thousands of antiques &
collectibles. Dining facili-
ties on premises. South of
Allentown, North of
Philadelphia & North-
east of Adamstown.

LUZERNE COUNTY

Ashley

Dallas

Exeter

Harvey's Lake

Hazleton

Kingston

Lehman

Luzerne

Plymouth

Shavertown

Sweet Valley

Sybertsville

West Pittston

White Haven

Wilkes Barre

Wyoming

LUZERNE COUNTY

Ashley

Action Auction Company
43 S. Main St.
(570) 822-8249
Multi-dealer shop &
auction house.

Dallas

Hitching Post Antiques
Tunkhannock Hwy.
(Rt. 309)
(570) 675-0721
Victoriana. Furn, china,
glass, jewlry, art, silver.

Major Antiques
Market St.
(570) 675-2991
Spec: primitive furn.

Things of Old
4 Carr Ave.
(717) 674-5461
Furn, toys, linens, glass,
clocks.

Travers Auction
66 Pine Crest Ave.
(570) 674-2631
Call for auction dates & times.

Exeter

Alley Antiques
164 Lincoln St., Rear
(570) 654-1469
Jewlry, pottery, art, glass,
silver, linens, metalwork.

The Dining Room Center
246 Rt. 11 (Wyoming Ave.)
570-655-5535
Multi-dealer co-op.

Harveys Lake

Back In Time Antiques
RR 1 Box 357
(717) 639-2666

Hazleton

Mariano's Furniture
1042 N. Church St.
(570) 455-0397
Antiq & vint furn. Glass,
vint clothing & china.

Remember When
21-23 W. Broad St.
(570) 454-8465
Spec: costume jewlry &
vint clothing, 1880-1960s .

Kingston

Betty A. Thompson
1407 Wyoming Ave.
(570) 287-1246
Vic furn, prims & glass.

Oblen Antiques
133 Division St.
(570) 283-5151
General line.

Lehman

Bess Barn Antiques
150 Market St.
(570) 675-1025
Clocks & Furn.

Luzerne

Collector's Corner
242 Main St.
(570) 288-3094

Plymouth

Antiques Warehouse
5 Smith Lane
(570) 779-2430
Furn & restoration.

Today's Treasures
10 E. Main St.
(570) 779-2929

Shavertown

Bay Window Shops
100 E. Overbrook Rd.
(570) 675-6400
Multi-dealer co-op.

Quilt Racque
183 N. Main St.
(570) 675-0914

Sweet Valley

Mountain View Barn
Route 118
Between Dallas & Benton
(570) 477-2483
Furniture. By chance or appt.

Sybertsville

Howel's Antique Flea Market
Route 93
(570) 788-1255

West Pittston

Antiques & Non
415 Wyoming Ave.
(570) 654-9585
Multi-dealer co-op.

Glass Factory
417 Wyoming Ave.
(570) 654-3310
Stained glass.

White Haven

Maggie Mae's
  Now & Then Shop
218 Main St.
(570) 443-0841

Wilkes Barre

AAG International
1266 Sans Souci Pkwy. #B
(570) 822-5300
Spec: Military items.
By appt.

Grazio's Antiques
6 Loomis Park
(570) 735-6680

Mike's Library
92 S. Main St.
(717) 822-7585
Books.

Olde Tyme Photos
111 Park Ave.
(570) 826-1434
Spec: historic photos
of NE PA.

Wyoming

Antiques by Carpet Concepts
58 Wyoming Ave.
(570) 693-7575
Furn, glass, china, porc
& toys.

Monument Antique Center
828 Wyoming Ave.
(570) 693-9309
General line.

Rielly & Jenks Inc.
79 Wyoming Ave.
(570) 693-5592
Early Am. pottery &glass.
18th & 19th c. furn & dec.

MONROE COUNTY

Blakeslee

Brodheadsville

Canandensis

Delaware Water Gap

East Stroudsburg

Long Pond

Marshall's Creek

Minisink Hills

Mountainhome

Saylorsburg

Sciota

Snydersville

Stroudsburg

Swiftwater

MONROE COUNTY

Blakeslee

Enchanted Cottage
Route 115
(570) 646-7464
Jewelry, glass & restored furn.

Maggie Mae's
Blakeslee Village
Shopping Center
Rts. 940 & 115
(570) 646-4888
Antiq & usd furn, art, glass,
china & books.

Pocono Auction
Rt. 115 & 940
(570) 646-6555
Call for auction dates & times.

Brodheadsville

Rinker Antiques
Village Edge Dr.
(570) 992-6957
Oak furn, old lighting,
prims & coll.

Canandensis

Marli's Arts & Antiques
RR 447
(570) 595-3876
Country furn, prints &
paintings.

The Village Gold &
  Silversmith
Rt. 447 @ light
(570) 595-3200
Jewelry.

Wooden Horse Antiques
Skytop Rd.
(570) 595-0303
Porc & early Am furn.

Delaware Water Gap

Tattered Elegance Antiques
Main St. (At the MArketplace)
(570) 424-8412
Porc, bisque & glass. Prims,
books & art.

East Stroudsburg

J & K Antiques
Independence Rd.
(570) 421-7524
Gen line. Spec: usd Lionel
trains.

Little Flea
766 Milford Rd.
(570) 424-2456
Furn, glass, china, books &
paper.

The Old Buggy Marketplace
Rt. 209 Marshall's Creek
(570) 588-4581
Multi-dealer center.

Long Pond

Cottage At Long Pond
Highway 115
(570) 646-9685
Country furn.

Marshalls Creek

Jean Yetter's Year
  Round Yard Sale
RR 5 Rt. 209
(570) 223-7511
Furn, glass, china
& vint clothing.

Log Cabin Antiques
RD 8 Creek Rd.
(570) 223-0307
Oak, primitive & Vic furn.

Pocono Bazaar, Inc.
Rt. 209 North
(570) 223-8640
Multi-dealer center
& flea market.

Minisink Hills

Buttermilk Falls Antiques
I-80, Exit 52, Rt. 209 N.
(570) 421-3326
Multi-dealer shop.

Country Things & Stuff
River Rd.
(570) 421-4447
Genral line.

Kerrs' Antiques
Old Mill Rd.
(570) 424-0838
Early lighting & tools.

Mountainhome

Mountainhome Antiques
Rt. 390
(570) 595-8581
Gen line. Spec: primitives.

The Other Woman
Rt. 191 & 390
(570) 595-7484
Vic, country, primitive &
Deco.

Saylorsburg

Apple Orchard Antiques
Route 115
(570) 992-9994

Sciota

Collector's Cove Ltd.
Route 33 & 29 S.
(570) 992-9161
Multi-dealer center.
Sundays only.

Corner Antiques
Business Rt. 209
(717) 992-4893
General line.

Whispers In Time
Fenner Ave.
(570) 992-9387
General line.

Yestertiques Antique Center
Rt. 209 & Bosserdsville Rd.
(570) 922-6576
Oak & Vic. furn. & dec.

Snydersville

Addded Touch
Bus Rt. 209 S.
(570) 992-7070
General line.

Wakefield Antiques
Bus Rt. 209 & Rim Rock Dr.
(570) 992-7226
General line.

Stroudsburg

Eleanor's Antiques
809 Ann Street
Stroudsburg, PA 18360
(570) 424-7724
General line.

Ibis Antiques
517 Main St.
(570) 424-8721
19th & early 20th c. furn &
dec.

Lea Katz Zubow
Route 209 S.
(570) 992-5462
General line.

Paper From The Past
300 Main St.
(570) 476-6240
Ephemera: postcards, peri-
odicals, newpaprs & mags.

Karen Larsen
Cherry Valley Rd. RD 1
(570) 992-4335
General line.

Lavender & Lace
350 Main St.
(570) 424-7087
Gen line. Spec: Vic.

Olde Engine Works
62 N. 3rd St.
(570) 421-4340
Multi-dealer co-op.

Olde Vinegar Works
70 Storm St.
570-421-4441
Multi-dealer co-op.

Swiftwater

Kelly Antiques
RT. 611
(570) 839-9389
Furn & dec.

NORTHAMPTON COUNTY

Bangor

Bath

Easton

Hellertown

Mount Bethel

Nazareth

Northampton

Portland

Richmond

Tatamy

Windgap

NORTHAMPTON COUNTY

Bangor

Carol's Collectables
136 Messinger St.
(610) 588-0333
Furn, oak, prims & smalls.

Clover Hill Dolls
81 Autumn Dr.
(570) 897-7034
Bisque dolls, pre-1920.

Hartzell's Auction Gallery
521 Richmond Rd.
(610) 588-5831
Call for auction dates & times.

Bath

Grandma Patty's Antiques
151 N. Chestnut St.
(610) 837-9633
Vic furn, glass, linens,
vint lighting.

Steckel House Antiques
Chestnut & Northampton St.
(610) 837-1660
Prims, stoneware, prints,
smalls, furn, ironware.

Easton

Barry' s New
    & Used Furniture
500 Northampton St.
(610) 250-0220
Gen line, usd & antiq.

Brick House Antiques
1116 Northampton St.
(610) 515-8010
Gen line.

Cottage Crafters
Northampton Crossing
(Rt. 33 & 248)
(610) 330-9903
Multi-dealer co-op.

Granny's Cupboard
200 Northampton St.
(610) 252-6766
Multi-dealer co-op.

Quadrant Book Mart
20 N. 3rd St.
(610) 252-1188
Books.

The Eagle's Nest
1717 Butler St.
(610) 258-4092
Stained glass lamps. Vic
-style linens & lace. China
crystal & silver.

Hellertown

Buddy K. Toys
20 Furham St.
(610) 838-6505
Toys.

Mount Bethel

Chris's Barn Antiques
Rt. 611
(610) 599-1064
Coll, usd furn, glass
& jewelry.

Country Doctor Antiques
772 S. Delaware Ave.
(Rt.611)
(610) 588-8995
Prims, toys, furn & coll.

Family Tree Antiques
Rt. 611
(610) 897-5683

Rum Corners Antiques
Potomac Street & Route 611
(570) 897-6073

Nazareth

Dotta Auction Co., Inc.
330 W. Moorestown Rd.
(Rt. 512)
(610) 433-7555
Call for auction dates & times.

Flamisch Antiques
694 Heyer Mill Rd.
(610) 759-6438
Oak, walnut & mahogony
furn. Glass & coll.

Gostony's Auction Center
1035 Bushkill Center Rd.
610- 759-5674/800-368-7761
Call for auction dates & times.

Nazareth Auction Center
Rt. 512
(610) 759-7389
Call for auction dates & times.

Old Red School House
543 Rose Inn Ave.
(610) 759-6622
Oak furn. By appt.

R & R Emporium
214 S. Main St
(610) 759-5610

Northampton

Carol Simcoe
2015 Main St.
(610) 262-7448
30's Ice Cream Parlor items.
Garden accents & art &coll.

Irons Antiques
223 Covered Bridge Rd.
(610) 262-9335
Country oak furn, prims,
quilts, folk art.

NORTHAMPTON COUNTY, PA

Northampton Coin
  & Jewelry Exchange
1918 Center St.
(610) 262-0759
Coll, coins & jewlry,
watches & Indian Artifacts

Portland

Graystone Collectiques
511 Delaware Ave. (Rt. 611)
(570) 897-7170
Country to classic furn
& smalls.

Knot Necessarily Antiques
501 Delaware Ave.
(570) 897-5606/897-7140
Oak furn, pinball machines,
RR mem, train & glass.

Indian Joe Curios
Delaware Ave.
No Phone

Kidd's Variety Depot
426 Delaware Ave.
(570) 897-0172
Antiq repro-all periods,
all styles.

Long Ago Antiques
Delaware Ave.
(570) 897-0407
Gen line,1800's - 1960's

Portland Antiques
Delaware Ave. (Rt. 611)
(570) 897-0129
Gen line, 1800's -1960's

Richmond

Richmond Antiques
Rt. 611
(610) 588-0861
Antiq lighting, toys,
furn & advertising.

Tatamy

A.B. C Barn
336 Bushkill St.
(610) 253-8295
Multi-dealer co-op.

Windgap

Gerry's Brass
  & Copper Finishing
464 Albert Rd.
(610) 863-9458
Vint lighting, gas, oil &
early electric. Restorer.

PIKE COUNTY

Greentown
Lake Teekuskung
Milford

PIKE COUNTY

Greentown

Singer's Antiques
RR 1 Box 405
(570) 676-3215

Lake Teekuskung

Teedytiques
at Lake Teekuskung
next to Woodlock Pines
(570) 685-7807
Spec: glass. Esp: Art Glass
& Vasoline glass

Milford

AAA Quality Antiques
100 Bennett Ave.
(570) 296-6243
Gen lin. Spec: oak frun.

Antiques of Milford
216 Broad St.
(570) 296-4258

Clockworks
319 Broad St.
(570) 296-5236
Clocks & watches.

Elizabeth Restucci's
214 Broad St.
(570) 296-2118
Jewelry.

Patina Antiques
320 Broad St.
(570) 296-1128
Antq & new furn
& dec.

Pear Alley Antiques
220 Broad St.
(570) 296-8919
General line.

School House Gallery
202 Broad St.
(570) 296-2223
Gen line. Spec: paintings,
prints & Majolica.

SCHUYLKILL COUNTY

Andreas
Frackville
Llewellyn
McKeansburg
New Ringold
Orwigsburg
Pottsville
Tamaqua

SCHUYLKILL COUNTY

Andreas

Red Barn Antiques
RR1 Box 2
(570) 386-4563

Frackville

Anna's Antiques
818 W. Pine St.
(570) 874-2094
General line.

Black Diamond Antiques
Schuylkill Mall
Rt 61 & I-81
(570) 874-7545
Multi-dealer mall.

Llewellyn

Antique & Collectible
    Cooperative
Rt 209
(570) 544-5520
Multi-dealer shop.

McKeansburg

McKeans Shop
S. Main St.
(570) 943-7752
General line.

New Ringold

Dog House
Water Tower Antique Mall
203 Feger St.
(570) 943-2398
Advertising.

Water Tower Antique Mall
203 Feger St.
(570) 943-2398
Multi-dealer mall.

Orwigsburg

Old County Seat
419 E. Market St.
(570) 366-2334
General line.

Pottsville

Bernie's Antiques
313 W. Market St.
(570) 622-7747

Blum Auction Service
2500 West End Ave.
(570) 622-3089
Call for auction dates & times.

Curious Goods
556 N. Centre St.
(570) 622-2173
Gen line. Spec: advertising &
beer related items.

Curran Collection
10 N. Centre St.
(570) 628-2244

Dave & Julies
    Then & Now
16 N. Centre St.
(570) 628-2838

Tamaqua

Hometown Coins
    & Collectibles
Rt. 309
(570) 668-6697
Coins & military objects.

WAYNE COUNTY

Beach Lake

Damascus

Equinunk

Hamlin

Hawley

Honesdale

Lake Ariel

South Sterling

WAYNE COUNTY

Beach Lake

Depression Glass Shop
Main St.
(570) 729-7393
Glass, lamps, clocks,
prints & coll.

Damascus

Log House Antiques
State Route 1025
Between Rts. 191 & 371
(570) 224-4805

Equinunk

Kellams Bridge Antiques
RR1
(570) 224-2781

Hamlin

Antique Musical Machines
RR 5
(570) 689-7263
Anything that plays music
automatically. By appt.

Glass Hat/Village Attic
Route 191
(570) 689-9524
Gen lin. Spec: glassware.

Hawley

Antiques & Collectibles
202 Main Ave.
(570) 226-9524
Art, pottery, miniatures,
china, glass, jewlry & furn.

Barbara's Books
730 Hudson St.
(570) 226-9021
Rare, Op books. Postcards
& prints.

Calla Lily Antiques
225 Bellemonte Ave.
(570) 226-7336

Castle Antiques &
Reproduction
515 Welwood Ave.
(570) 226-8550
Antiq & repro furn.

Country Classics Antiques
209 Belmont Ave. (Rt. 6)
(570) 226-8853
Country furn & dec.

Decorator's Den &
Resale Company
Route 6
(570) 226-0440

Hawley Antique Exchange
209 Belmont Ave. (Rt. 6)
(570) 226-1711
Multi-dealer co-op.

Hawley Antique Center
318 Main Ave.
(717) 226-8990
Multi-dealer co-op.

Loft Antiques
Rt. 590
(570) 226-685-4267
19th & early 20th c. furn,
prints, china, & glass.

Richmond Antiques
Rt. 590
(570) 226-5222
Gen line. Spec: old post-
cards, stamps, advertis-
ing & other ephemera.

Timely Treasures
475 Welwood Ave. (Rt. 6)
(570) 226-2838
Furn & dec.

Honesdale

Annn Lynch
410 Broad St.
(570) 253-6732
Early 19th c. Am country furn.

Morobito Auction Company
Rt. 6 & 652
(570) 253-7288
Call for auction dates & times.

Robert Williams Antiques
Rt. 191 2 mi. N. of Honesdale
(570) 253-4564
18th & 19th c. country furn.

Schroeder's Antiques
2 mi W. of Honesdale
(570) 253-0637
Glass, china, small furn & dec.

The Country Auction
4 mi. S. of Honesdale
(570) 253-6313
Call for auction dates & times.

Used Furniture Gallery
Rt. 6 & 652
(570) 253-7288
Gen line.

Lake Ariel

CYS Unusual Antiques
144 Maple Ave.
(570) 698-8635
Toys & unusual antiques.

Doug Schmitt Antiques
Tresslarville Rd.
(570) 698-6694

South Sterling

Nancy's Barn & Gift
Rt. 191
(570) 676-3032
Gen line.

WYOMING COUNTY

Laceyville
Nicholson
Tunkhannock

WYOMING COUNTY

Laceyville

Indian Hill Antiques
Rt. 6
(570) 869-1850
Furn, prims, jewlry,
glass & advertieing.

Nicholson

Rivenburg Auction Gallery
Rt. 11
(570) 942-6622
Call for auction dates & times.

Tunkhannock

Apple Wagon Antique Mall
Rt. 6
(570) 836-8713
Multi-dealer shop.

Bygones Antiques
8 W. Tioga St.
(570) 836-5815
China, glass, jewelry,
coll & furn.

Dale Myers Antiques
Rt. 29
(570) 836-1582
General line.

K's Mercantile
Rt. 29 (6 miles S. of town)
(570) 836-4420
General line.

La Torre's Antiques
Rt. 6
(2.5 miles W. of town)
(717) 836-2021
Roseville pottery & clocks.

Old Store
Historic Rt. 6
(570) 836-6088
Gen eral line.

Silver Sleigh Antiques
Bowmans Creek & Rt. 29
(570) 298-2360
General line.

W D Kreckman Antiques
139 State Rt. 1001
(570) 836-4076
Pottery, furn, coll, china
& glass.

YORK COUNTY

Brogue
Dallastown
Delta
Dillsburg
Dover
Etters
Felton
Glen Rock
Hanover
Hellam
Lewisberry
Menges Mill
Mt. Wolf
New Park
Railroad
Red Lion
Shrewsbury
Stewartstown
Thomasville
Yoe
York

YORK COUNTY

Brogue

Country Traditions
Collinsville Rd.
(717) 927-8047
Country oak furn & coll.

Dallastown

Bob's Antiques
209 E. Main St.
(717) 244-6810
Oak furn.

Park Hill Reflection
370 E. Main St.
(717) 246-3936

Delta

Calico Medley
823 Main St.
(717) 456-7207
Gen line. Spec: Oak furn.

Dillsburg

B & J Antique Mall
14 Franklin Church Rd.
(Off Rt. 15 S.)
(717) 432-7353
Multi-dealer shop.

Spring House Antiques
117 N. Baltimore St.
(717) 432-5053
General line of antiques,
with a flavor of Victor-
ian, displayed in a
Victorian house
(2 floors) Open Wed-
Sat 10-5 and Sun 1-5.

Dover

Olde Country Things
5501 Carlisle Rd.
(717) 292- 6251

Etters

L & B Antiques & Things
2365 Old Trail Rd.
(717) 938-0788
Furn, glass, smalls,
jewlry& coll.

The Barn
1285 Pines Rd.
(717) 938-8001
General line.

Felton

Louis G. Schmidt
298 Cross Mill Rd.
(717) 993-9028
Tools & ironware.

Glen Rock

Cold Spring Antique Mall
55 Main St.
(717) 235-8560
Multi-dealer co-op.

Hanover

Black Rose
At North Hanover Mall
115 Carlisle St.
(717) 632-0589
Multi-dealer co-op.

Hanover Theatre Antiques
37 Frederick St.
(717) 633-1148

Longhouse Antiques
1521 Carlisle Pike
(717) 633-1994

Markle's Antique Shop
1949 Baltimore Pike
(717) 637-7897
General line.

Nancy's Now & Then
1020 Beck Mill Rd.
(717) 632-9555

Richard Ownen's
234 Frederick St.
(717) 630-8176
19th c. furn & dec.

Route 94 Antiques
506 S. Franklin St.
(717) 633-5841
Prims & country store ad-
vertising.

Times Passed
9 Center Square
(717) 630-8262
Coll & Folk Art.

Hellam

Nubbintown Mill
Krevtz Creek Rd.
(717) 757-3154

Lewisberry

Lewisberry Antiques
& Craft Company
206 Market St. (Rt. 177)
(717) 938-3200
Multi-dealer shop.

Menges Mill

Colonial Valley
Flea market
Rt. 116
(410) 472-2701
Sunday flea markets.

Mt. Wolf

Little House At
Lieberknecht
245 Chestnut St. Ext.
(717) 266-4410

New Park

New Park Cow Palace
Marsteller Rd.
(717) 993-0147
Sat & Sun flea markets.

Railroad

Railraod General Store
4 E. Main St.
(717) 235-3360

Red Lion

Angie's Country Corner
680 Chapel Church Rd.
(717) 244-8783
General line.

Antiques On Main Street
30 N. Main St.
(717) 246-8026
Gen line, early 1800s-1950s.

Family Heirloom Weavers
(717) 246-2431
Repair, restore & sell textiles.

**Red Lion Antique Center
59 S. Main St.
(717) 244-8126
Open Tues-Sat 10-5,
Sun 12 Noon-5, Closed
Mondays. Featuring
clocks, glassware, prima-
tives, jewelry, reference
books, Howard products
and used books.**

Auction Hall. Stop by.

Southwood Antiques
Springwood Rd. & Locust St.
(717) 244-0979
Oak, walnut & mahogany,
1800's-1900's. All styles.

Shrewsbury

A Place In Time
39 E. Forrest Ave.
(717) 235-9183
General line.

Another Time Vintage Apparel
49 N. Main St.
(717) 235-0664
Antiq & vint clothing,
Vic-1950s.

**Antiques on
Shrewsbury Square
2 N. Main St.
(717) 235-1056 or 2006
Premier 3,000 sq. ft. shop,
all antiques, open daily
10 to 5. See our 130 year
old Tinsmithing shop.
One mile West of
exit 1 off I-83.**

Forget-Me-Not
42 N. Main St.
(717) 235-0737
Prims, country furn, glass &
coll.

Full Count Antiques
21 N. Main St.
(717) 235-4200
Multi-dealer co-op.

Kristy's of Shrewsbury
19 S. Main St.
(717) 235-8577

Olde Towne Antiques
10 N. Main St.
(717) 227-0988

Shrewsbury Antique Center
65 N. Highland Dr.
(717) 235-6637
Multi-dealer co-op.

Sixteen North
Main Antiques
16 N. Main St.
(717) 235-3448
Furn & dec. Orig restored
telephones.

Village Studio Antiques
13 N. Main St.
(717) 227-9428

Village Treasures
3 A Main St.
(717) 235-5111
Spec: Toys.

Long's Antiques
36 N. Main St.
(717) 235-9170
Vic & Empire furn.
Coll & prints.

Patrick's Antique Emporium
8 S. Main
(717) 235-9049
Multi-dealer co-op.

Main St. Exchange
23 S. Main
(717) 235-0805

Stewartstown

Liz's Antiques
6876 Hickory Rd.
(717) 993-3241
General line.

Thomasville

Helen's Antiques
R1 Box 107 (10 mi. West of York
(717) 225-5121
General line.

Yoe

Dora's Antiques
69 N. Main St.
(717) 456-7207
Furn & coll.

York

1st Capital Antiques
736 E. Market St.
(717) 845-4255
19th & 20 th c. furn.
Dep glass, prims & dec.

Alley Cats
34 West Clark Ave.
(717) 854-6719
Spec: vint clothing,
late 1800's-1950's.

Antique Center of York
190 Arsenal Rd.
(717) 846-1994
Multi-dealer co-op.

Armory Antiques
380 W. Market St.
(717) 845-3960
Firearms, militaria, glass,
china & pottery.

Dec-Art Antiques
1419 W. Market St.
(717) 854-6192

Dennis's Antiques
1779 W. Market St.
(717) 845-2418
18th, 19th & 20th c.
furn & dec.

Historic York Inc.
Architectural Warehouse
224 N. George St.
(717) 854-7152
Salvaged architectural
pieces.

J & J Pitt
2406 N. Sherman Ave.
(717) 755-4535
Spec: vint furn & coll.

Kathryn's Place
38 N. George St.
(717) 846-4015
General line.

Kelly's Used Furniture
228 W. Market St.
(717) 848-1023

Kennedy's Antiques
4290 W. Market St.
(717) 792-1920
General line.

Kindig Antiques
325 W. Market St.
(717) 848-2760

Leon Ness Jewelry Barn
2695 S. George St.
(717) 741-1113
Jewlry, fine & costume,
1850-1950.

Mary Mac's Antiques
130 W. Market St.
(717) 755-5741

My Romance Antiques
2389 E. Prospect St.
(717) 757-3177

Ralph's Place
4350 W. Market St.
(717) 792-5531
Antiq, new & usd furn.

Toni's Antiques
5210 N. Susquehanna Trail
(717) 266-3435

Wish-N-Want
4230 N. Susquehanna Trail
(717) 266-5961
General line.

York Emporium
343 W. Market St.
(717) 846-2866
Co-op. Spec: usd
& rare books.

NEW JERSEY

Atlantic County
Bergen County
Burlington County
Camden County
Cape May County
Cumberland County
Essex County
Gloucester County
Hudson County
Hunterdon County
Mercer County
Middlesex County
Monmouth County
Morris County
Ocean County
Passaic County
Salem County
Somerset County
Sussex County
Union County
Warren County

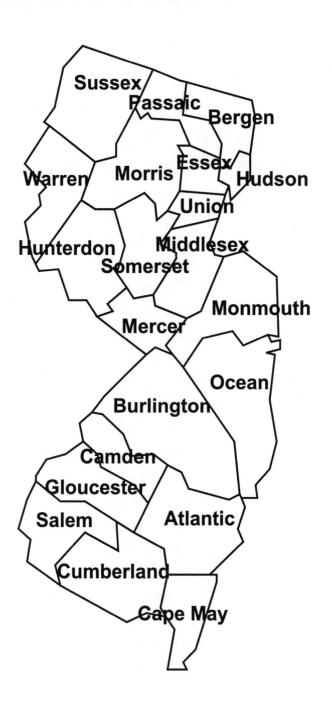

New Jersey Counties

ATLANTIC COUNTY

Absecon
Atlantic City
Egg Harbor
Hammonton
Margate
Mays Landing
Mizpah
Oceanville
Pleasantville
Richland
Scullville
Smithville
Somers Point
Sweetwater
Ventnor
West Atlantic City

ATLANTIC COUNTY NEW JERSEY

Absecon

Cobweb Corner & Seascape
6th Ave. & White Horse Pike
(609) 748-2522
Gen line: 75,000 items.

Atlantic City

Bayside Basin Antiques
800 N. New Hampshire
Historic Gardener's Basin
(609) 347-7143
Gen line. Spec: art, Am
Indian artifcts & Or rugs.

Ed's Used Furniture & Antiques
915 Atlantic Ave.
(609) 344-9758

**Princeton Antiques
  Bookshop
2915, 2917, 2931 & 2933
Atlantic Ave.
(609) 344-1943
FX:344-1944
Five shops full of: oils,
watercolors, oriental rugs
& ceramics, china,Am &
Euro pottery, lamps & furn.
SPEC: 240,000 BOOKS IN
STOCK & OFFER BOOK
LOCATING SERVICE;
75% chance of finding books
w/in 45 days. Est. 1967.
Website: www.princetn.com
e-mail:princetn@earthlink.net
By Appt. Only**

Egg Harbor

Heinholdt Books
1325 W. Central Ave.
(609) 965-2284
Out of print books. Spec: NJ
& local history publications.

Hammonton

Almost New
133 Bellevue Ave. (Rt. 54)
(609) 704-9221
Used furn.

The Last Stop
N. Egg Harbor Rd.
(609) 561-7201
Consignment shop.

Silver Plating
  of South Jersey
503 White Horse Pike
(609) 567-2239

Margate

The Estate Sale
8001 Ventnor Ave.
(609) 823-3209
Consignment shop.

Mays Landing

Gravelly Run Antiquarians
5045 Mays Landing Rd.
(609) 625-7778
Books only.

Mizpah

The Potpourri Gallery
6953 Rt. 40 (Harding Hwy.)
(609) 476-2667
Late 18th c.-1930's furn,
glass & mantel clocks.

Oceanville

Seafarer Antiques
Rt. 9 & Lilly Lake Rd.
(609) 652-9491
Spec: maritime/nautical.
Custom furn from ship salvg.

Pleasantville

Consignment Galleries
10 E. Verona Ave.
(Black Horse Pike)
(609) 646-5353
Consignment shop.

Doc's Furniture Mart
881 Black Horse Pike
(609) 641-5079
Gen line: new, usd & antiq.

Moni Mire Gift Attic
1008 S. New Rd.
(609) 646-7841
1920s-1930s: glass, furn,
china & prints.

Richland

Goodstuff's
1343 Harding Hwy. (Rt.40)
(856) 697-8500
General line.

Scullville

The Red Garagee
1769 Rt. 559
Mays Landing-Somers Pt. Rd.
(609) 653-0097

Smithville

Country Folk
Rt. 9
(609) 652-6161
Country & Vic furn.
Architecturals.

**Days of Olde
110 S. Rt. 9
(1 mile S. of Historic
Smithville & 9 miles N. of
Atlantic City.)
(609) 652-7011**

Largest co-op in South Jersey; 16,000 sq. ft. of quality antiques & collectibles. 75+ dealers. Open 7 days, 11-5.

Rose of Sharon Antiques
Village Green at Smithville
615 E. Moss Mill Rd.
(609) 652-6300

The Town of Historic Smithville
& The Village Greene
Rt. 9 & Moss Mill Rd.
(609) 652-7777
A variety of antique shops
housed in historic buildings.

Somers Point

A Antiques & Estate Buyers
811-817 Shore Rd.
(609) 927-7897

Anything Collectible
812-B Shore Rd.
(609) 927-3809

Olde Bay Shoppe
Mays Landing Rd.
(609) 927-8081

Sweetwater

Shops at Sweetwater Casino
7th Ave. (Off Rt. 643)
(609) 965-4222
Multi-dealer co-op.

Ventnor

Antiques and More
6405 Ventnor Ave.
(609) 823-8889

Black Bird Antiques
6510 Ventnor Ave.
(609) 823-0233
Fr, Eng & Germ porc. Cut
glass, colored glass. Jewlry.

West Atlantic City

Beacon Street Shops
7006 Black Horse Pike
(609) 646-9382
Gen line. Spec: antiq & repro
lighting. Stained glass.

BERGEN COUNTY

Allendale
Bergenfield
Bogota
Cliffside Park
Closter
Englewood
Fairview
Garfield
Glen Rock
Hackensack
Hasbrouck Heights
Hillsdale
Ho Ho Kus
Lodi
Lyndhurst
Mahwah
Midland Park

Montvale
Moonachie
Norwood
North Bergen
Oakland
Oradel
Paramus
Ramsay
Ridgefield
Ridgewood
River Edge
Rutherford
Saddle River
Teaneck
Tenafly
Westwood
Wyckoff

BERGEN COUNTY NEW JERSEY

Allendale

Now & Then
140 W. Allendale Ave.
(201) 934-1440
General line.

Bergenfield

Ambiance Antiques
by Larry A. Wenzel
79 N. Washington Ave.
(201) 385-1111
General line.

Antique Corner
50 W. Church St.
(201) 384-8001
General line.

Old Curiousity Shop
100 Portland Ave.
(201) 387-7799
Multi-dealer shop & auction
house. Call for dates & times.

The Book Stop
52 S. Washington Ave.
(201) 384-1162
Rare & out of print books.

Bogota

Advalorem Books
14 E. Fort Lee Rd.
(201) 525-1828
Books only.

Cliffside Park

Stan's Antiques
583 Anderson Ave.
(201) 945-4679
Furn, glass & paintings.

Closter

Antique D'Zynes
70 Herbert Ave.
(201) 768-8844
19th c. Fr furn & dec.

Canterbury Mews Gallery
105 Closter Plaza
(201) 767-2300
Furn, porc, glass & paintngs.

Englewood

Antiques By Ophir Gallery
33 Park Place
(201) 871-0424
Spec: Tiffany & Art Nouveau.

Bizet Antiques
& Unusual Finds
6 S. Dean St.
(201) 568-5345
Antiqs & unusuals, Vic-1940's.

Chelsea Square Inc.
10 Depot Square & Dean St.
(201) 568-5911
Fr country pine furn & dec.

Crown House Antiques
39 E. Palisade Ave.
(201) 894-8789
19th & 20th c. Eng & Fr
furn. Pottery,1920's & 1930s.

Jewel Spiegel Galleries
49 N. Dean St.
(201) 871-3577
Furn, prints & coll.

Portobello Road Antiques
491 Grand Ave.
(201) 568-5559
20th c. Dec, toys & coll.

Rose Hill Auction Gallery
35 S. VanBrunt St.
(201) 816-1940
Call for auction dates & times.

Royal Galleries Antiques
66 E. Palisade Ave.
(201) 567-6354
Am paintings, 19th & 20th c.
Am & Eng silver & Euro porc.

Starr
1 Grand Ave.
(201) 568-9090/800-995-5784
Antiq & new oriental rugs.

The Book Store At Depot
Square
8 Depot Square
(201) 568-6563
Rare & out of print books.

Global Treasures
120 Grand Ave.
(201) 569-5532
19th & 20th c. art & furn.

Fairview

Art 'N Things By Sorrentino
133 Anderson Ave.
(201) 943-2288
Toys & models.

Garfield

Bedlam Brass Beds
& Antiques
530 River Dr.
(973) 546-5000
Spec: antiq brass beds & brass
replacement parts.

Glen Rock

The Jewel Table
877 Prospect St.
(201) 612-9027

BERGEN COUNTY, NJ

Hackensack

Grandma's Attic
23 Banta Place
(201) 487-0393
Furn, porc, Dep & Art glass.

Hasbrouck Heights

Antique Boutique
313 Blvd. Rd.
(201) 393-0110
Furn & collectibles.

Hillsdale

The Book Shop
430 Hillsdale Ave.
(201) 391-9101
Usd & out of print books.

Ho Ho Kus

Aviary Antiques
622 N. Maple Ave.
(201) 652-0002
Furn, sterling, china,glass,
prints, mirrors & oils.

Camelot Antiques
9 N Franklin Tpk.
(201) 444-5300
General line.

Discovery Antiques
620 N. Maple Ave.
(201) 444-9170
Cont. furn, & access.
Sterling & jewelry.

Regal Antiques LTD
181 E. Franklin Tpk.
(201) 447-4190
19th & 20th c. Cont. furn &
dec.

Lodi

N. Richman & Associates
509 Westminster Place
(973) 772-9027
Antiq & usd furn. Sat only.

Lyndhurst

Stamps & Coins & Things
306 Valley Brook Ave.
(201) 933-4499
Out of print books.

Mahwah

Granny's Attic Antiques
142 Franklin Tpk.
(201) 529-5516
Gen line. Spec:
Fr, Dutch & Eng.

Midland Park

Bergen Caning & Supply
230 Godwin Ave.
(201) 445-6888
Gen line. Spec: cane &
rush chairs.

Brownstone Mill Center
Paterson Ave. & Goffle Rd.
(201) 445-3074/ 652-9602
Multi-dealer shop.

GF Warhol & Company
18 Goffle Rd.
(201) 612-1010
18th & 19th c. dec
arts, furn & access.

The Blue Barn
60 Goffle Rd.
(201) 612-0227

Time Will Tell
Godwin Plaza
644 Godwin Ave.
(201) 652-1025
Clocks

Tuc-D-Away Antiques
229 Godwin Ave.
(201) 652-0730
Country antiqs & primitives.

Montvale

Montvale Antique Mall
30 Chestnut Ridge Rd.
(201) 391-3940
Multi-dealer co-op.

Moonachie

A.R. K Antiques
1 Anderson Ave.
(201) 224-9500/800-224-6722
Wholesale only. Importers of
Euro antiqs & repros.

North Bergen

Park Antiques
9001 River Rd.
(201) 943-7828
18th & 19th c.
Decorative arts.

Norwood

Elsie Jenriche
505 Broadway
(201) 768-1046

Oakland

Summer Kitchen Antiques
3 Dogwood Dr. (Rt. 202)
(201) 651-1978/891-2997
Spec: 18th & 19th c. Furn.
Pewter always in stock.

Oradel

All American Antiques
650 Lotus Ave.
(201) 599-2395

Paramus

Country Cottage Gifts
578 Paramus Rd.
(201) 447-1122
Furn, jewelry, clocks,
paintngs & dec.

Ramsay

Carriage House Antiques
54 E. Main St.
(201) 327-2100
Gen line.

Golden Triangle Stamp & Coin
141 E. Main St.
(201) 825-3456
Stamps & coins.

William Minery Antiques
259 Grove St.
(201) 825-8027
Antiq. & usd. furn, paintngs,
oriental rugs, glass & porc.

Ridgefield

Cello Antiques
611 Bergen Blvd.
(201) 945-5577

Ridgewood

Antiques of Ridgewood
8 Franklin Ave.
(201) 652-9070
19th c. Euro furn, porc,
lighting & dec.

BeautifulThings
From The Past
419 Goffle Rd.
(201) 670-7090

Boyds Ltd.
580 North Maple Ave.
(201) 493-1499

Boyds Ltd. II
76 East Ridgewood Ave.
(201) 493-8230

Habitat Antiques
795 E. Glen Ave.
(201) 447-2111
17th & 18th c. Am. furn, porc
& dec. Architecturals.

Hahn's Antiques
579 Goffle Rd.
(201) 251-9444
Turn of the cent. Am oak furn.

Irish Eyes Imports
1 Cottage Place & E.
Ridgewood St.
(201) 445-8585
Gen line of Irish imports.

Ivory Tower Inc.
38 Oak St.
(201) 670-6191

Ridgewood Furniture
Refinishing
166 Chestnut St.
(201) 652-5566
Furn & smalls.

River Edge

Brier Rose Books
26 River Edge Rd.
(201) 967-1111
Books only.

Rutherford

American Coin Exchange
217 Patterson Ave.
(201) 933-2000
Coins & precious metals.

Morgan Marguerite Studio
6 Highland Cross
(201) 939-7222

Saddle River

Antiques of Saddle River
3 Barnstable Ct.
(201) 236-0099
19th c. Euro furn, porc,
lighting & dec.

Flashback Antiques
4 Barnstable Ct.
(201) 236-9881
19th c. Euro furn, porc,
lighting & dec.

Richard C. Kyllo Antiques
210 W. Saddle River Rd.
(201) 327-7343

Yesterday's Treasures
7 Barnstable Court
(201) 825-1420

Baldini Ricci Galleries
24 Industrial Ave.
(201) 327-0890

Teaneck

Dason Lighting Inc.
1348 Teaneck Rd.
(201) 837-7831
Lighting.

Park Avenue Books
244 Park Ave.
(201) 836-0007
Books. By appt. or
mail order.

Tenafly

A Gilded Cage
145 Dean Dr.
(201) 871-3002

Westwood

Gardner's II Antiques
349 Broadway Ave.
(201) 664-0612
Gen line.

Westwood Antique Center
273 Westwood Ave.
(201) 666-8988
Multi-dealer shop.

Wyckoff

Cheerful Heart
353 Franklin Ave.
(201) 891-6991
Country primitives.

L'Eglise
630 Wyckoff Ave.
(201) 891-3622
17th -early 20th c. furn & dec.

BURLINGTON COUNTY

Bordentown
Burlington
Cinnaminson
Columbus
Crosswicks
Hainesport
Maple Shade
Medford
Moorestown
Mount Holly
Mount Laurel
Pemberton
Rancocas
Vincentown

BURLINGTON COUNTY NEW JERSEY

Bordentown

Shoppe 202
202 Farnsworth Ave.
(609) 298-1424
Gen line. Spec: oak furn.

Burlington

H.G. Sharkey & Co.
306 High St.
(609) 239-0200
Jewlry, pottery, porc.
collectibles & art.

High Street Exchange
337 High St.
(609) 239-3044
Multi-dealer shop.

Philip's Furniture
347 High St.
(609) 386-7125/429-3869
Furn, smalls & collectibles.

Cinnaminson

River Road Antiques
1101 River Rd. (Broad St.)
(856) 829-0522
General line.

Columbus

Columbus Farmers Market &
Flea Market
Rt. 206 S.
(609) 267-0400
Flea market Thurs, Sat & Sun
Dawn till 1:30. Indoor shops,
Thurs-Sun.

Georgetown Station
35 Chesterfield Rd.
(609) 298-0089
Furn, dolls, beaded handbags
& smalls.

Living History Shop
18 Tower Dr.
(609) 261-2649

Crosswicks

Jack & Mary's Antiques
467 Main St.
(609) 298-2035
Gen line.

Hainesport

Country Antique Center
Rt. 38
(609) 261-1924/800-264-4694

Over 100 dealers.
Featuring: Primitives,
jewelry, cut glass,
Depression glass, Heisey,
Roseville & Furniture.
Open 7 days, 10AM to 5PM.

Ebenezer's Antiques
2245 Rt. 38
(609) 702-9447
E-mail:
ebenezer@nothinbut.net
Buy & Sell: Victoriana,
Primitives & Porcelains.
Spec: furniture, 1840-1920.

Never Again &
Fox Hill Antique Center
2123 Rt. 38
(3 miles East of I-295)
(609) 518-0200
Two shops selling a mix
of Victorian furniture,
European and German
porcelain & fine glass.
Largest selection of Bride's
baskets. E-mail:
Ogurney@bellatlantic.com

Rupp's Antiques
2108 Rt. 38
(609) 267-4848
Vic, traditional & period
furn & smalls.

The Browse Around Shop
1366 Rt. 38
(609) 262-0274
Antiq, new & repro furn.
Smalls.

Maple Shade

Cherry Hill Liquidators, Inc.
105 W. Main St.
(856) 321-0742
Vic & Deco furn.

Medford

Arbor Gate Antiques
16 S. Main St.
(6090 654-1200
Antiqs, collectibles,
fine furn & dec.

Mill House Antiques
Church Rd. & Lenape Tr.
(609) 953-1402

Medford Village Antiques
Gallery
32 N. Main St.
(609) 654-7577
Multi-dealer shop.

Recollections
6 N. Main St.
(609) 654-1515
General line.

Spirit of '76
49 N. Main St.
(609) 654-2850

The Way We Were
4 N. Main St.
(609) 654-0343
Jewlry & watches, 1920-1940.

Toll House Antiques
160 Old Marlton Pike
Medford, NJ
(609) 953-0005
Furn, access, pottery
& folk art.

The Swan
1 N. Main St.
(609) 654-5252

Yesterday & Today Shop
Lakes Shopping Center
668 Stokes Rd.
(609) 654-7786
Antiq & repro furn. Jewlry.

Vintage in the Village
26 S. Main St.
(609) 654-4707
Gen line. Furn, china,glass
& hand painted furn.

Moorestown

Country Peddler Antiques
111 Chester Ave.
(856) 235-0680
Furn, glass & repro
Persian rugs.

George Wurtzel Antiques
69 E. Main St.
(856) 234-9631
Antiq & vint. jewlry,
watches & sterling.

Kingsway Antiques
527 E. Main St.
(856) 234-7373
Coll, china. Porc, medals & furn.

Mount Holly

Arcade Antiques
44 High St.
(609) 265-1200
Multi-dealer co-op.

Bill's Bargains
15 King St.
(609) 261-0096
New & usd furn.

Center Stage Antiques
41 King St.
(609) 261-0602
Furn.

Mount Laurel

Collector's Express
104 Berkshire Dr.
(856) 866-1693

Pemberton

Encore Antiques
108 Hanover St.
(609) 726-0061

Grist Mill Antique Center
127 Hanover St. (Rt. 616)
(609) 726-1588
Multi-dealer shop.

The Alphabet Owl
12 Pemberton-Juliustown Rd.
(609) 894-2335

Rancocas

Carpet Baggers
208 Creek Rd.
(856) 234-5095
Spec: dolls & lampshades.
Doll hosp.

Creek Road Antique Centre
123 Creek Rd.
(856) 778-8899
Multi-dealer co-op.

Spencer's Indoor Antique
Market
116 Creek Rd.
(856) 778-2065/222-9555
Indoor & outdoor multi-
dealer market.

Vincentown

Allen's Auction Barn
231 Landing St.
(609) 267-8382
Call for auction dates & times.

Antique Phonograph
 & Record Center
2127 Hwy. 206 N.
(609) 859-8617
Phonographs & records.

CAMDEN COUNTY

Audubon
Barrington
Berlin
Collingswood
Gibbsboro
Haddon Heights
Haddonfield
Merchantville
Pennsauken
Runnemeade
Westmont

CAMDEN COUNTY NEW JERSEY

Audubon

Treasures in the Attic
57 East Kings Hwy.
(856) 546-1444
Consignment shop.

Barrington

Grandmom Applegate's
107 Clements Bridge Rd.
(856) 672-0432
Gen line. 19th & early
20th c. Am. Art.

Potpourri Antiques
113 Clements Bridge Rd.
(856) 547-3611
Multi-dealer co-op.

Berlin

Antiques Plain & Fancy
180 Haddon Ave.
(856) 767-4805

Wilma Saxton, Inc.
37 Clementon Rd.
(856) 267-8029
Sterling silver & plate,
Deco-present.

Winters' Gun Specialties
66 W. White Horse Pike
(856) 767-0349
Antiq guns & access.

Collingswood

Collingswood Antiques
812 Haddon Ave.
(856) 858-9700
Vic & Country furn & access.

Ellis Antiques
817 Haddon Ave.
(856) 854-6346
Fine & costume jewlry.
Gen line & Vic. furn.

The Yesteryear Shop
788 Haddon Ave.
(856) 854-1786
Vintage glass, china, jewlry
& linens.

Gibbsboro

Gibbsboro Book Barn & Bindery
10 Washington Ave.
(856) 435-2525
OP & 1st ed. books.

Haddon Heights

Haddon Heights Antiques Center
Clements Bridge Rd.
   & E. Atlantic Ave.
(856) 546-0555
Multi-dealer co-op, 80 dlrs.

Haddonfield

Haddonfield Gallery
1 Kings Court
(856) 429-7722

Owl's Tale
140 Kings Highway East
(856) 795-8110
Gen line, period-1920s.
Spec: Estate jewlry.

The Haddonfield Antique Center
9 Kings Hwy. East
(856) 429-1929
Multi-dealer co-op, 25 dlrs.

Two in the Attic
3 Kings Court
(856) 429-4035
Gen line.

Merchantville

Between The Covers
   Rare Books
35 Maple Ave.
(856) 665-2284
Books only.

Green Marquee Antiques
21 N. Centre St.
(856) 910-0055
General line.

Pennsauken

Memories Past
7725 Maple Ave.
(856) 317-0662
Spec: linens. Vic. china
& furn.

Slots by Bob Levy
2802 Centre St.
(856) 663-2554
Vintage slot machines.

Runnemeade

AAA Antiques
11 N. Black Horse Pike
(856) 939-3939
Gen line. Spec: toys.

Antiques & Coin Unlimited
Black Horse Pike
(856) 931-3131
Gen line. Spec: jewelry.

Westmont

West Jersey B-Thrifty Shop
225 Haddon Ave.
(856) 854-1003
Thrift shop.

CAPE MAY COUNTY

Avalon
Beesley's Point
Cape May
Cape May Courthouse
Cold Spring
Dias Creek
Marmora
Ocean City
Palermo
Rio Grande
Seaville
Stone Harbor
Swainton
Tuchahoe
Villas
West Cape May
Wildwood

CAPE MAY COUNTY NEW JERSEY

Avalon

Antiques, etc.
20th & Ocean Dr.
(609) 967-5500
Multi-dealer shop.

Beesley's Point

Beesley's Point Antiques
715 N. Shore Rd. (Rt. 9)
(609) 390-3732/390-1691
General line.

Cape May

A Rose is a Rose
656 Washington St.
(609) 884-1380
Spec: Vic. Smalls.

Aleathea's Antique Shop
Inn of Cape May Lobby
Ocean St. & Beach Dr.
(609) 884-3500

Antique Doorknob
600 Park Blvd.
(609) 884-6282

Artisan's Alcove
523 Lafayette St.
(609) 898-0202
Spec: estate jewelry.

Cape Island Antiques
609 Jefferson St.
(609) 884-6028
Spec: Vic. furn.
Brass & silver.

Finishing Touches
678 Washington St.
(609) 898-0661
1890's-1920 lighting.

K's Used Furniture
  & Flea Market
Bayview Rd. & Rt. 9
(609) 465-9767
Indoor market & flea.

Laurels
24 Decatur St.
(609) 898-1004

Mary Ann's Antiques
511 Washington St. Mall
(609) 898-8786
Estate jewelry & coll.

Millstone Antiques
742 Seashore Rd. at Cox Lane
(609) 884-5155
General line, 1860s-1940s.

Nostalgia Shop
408 Washington St.
(609) 884-7071
Smalls, lamps & small furn.

Out of the Past Antiques
727 Beach Ave.
(609) 884-3357

**Sea Horse Antiques
Rt. 9 & Second Ave.
(609) 884-8866
Over 80 dealers. We
buy, sell & trade. Dealer
space available. Open
year round. 1/4 mile from
base of Cape May bridge,
on right hand side.**

Stephanie's Antiques
318 Washington St.
(609) 884-0289
General line.

**Tabby House Antiques
& Comfortables
479 W. Perry St.
(609) 898-0908
18th & 19th c. furnishings & accessories. Also featuring LT. Moses Willard Lighting.**

The Clock Works
600 Park Blvd.
(609) 898-8777
Clocks & watches.

Triple Five Shop
555 Elmire St.
(609) 884-5864

Victorious Antiques
Congress Hall
251 Beach Dr.
(609) 898-1777/884-1777
Jewelry. Spec: antiq engagement rings.

Cape May Courthouse

Golden Pond Antiques
2089 Rt. 9 North (Clermont)
(609) 624-0608

The Gingerbread House
Rt. 9 North (Swainton)
(609) 465-9234

Victorian Cottage Antiques
20 N. Main St.
(609) 465-2132

Cold Spring

House of Old
731 Townbank Rd.
(609) 884-1458
1920s furn. Tools. China.

Dias Creek

Ken's Antiques
& Furniture Restoration
22 Rt. 47 N.
(609) 463-8987

Marmora

Fred Peech Antiques
1008 S. Shore Rd.
(609) 390-1873
General line: Am & Eng,
mid 1700-1900.

Ocean City

Avant Garden
742 Haven Ave.
(609) 399-7860

**Back In Time Antiques,
Used Furniture
& Consignment
1337 West Ave.
(609) 399-2234
Antiques & quality used
furniture. Auction gallery.
Buying one piece to entire**
estates. **Have antiques?
We will travel to your
location.
Open 10-5 daily.
Closed Wednesdays.**

B's Fantasy
8th & Asbury
(609) 398-9302
General line.

Kay Jay's Doll Emporium
18 East 9th St.
(609) 399-5632
Spec: dolls & doll hospital.

Joseph's Antiques
908 Asbury Ave.
(609) 398-3855/398-2984
General line.

Only Yesterday
1108 Boardwalk
(609) 398-2869
Gen line, 20th c. nostalgia
& coll.

Only Yesterday
1137 Asbury Ave.
(609) 398-5128
Gen line, 20th c. nostalgia
& coll.

Toyrareum
1101 Asbury Ave.
(609) 391-0480

Yesterday's Best
2748 Asbury Ave.
(609) 391-9042
Gen line. Spec: Vic,
Edwardian & Art Nouveau

Palermo

Rail Road Crossing Antiques
1143 Shore Rd.
(609) 390-1833

Rio Grande

Rodia Used Furniture
2500 Rt. 9 South
(609) 465-5865

Seaville

Grandma's Attic Co-Op
3071 Rt. 9
(609) 624-1989
Multi-dealer co-op.

The Antiquarian
3050 Rt. 9
(609) 624-0878
General line.

Stone Harbor

Stephen Christopher's
255 96th St.
(609) 368-0575

Swainton

Oak Tree Antiques
1401 Rt. 9 N.
(609) 465-1592

**Mallard Lake Antiques
1781 Rt. 9 North
(609) 465-7189
European Porcelain
(Limoges, German or
English). American &
European glass (cut to
Depression and every-
thing in between).**

**The August Farmhouse
Antiques
1759 Rt. 9 N.
(609) 465-5135/465-5235
Formal decorative
antiques: furniture, glass,
silver, crystal, mirrors &
lamps. Antique and vin-
tage furnishings and
accessories. Victorian to
Art Deco.**

The Dutch Rose
Rt. 9 N
(609) 463-0844
Am country primitives: linens,
cupboards & kitchen items .

Tuckahoe

The Four Y's
2371 Mosquito Landing Rd.
(Rt.50)
(609) 628-2721
Glass, china,bottles &
figurines.

Tuckahoe Station Antiques
2261 Rt. 50
(609) 628-2372

Yesteryear
2235 Rt. 50
(609) 628-2478
Gen line. Spec: Victorian.

Yesteryear Two
2245 Rt. 50
(609) 628-2384
Comic books, baseball mem
& coll.

Villas

St. Anthony's Estate Tag Sale
901 Bayshore Rd.
(609) 889-2599
General line.

West Cape May

Bogwater Jim Antiques
201 N. Broadway
(609) 884-5558
Spec: Pond boats.

Bridgetowne Antiques
523 Broadway
(609) 884-8107
Gen line. Spec: garden &
architecturals.

Promises Collectibles
301 N. Broadway
(609) 884-4411
General line.

**Rocking Horse Antiques
Center
405 W. Perry St.
(609) 898-0737
Over 60 dealers.
Retail & Wholesale.
Dealer space available.
Open 7 days a week,
year round.**

Wildwoood

**Welcome Home
3901 Pacific Ave.
(609) 523-6600
Large selection of
antique & collectible
furniture. Full service
furniture restorations.
Hours: Summer daily, 10-5.
Winter: closed Tues. & Wed.**

CUMBERLAND COUNTY

Bridgeton
Deerfield
Fairton
Greenwich
Heislerville
Mauricetown
Millville
Shiloh
Vineland

Antiques and Collectibles

The Squirrel's Nest

HOURS THURSDAY THRU SATURDAY
11A.M. TO 4 P.M.

(856) 455-6594
(856) 451-1206

680 SHILOH PIKE
BRIDGETON, NJ 08302

Bridgeton

The Squirrel's Nest
680 Shiloh Pike (Rt. 49)
(856) 455-6594/451-1206
Antiques & collectibles.
Old & new books. Bottles,
small furniture, glassware
& pottery. Open Thursday
thru Saturday, 11 am-4pm.

Tracy's Corner
62 N. Laurel St.
(856) 455-2160

Deerfield

Deerfield Village
1530 Rt. 77
(856) 451-2143
15,000 sq. ft. Large inven-
tory of furniture. Clean &
well lighted displays.
Ample off street parking.
Clean restrooms.
Open Thursday thru
Monday, 10am to 6pm.

Fairton

Carriage House Signs 'n Things
Bridgeton-Fairton Rd.
(856) 455-6400

Greenwich

The Griffin
Greate St.
(856) 451-5867

Heislerville

Wood Pump Antiques
206 Main St.
(856) 785-0237
Gen line of country.

Mauricetown

Boxwood & Ivy Antiques
9087 Highland St.
(856) 785-1246
Furn, cut glass, Majolica,
Interior dec.

Mary's Antiques
9070 Highland St.
(856) 785-2686

Maurice River Antiques
1207 Front St.
(856) 785-9428
Country & Vic furn, glass
& pottery.

The Cook House Antiques
9533 Highland St.
(856) 785-1137
General line.

Tulip Tree Antiques
South St.
(856) 785-0850

Millville

Wind Chimes Book
    Exchange
210 High St.
(856) 327-3714
Usd, OP & 1st ed books.

Shiloh

**Shiloh Antique Shoppe
11 S. Main St.
Rt. 49 at blinker light
(856) 453-1800
1,500 sq. ft. of fine country antiques. Period to
Primitive: furniture,
quilts, architecturals, pottery, tin, copper, iron and
more. Daily 10-5. Some
by chance.**

Vineland

Rose Petal Treasures
1199 S. Main Rd.
(856) 794-8300

U Sell Flea Market
Vineland Area
(856) 691-1222
Call for hours & Directions.

ESSEX COUNTY

Belleville

Caldwell

Cedar Grove

East Orange

Irvington

Maplewood

Millburn

Montclair

Roseland

South Orange

Verona

West Orange

ESSEX COUNTY NEW JERSEY

Belleville

Second Hand Rose
203 Washington Ave.
(973) 759-0019
Spec: smalls.

Caldwell

Anne Filkin
328 Bloomfield Ave.
(973) 228-9038

Book Heaven
Box 371
(973) 228-5927
Rare & OP books.

Cedar Grove

The Mulberry Bush
496 Pompton Ave.
(973) 239-9357
Gen line, 1850-1940's.

East Orange

Antiques Etc.
194 Central Ave.
(973) 678-0011
Furn, dec & lighting.

Irvington

Alice's Antiques
1264 Springfield Ave.
(973) 372-6612

Antiques, Lace & Things
125 Springfield Ave.
(973) 416-2177

Maplewood

Bee & Thistle Antiques
89 Baker St.
(973) 763-3166
Porc, crystal, glass & silver.

On Track Antiques
Maplewood Ave. &
Depot Place
(973) 763-4514
Period glass, silver, rugs,
books, furn & art. By appt.

Renaissance Antiques
410 Ridgewood Rd.
(973) 761-7450
19th & 20th c. mahogany
& oak furn, botanicals & dec.

Millburn

Forgotten Times
27 Main St.
(973) 376-4148
Euro furn, lamps &
tapestries.

Montclair

American Sampler Inc.
26 Church St.
(973) 744-1474
Antiq & repro furn,
Folk art & dec.

Dobbs Ltd.
20 Chuch St.
(973) 744-1474
Vic repr & antiq furn,
dec & jewelry.

Antique Star
627 Bloomfield Ave.
(973) 746-0070
Furniture & clocks.

Bill Sablon Antiques
411 Bloomfield Ave.
(973) 746-4397
Furn, silver, lamps, rugs,
paintngs & architecturals.

Browser's Nook
322 Orange Rd.
(973) 744-1619
Antiq & usd furn. & dec.

Chameleon Antiques
97 Walnut St.
(973) 655-9190

Class Act Antiques
415 Bloomfield Ave.
(973) 746-9543
General line.

Earl Roberts Antiques
17 S. Fullerton Ave.
(973) 744-2232

Edward's Antiques
55 N. Fullerton Ave.
(973) 783-9352
Coll to period furn & dec.

Fly by Night Gallery
425 Bloomfield Ave.
19th c. restord Modern furn.
20th c. furn & dec.

Gallery of Vintage
504 Bloomfield Ave.
(973) 509-1201

Garage Sale
194 Claremont Ave.
(973) 783-0806
Spec: 20th c. usd bedrm
& dining rm sets.

Georgiana Stockel
80 S. Mountain Ave.
(973) 744-5642

J & J Antiques
46 Fairfield St.
973-744-8386
Antiq & usd furn,
glass & pottery.

Jackie's Antiques
51 North Fullerton Ave.
(973) 744-7972

Maps of Antiquity
Montclair Area
(973) 744-4364
Antiq maps. Appt only.

Martin William Antiques
41 Church St.
(973) 744-1149
19th & early 20th c. furn
& repro/custom furn &
dec access.

Mary Wood Estate Sales
94 Yantacaw Brook Rd.
(973) 783-2942/783-9352

Milt's Antiques
662 Bloomfield Ave.
(973) 746-4445
Spec: antiq & usd furn
& sterling.

Montclair Antique Center
34 Church St.
(973) 746-1062

Montclair Book Center
221 Glenridge Ave.
(973) 783-3630
New, used, rare & OP
books. Spec: NJ history.

Noel's Place
173 Glenridge Ave.
(973) 744-2156
New, used & antiq furn
& dec.

Past & Present Resale
416 Bloomfield Ave.
(973) 746-8871
Furn, pottery, glass &
collectibles to the 1950s.

Patterson Smith
23 Prospect Terrace
(973) 744-3291
Books, by appt.

Persia Oriental Rugs, Inc.
500 Bloomfield Ave.
(973) 744-3731
New, usd & antiq
Oriental rugs.

Station West Antiques
225 Glenridge Ave.
(973) 744-9370
General line

The Ivory Bird Antiques
555 Bloomfield Ave.
(973) 744-5225
Spec: Eng furn & dec.
Oriental & Fr furn, smalls

The Way We Were Antiques
15 Midland Ave.
(973) 783-1111
General line.

Threadneedle Street
195 Bellevue Ave.
(973) 783-1336
Spec: Eng antiques.

Trent Antiques
436 Bloomfield Ave.
(973) 783-4676
General line.

Yesterday's Books
& Records
559 Bloomfield Ave.
(973) 783-6262
Spec: jazz records, books.

Roseland

Roseland Group
174 Eagle Rock Ave.
(973) 618-1288

South Orange

Aaltglen's Galleries
461 Irvington Ave.
(973) 762-7200

Alan Angele
Popular Culture
350 Turrell Ave.
(973) 378-5822
Books only.

Carrie Topf Antiques
50 W. South Orange Ave.
(973) 762-8773
General line.

Verona

June Emrich Antiques
282 Bloomfield Ave.
(973) 857-9144

West Orange

In Days of Old
173 Main St.
(973) 325-7955

GLOUCESTER COUNTY

Bridgeport

Clarksboro

Gloucester

Malaga

Mickleton

Mullica Hill

Newfield

Pitman

Repaupo

Turnersville

Williamstown

Woodbury

GLOUCESTER COUNTY NEW JERSEY

Bridgeport

Raccoon Creek Antiques
20 Main St.
(856) 467-3197
Americana & Folk art.
Spec: orig surface & paint.

Clarksboro

Boggs Boynton Antiques
186 Timberlane Rd.
(856) 224-1165

Jansen's
E.Greenwich Indust Park
Timberlane Rd.
Reproductions.

Karl Dreibach & Company
186 Timberlane Rd.
(856) 224-0266

The Barn
E. Greenwich Indust Park
Timberlane Rd B-7
(856) 423-3227

Gloucester

Fanatic Collector's Co-op
Rt. 130 N
(856) 456-6542
Multi-dealer.

Malaga

Mike's Used Furniture
559 Rt. 47S
(856) 694-3005/694-0635
Usd furn, antiqs & coll.

Verne C. Streeter
Rt. 40 & Malaga Park Dr.
(856) 694-4163

Mickleton

Dutch Auction Sales
356 Swedesboro Ave.
(856) 423-6800
Call for auction dates & times.

Mullica Hill

Antiquities
43 S. Main St.
(856) 478-6773
18th & 19th c. Am
furn, art & dec.

Carriage House
62 N. Main St.
(856) 478-4459
Furniture.

Debra's Dolls
20 N. Main St.
(856) 478-9778
Dolls & related access.

Doll & Toys
34 S. Main St.
(856) 478-6137
Dolls & toys.

Elizabeth's
32 N. Main St.
(856) 478-6510
Furn. & metalwares.

June Bug Antiques
44 S. Main St.
(856) 478-2167/646-7841
Country primitives, quilts,
tin & dec.

Lynne Antiques
49 S. Main St.
(856) 223-9199
Furn & smalls.

Main Street Books
26 S. Main
(856) 223-1189
Usd, OP & collctble books.

Mame's on Main Street
13 S. Main St.
(856) 223-0555
Furn, decorative access & collectibles.

Mullica Hill Art Glass
53 S. Main St.
(856) 478-2552

Murphy's Loft
53 N. Main St. (Rt 322)
(856) 478-4928
Books, prints, paper,
maps & magazines.

Raccoon's Tale
6 High St.
(856) 478-4488
Am pottery, china & glass.

Sugar & Spice Antiques
45 Main St.
(856) 478-2622
Vic furn & dec.

The Antique Corner
45 N. Main St.
(856) 478-4754
Furn & smalls.

The Antique Warehouse
2 S. Main St.
(856) 478-4500
Multi-dealer mall.

The Clock Shop
45 S. Main St.
(856) 478-6555
Clocks.

The Front Porch Antiques
21S Main St.
(856) 478-6556
Furn: oak, mahog & walnut.
China, prints & dec access.

The Hartman Collection
43 S. Main St.
(856) 478-9595
19th & early 20th c. furn & dec.

The King's Row Antique Center
46 N. Main St.
(856) 478-4361
A great selection of quality antique furnishings, accessories & collectibles from many dealers. New merchandise daily. Open 7 days, 11-5. Quality antiques bought & sold.

The Old Gray Mare
54 S. Main St.
(856) 478-6229
Country furn, lighting & art.

The Old Mill Antique Mall
1 S. Main St. (Rt. 45)
(856) 478-9810
50 dealers under one roof. Three floors of antiques & collectibles. Open 7 days a week 11-5.

The Old Post Shoppes
50 S. Main St.
(856) 478-2910
General line.

The Queen's Inn Antiques & Cafe
48 N. Main St.
(856) 223-9434
www.mullicahill.com/queensinn. Country furnishings.

The Royal Crescent
37 S. Main St.
(856) 223-0220

The Sign of St. George
30 S. Main St.
(856) 478-6101
Furn. & jewelry.

The Treasure Chest
50 S. Main St.
(856) 468-4371

The Yellow Garage
66 S. Main St.
(856) 478-0300
Multi-dealer co-op.

THE OLD MILL ANTIQUE MALL
45 Dealers on 3 Floors
Open 11 to 5 Daily

Pottery, Glass, Toys, Sports
Ephemera, Tools, Dolls
Jewelry, Insulators, & Furniture

1 S. Main Street, (Rt. 45)
Mullica Hill, NJ 08062
856-478-9810
Dealer Inquiries Welcome

Newfield

Raven's Antiques
1888 (Rt. 40)
(856) 697-3622
Tools, bottles & glass.

The Old Barn
226 N. West Blvd.
(856) 697-3242
Antiq & coll.
Spec: S. Jersey glass.

Pitman

Foley's Idle Hour
162 S. Broadway Ave.
(856) 582-0510
Old, new, rare & OP books.

Repaupo

S & S Auctions
Repaupo Station Rd.
(856) 467-3778
Call for auction dates & times.

Turnersville

Antique Trains
Greentree Rd & Lantern Lane
(856) 589-6224
Trains, 1905-present.

Williamstown

Ternay's Antiques
1665 Glassboro Rd.
(856) 881-4527
General line.

George's Fault
1708 S. Blackhorse Pike
(856) 262-4900
Multi-dealer shop.

Woodbury

Posh Pomegranate
66 S. Broad St. (Rt.45)
(856) 853-1544
Multi dealer co-op, 40 dealers. 17,000 sq. ft. Dealers welcome.

HUDSON COUNTY

Bayonne
Bergen
Hoboken
Jersey City
North Bergen
Secaucus
West New York

HUDSON COUNTY NEW JERSEY

Bayonne

Antiques by Angela & Deborah
922 Broadway (44th St.)
(201) 823-1148
Gen line,1800-1940s. Spec:
bed & dining rm sets.

Bargain Hunter's Den
444 Avenue C
(201) 339-7026
Usd. furn.

Castle Clock Shop
745 Broadway
(201) 823-1160
Clocks & railroad watches.

Bergen

Now & Then
140 Allendale Ave.
(201) 934-1440
Consignment shop.

The Tickled Pink Petunia
6718 Park Ave.
(201) 869-5829
Spec: glass & jewelry.

Hoboken

Adelaide Claiborne Collections
40 Hudson Place
(201) 659-5018
Spec: 1920s-1950s Platinum
Era Engagement & wed rings.

E. Greene
327 Washington St.
(201) 659-8033
Maps & prints.

Erie Street Antiques
533 Washington St.
(201) 656-3596
19th & 20th c. furn.
Spec: Am Vic.

Clary & Co. Antiques Ltd.
327 Washington St.
(201) 792-7442
Furniture & lighting.

Fat Cat Antiques
57 Newark St.
(201) 222-5454
Vint jewelry. Vint coll.

Ferenc Antiques & Collectibles
703 Garden St.
(201) 798-2441
Lighting, glass, jewlry &
vint clothing.

House Ware Inc.
628 Washington St.
(201) 659-6009
Vint & new furn.

Hoboken Antiques
511 Washington St.
(201) 659-7329
Gen line: old & antiq.

Little Cricket Antiques
1200 Washington St.
(201) 222-6270
Cottage style furn, textiles &
access. Vint jewlry.

The Mission Position
1122 Washington St.
(201) 656-3398
Spec: Arts & Crafts period.

The Old Time House
402 Grand St.
(201) 222-6167
Gen line. Spec: Clocks & Art
Deco statues.

United Decorating Co. Inc.
421 Washington St.
(201) 659-1922
Spec: old postcards, photos,
political items, local mem.

Jersey City

Cliff's Clocks
400 7th St.
(201) 798-7510

L & L Antiques
1170 Summit Ave.
(201) 656-6928

Portfolio Inc.
498 Jersey Ave.
(201) 332-1311

Retro Antiques
3514 John F. Kennedy Blvd.
(201) 656-6139

North Bergen

Park Antiques
9001 River Rd.
(201) 943-7828
18th & 19th c. Fr, Eng
& Am furn & dec.

Secaucus

Antique Depot
100 Dorigo Lane
Secaucus, NJ
(201) 392-1828
General line.

West New York

The Tickled Pink Petunia Two
6708 Park Ave.
(201) 869-6100
Vic-Deco furn, lamps,
mirrors & prints.

HUNTERDON COUNTY

Annandale

Califon

Clinton

Flemington

Frenchtown

Glen Gardner

Lambertville

Lebanon

Oldwick

Pittstown

Pottersville

Ringoes

Rosemont

Whitehouse Station

HUNTERDON COUNTY NEW JERSEY

Annandale

Everything Country
1451 Rt. 22
(908) 236-2495
Gen line of Primitives,
late 1800-early 1900.

Golden Rainbow
96 Beaver Ave.
(908) 730-6603
Usd. furn, vint canoes
& row boats.

Califon

44 Main Street Antiques
44 Main St.
(908) 832-2910

The Fox Room
R.R. 1 Box 313
Beacon Light Rd.
By appt. 800-833-7135
Horse related items.
Jewlry & coll.

Clinton

Art's Resale
1751 Rt. 31 N.
(908) 735-4442
General line.

Memories
21 Main St.
(908) 730-9096

Paddy-Wak Antiques
19-1/2 Old Hwy. 22
(908) 735-9770

Rockinghorse Antiques
Rt. 57 Port Murray Lane
(908) 689-2813
General line.

The Clinton Antique Center
21 Main St.
(908) 730-9096

Weathervane Antiques
18A Main St.
(908) 730-0877
Multi-dealer shop.

Flemington

Consignment Collections
9 Central Ave.
(908) 788-0103

Main Street Antique Center
156 Main St.
(908) 788-6767
Multi-dealer co-op.

Popkorn Antiques
3 Mine St.
(908) 782-9631
Spec: Am pottery & glass.

Quiet Rainbow
17 Church St.
(908) 284-1255

The Hunterdon Exchange
155 Main St.
(908) 782-6229
Consignment shop.

The Little House of Treasures
755 Rt. 202
(908) 806-6262
Furn, glass, tools & silver,
1890s-1940s.

Antique, Thrift & Gift
39 Mine St.
(908) 788-8553
Gen line antiq. vint & usd,
mid 1800s- present.

Frenchtown

Brook's Antiques
24 Bridge St.
(908) 996-7161

Frenchtown House
15 Race St.
(908) 996-2482

JM Home
29 Bridge St.
(908) 996-0442
Gen line, repro furn & dec.

Moon River Antiques, etc.
17 Race St.
(908) 996-8854
Antique furn & toys.

Running Fox Antiques
49 Bridge St.
(908) 996-7391

Star Base 38
38 Bridge St.
(908) 996-1070
Art & antiqs.

Stone Company Antiques
8 Race St.
(908) 227-6569
Gen line, late 1800s- early 1900s.

Treasures & Pleasures
106 Harrison St.
(908) 996-0999
Spec: 40s & 50s household
coll & newly painted old furn.

Variete
43 Bridge St.
(908) 996-7876
Spec: primitives & tabletop.

WoodsEdge
36 Bridge St.
Am furn & dec.

Glen Gardner

Hunt House Antiques
Rt. 31
(908) 537-7044
General line, 18th c.-20thc.
Spec: country prim & formal.

Lambertville

America Antiques
S. Main St.
(609) 397-6966
Gen line. Cont, Euro & Am,
19th & 20th c. furn & dec.

Antiques by Rossi
285 S. Main St.
(609) 397-1599

Archangel Antiques
43 N. Union St.
(609) 397-4333
Multi-dealer co-op.

Artfull Eye
12 N. Union St.
(609) 397-8115
Gen line furn & dec. Spec:
fine art, 1850-1950.

Best of France Antiques
204 N. Union St.
(609) 397-9881

Blue Raccoon
6 Coryelle St.
(609) 397-1900
Primitives & painted
country pieces.

Bridge Street Antiques
15 Bridge St.
(609) 397-9890
Multi-dealer co-op.

Brion Galleries
1293 Rt. 179
3 miles NE of Lambertville
downtown
Art, sculps, collectibles &
old English stained glass.

Broadmoor Antiques
6 N. Union St.
(609) 397-8802
Multi-dealer gallery.

Castor Jewelry
3 N. Union St.
(609) 397-0809
Jewelry.

Center City Antiques
11 Kline's Court
(609) 397-9886
Multi-dealer co-op.

Coryell Street Antiques
51 Coryell St.
(609) 397-5700
Art & period furn. Spec:
desks,clocks, KY rifles.

David Rago's Auction
333 N. Main St.
(609) 397-9374.
Call for auction dates & times.

E.H. Limited
8 Bridge St.
(609) 397-4411
Sterling, Sheffield, bronzes,
enamels, chandeliers & furn.

Fran Jay Antiques
10 Church St.
(609) 397-1571
20th c. Am. glass, toys &
postcards.

Friarswood Antiques
36 Coryell St.
(609) 397-2133
Spec: Am porc.

Garden House Antiques
39 N. Union St.
(609) 397-9797
Gen line. Spec: 19th &
20th c. Dec arts.

Gloria N. Greenwald
   Antiques & Folk Art
45 Clinton St.
(609) 397-9424
Early 18th & 19th c. Am
painted furn, folk art & dec.

Golden Nugget Antique
   Flea Market
Rt. 29
(609) 397-0811
Indoor & outdoor, year
round. Call for times.

Greenbranch Antiques
3 Lambert Lane
(609) 397-1225

H. & C. Eick Antiques
54 N. Union St.
(609) 397-8485
18th & 19th c. formal Fr,
Eng. & Am furn & dec.

H K H Inc.
14 Church St.
(609) 397-4141

Helena Castella Antiques
14 Bridge St.
(609) 397-7274
18th & 19th c. Am, It,
Eng, & Fr. furn & dec.

Heritage Antique Lighting
67 Bridge St.
(609) 397-8820
Spec: repro lighting.

Howard Mann Art Center
45 N. Main St.
(609) 397-2300
Fine art.

JH Home, Ltd.
7 N. Union St.
Lambertville, NJ
(609) 397-9400
Gen line, repro furn & dec.

JRJ Home
24 N. Union St.
(609) 397-3800
Gen line, repro furn & dec.

Jack's Furniture & Antiques
56 Coryelle St.
(609) 397-2632

Jim's Antiques
   Fine Art Gallery
9 Lambert Lane
(609) 397-7700
Specializing in
Pennsylvania
Impressionists, mainly
the New Hope School.
We feature works by:
Redfield, Garber,
Folinsbee, Leith-Ross,
Spencer, Sotter, Snell,
Nunaker, Coppedge, RAD

Miller, Lathrop, M.E. Price, & Martha Walter, with a collection of sculptures by Harry Rosin, and much more. Always over 120 works on display. Hrs: Wed-Fri 10:30-5:00, Sat-Sun 10:30-6. Closed Mon-Tues.

Jim's Antiques Ltd.
6 Bridge St.
(609) 397-7700
Exciting antiques gallery brimming with 7,000 sq. ft. of exquisite objects d'art, porcelains, bronzes, 18th, 19th & 20th c. paintings, estate silver & jewelry, vintage watches, furniture, toys, art glass & pottery, native American items - all of exceptional quality. Hours: Wed-Fri 10:30-5:00, Sat-Sun 10:30-6. Closed Mon-Tues.

Joan Evans Antiques
48 Coryelle St.
(609) 397-7726

Karen & David Dutch
22 Bridge St.
(609) 397-2288
19th c. Am furn & dec. Spec: desks, bookcases, & dining rm.

Kelly McDowell Antiques
38 Coryelle St.
(609) 397-4465
Spec: 18th c.-1940s jewelry. Fine art & dec.

Lambertville Antique Market
1864 River Rd.
(609) 397-0456
Over 100 vendors outdoors every Wed & Sat & Sun. Rain or Shine year round. Three buildings containing over 60 showcases & 5 individual shop dealers. Restaurant on premises. LOCATED: 1-1/2 miles South of Lambertville on Rt. 29

Lambertville Gallery of Fine Art
20 N. Union St.
(609) 397-4121
Fine art.

Lambertville Stained Glass
28 Coryell St.
(609) 397-8155
Contemp & traditional stained glass.

Left Bank Books
28 N. Union St.
(609) 397-4966
Books only.

Lovrinic Antiques
15 N. Union St.
(609) 397-8600
18th & 19th c. Am furn.

Meld
53 N. Union St.
(609) 397-8487/8600
20th c. Fr: furn,art glass, lamps, mirrors & ad posters.

Mill Crest Antiques
72 Bridge St.
(609) 397-4700
Linens, textiles & china. Fr & Am quilts.

Miller-Topia Designers
35 N. Union
(609) 397-9339
Importers: Eng, Fr, Welsh & Am furn & dec.

Olde English Pine
202 N. Union St.
(Corner of Elm & N. Union)
(609) 397-4978
Imported Eng country pine furn.

Oxus River
25 Ferry St.
(609) 397-5690
Spec: Asian antiques, Folk art & Oriental rugs.

**Park Place Antique
Jewelry
6 Bridge St.
(609) 397-0102**
Fine antique and estate
jewelry. Spec: period dia-
mond engagement rings.
Signed items:Tiffany,
Webb, and Van Cleef &
Arpels. Fine period pieces:
Victorian, Edwardian, Art
Deco, Retro Modern &
Platinum Era. Purchase
single items or entire col-
lections.

Perrault -Rago Gallery
17 S. Main St.
(609) 397-1802
Am & Eng Arts & Crafts
furn & dec.

Passiflora
54 Coryell
(609) 397-1010

Pedersen Gallery
17 N. Union
(609) 397-1332

Peter Wallace Antiques
5 Lambert Lane
(609) 397-4914

Phoenix Books
49 N. Union St.
(609) 397-4960
OP & Usd books.

Porkyard Antiques
8 Coryell St.
(609) 397-2088
Multi-dealer shop.

Portico
48 Coryell St.
(609) 397-6353
Country items, repro & dec.

Prestige Antiques
287 S. Main St.
The Laceworks Bldg.
(609) 397-2400
Importers of Fr & Eng furn.
Spec: formal & country.

Robert H. Yaroschuk
10 N. Union St.
(609) 397-8886
Furn & dec.

Robin's Egg Gallery
24 N. Union St.
(609) 397-9137
Period furn, paintings &
architecturals.

Rossi Antiques
285 S. Main St.
(609) 397-1599

Stefon's Antiques
29 Bridge St.
(609) 397-8609
18th c.-1940s: Sterling, crystal,
small furn & porc.

Taylor's Country Store
28 N. Union St.
(609) 397-8816

The 5 & Dime
40 N. Union St.
(609) 397-4957
1900-present coll toys.

The Drawing Room Antiques
36 S. Main St.
Lambertville, NJ
(609) 397-7977
18th & 19th c. furn & dec.

The Old Carriage House
51 Bridge St.
(609) 397-3331
Am. furn & dec .

The Orchard Hill
Collection
22 N. Union St.
(609) 397-1188
Dutch Colonial furn. & dec.
Spec: cupboards.

The People's Store
28 N. Union St.
(609) 397-9808
Multi-dealer co-op.

Undercover Underfoot
12 Church St.
(609) 397-0044

Weaver Antiques &
Fine Furnishings
9-B Church
(609) 397-4171

Lebanon

Jantiques
1261 Rt. 31
(908) 735-4009

Lebanon Antique Center
1211 Rt. 22
(908) 236-6616
General line.

Oldwick

Collections
152 Oldwick Rd. (Rt. 523)
(908) 439-3736
General line.

Keeping Room Antiques
53 Main St. (Rt. 517)
(908) 439-3701
Primitive furn & dec. Spec:
primitive painted cupboards.

The Magic Shop
60 Main St.
(908) 439-2330
General line.

Pittstown

Jan's Vintage Textiles
At the Sky Manor Airport
(908) 996-1000
Textiles.

Provenance Auction Associates
Sky Manor Rd.
(908) 996-7505
Call for auction dates & times.

Pottersville

Moonlight Mile Antiques
10 Black River Rd.
(908) 439-3337

The Mill
Fairmount Rd. (East)
(908) 439-2724/439-3803
Books & prints.

Ringoes

Ted Allgair Antiques
Rt. 31
(609) 466-9296
19th & early 20th c. furn.
Early pottery. Stained glass

Rosemont

Lots of Time Shop
78 Rt. 519
(Stockton-Kingwood Rd.)
(609) 397-0890
Clocks & clock repair.

Whitehouse Station

Whitehouse Station
Old Highway Antiques
406 Rt. 22 West
(908) 534-1822

MERCER COUNTY

Hamilton Township
Hightstown
Hopewell
Princeton
Trenton

MERCER COUNTY NEW JERSEY

Hamilton Township

Greenwood Antiques
1918 Greenwood Ave.
(609) 586-6887
Am. Paintings & OP art books.
By appt.

Hightstown

Empire Antiques
278 Monmouth St.
(609) 426-0820
Gen line: antiq, usd, repro &
import. Call for auction dates
& times.

The Timekeeper Antiques
780 York Road (Rt. 539)
(609) 448-0269
Oak & walnut furn & clocks.

Olde Country Antiques
346 Franklin St.
(609) 448-2670
18th & 19th c. primitives, oil
lamps, early furn & coll.

Hopewell

Brian Gage Antiques
33 W. Broad St.
(609) 466-1722
Furniture & dec items.

Camelot Antiques
& Interiors...
31 West Broad St.
(609) 333-1033
Eclectic mix of Euro, Asian
& Primitives, artworks,
Oriental rugs, lamps, mir-
rors, clocks, collectibles &
architecturals. Unique &
unusual finds for your castle.
Buy-Sell. Estates purchased.
www.camelotantiques.com

Hopewell Antique Center
35 W. Broad St.
(609) 466-2990
Multi-dealer co-op.

Hopewell Antique Cottage
8 Somerset St.
(609) 466-1810
Late 19th & early 20th c. formal
furn. Spec: dining rooms.

Hopewell Antique Paper
& Collectibles Center
#1 Railrod Place
(609) 466-0303

On Military Matters
31 W. Broad St.
(609) 466-2329
Books.

Pennfield Antiques
47 W. Broad St. (Rt. 518)
(609) 466-0827
Vic furn, lighting & mirrors.

Sallies Antiques
33 W. Broad St.
(609) 466-7449
Am cut glass, Venetian glass,
china & sterling.

Tomato Factory Antique
Center
Hamilton Ave. (At end of
street)
(609) 466-9833
Multi-dealer center.

Princeton

Bryn Mawr Bookshop
Arts Council
102 Witherspoon St.
(609) 921-7479
Rare, 1st ed & OP books.

Collectors' Editions
P.O. Box 7005
Princeton, NJ
(609) 520-1669
Books: photography & dec
arts only. Catalog avail.

East & West Antiques
4451 Rt. 27
(609) 924-2743
Spec: Chinese furn & dec.

Eye For Art
6 Spring St.
(609) 924-5277

Gilded Lion
4 Chambers St.
(609) 924-6350

Skilman Furniture
212 Alexander St.
(609) 924-1881
Usd furn.

Tamara's Things
4206 Quaker Bridge Rd.
(609) 452-1567

The Silver Shop
59 Palmer Square W.
(609) 924-2026

Witherspoon Art & Book
12 Nassau St.
(609) 924-3582
Used books.

Trenton

Antiques by Selmon
10 Vetterlein Ave.
(609) 586-0777

Armies of the Past Ltd.
2038 Greenwood Ave.
(609) 890-0142
Military items. Civil War-
Vietnam. Sat or by appt.

Canty Inc.
1680 N. Olden Ave.
(609) 530-1832
Usd. & antiq. furn.

Searchmon
1027 S. Broad St.
(609) 394-0099

MIDDLESEX COUNTY

Cranbury

East Brunswick

Edison

Fords

Highland Park

Jamesburg

Metuchen

New Brunswick

North Brunswick

Pennington

Perth Amboy

Piscataway

Woodbridge

MIDDLESEX COUNTY NEW JERSEY

Cranbury

Adams Brown Company
26 N. Main St.
(609) 655-8269
By appt.

Anthony's Cranbury Antiques
60 N. Main St.
(609) 655-3777
Jewelry. Spec: formal Vic
furn, porc & art glass.

Cranbury Book Worm
54 N. Main St.
(609) 655-1063
Rare books.

David Wells Antiques
55 N Main St.
(609) 655-0085
Gen line.

East Brunswick

LB Military Goods
290 Rt.18
(732) 238-6011
Military items, WWI-Korea
& Vietnam.

Edison

Edison Hall Books
5 Ventnor Dr.
(732) 548-4455
Art, pottery, 1st eds by appt.
or mail order only.

Fords

Bargain Market
491 New Brunswick Ave.
(732) 738-5077
Antiq & usd furn.

Highland Park

Karwen's Antiques
68 Raritan Ave.
(732) 828-5575
Gen line. Spec: vintage
costume jewelry.

Neil's Classic Novelty
   Emporium
179 Woodbridge Ave.
(732) 572-3286
Gen line, usd furn & antiqs.

Rutgers Gun Center
127 Raritan Ave.
(732) 545-4344
Firearms & access. Spec:
books on firearms.

Jamesburg

Barbara's Unique Antique
   Boutique
35 E. Railroad Ave.
(732) 521-9055
Smalls & small furn.
Spec: jewelry.

Metuchen

Boro Art Center
505 Middlesex Ave.
(732) 549-7878

Metuchen Antique Shop
267 Central Ave.
(732) 603-9724

New Brunswick

Aaron Aardvark & Son
119 French St.
(732) 246-1720
Gen line. Spec: 18th, 19th
& 20th c. furn.

Amber Lion Antiques
365 George &
Paterson Sts.
(732) 214-9090
Gen line 18th c.-1950s.

American Antiques Auction
1050 George St.
(732) 247-6767
Call for auction dates & times.

Gallen Furniture
162 Church St.
(732) 846-3695
Old & new furniture.

Somewhere In Time
365 George St.
(732) 247-3636
Gen line, Vic-1970s.

North Brunswick

Davidson Mill Village
2430 Rt. 130
(732) 940-8600
General line.

Pennington

S&S Collectibles
2516 Pennington Rd.
(609) 737-3040
Wholesler, furn & lighting.

Perth Amboy

Crystal Shoppe Antiques
289 High St.
(732) 442-2704

Maid of Perth
211 Front St.
(732) 442-4472

New Jersey Wholesale
450 Market St.
(732) 442-4242
18th c. repro furn.

Piscataway

Becky's Antiques
500 New Market Rd.
(732) 968-6227
Gen line. Spec: Vic furn.

Woodbridge

Nana's Attic
114 Main St.
(732) 855-1121

MONMOUTH COUNTY

Allentown
Asbury Park
Atlantic Highlands
Avon By The Sea
Belmar
Brielle
Deal
Eatontown
Englishtown
Fair Haven
Farmingdale
Freehold
Highlands
Holmdel
Howell
Keyport
Little Silver

Locust
Long Branch
Manalapan
Manasquan
Marlboro
Middletown
Millstone
Red Bank
Rumson
Sea Girt
Spring Lake
Wall
Wanamassa
West Belmar
West End

MONMOUTH COUNTY NEW JERSEY

Allentown

Brown Bear's Antiques
24 South Main St.
(609) 259-0177
Furniture & art.

Veronica's Cottage
40 S. Main St.
(609) 259-6640
Gen line, vint & antiq.

Asbury Park

Ann Tiques
1022 Main St.
(732) 869-0347

Antic Hay Rare Books
P.O. Box 2185
Asbury Park, NJ 07712
(732) 774-4590
Rare, fine & OP books.
Mail order & internet only.

House of Modern Living
701 Cookman Ave.
(732) 988-2350
1950s-70s furn & access.

Of Rare Vintage
718 Cookman Ave.
(732) 988-9459
1920s-40s furn & access.

Olde England Antiques
  Paul Mitchell Antiques
901 Main St. (Corner 1st Ave.)
Asbury Park, NJ
(732) 988-6686/998-6686

Wm. Barron Galleries
504 Main St.
(732) 988-7711
Call for auction dates & times.

Atlantic Highlands

East House Antiques
Rt. 36 & Sears Ave.
(732) 291-2147
Gen line.

Avon By The Sea

Country By the Sea
515 Sylvania Ave.
(732) 776-6671
Multi-dealer co-op.

Belmar

Aajeda Antiques
1800 F St.
Corner 18th & Main Sts.
(732) 502-3131

The Antique Connection
404 5th Ave.
(732) 681-3970

Brielle

Brielle Antique Center
Union & Green Lanes
at the River
(732) 528-8570
Multi-dealer co-op.

Chappie's Antiques & Collectibles
406 Higgins Ave.
(732) 528-8989
Gen line. Spec: vin doll
houses & miniatures.

Escargot Books
503 Rt. 71
(732) 528-5955
Usd & rare books.

Relics
605-R Rt. 71
(732) 223-3452

Deal

Surrey Lane Antiques
Footnotes Plaza
280 Norwood Ave.
(732) 531-6991
General line.

Eatontown

Earth Treasures & Jewelers
Office Max Plaza
Between Rt. 35 S & 36 W
(732) 542-5444
Estate jewelry.

Antique Treasure Haven
152 Main St.
(732) 544-5665
Spec: dining room sets.

Englishtown

Englishtown Auction Sales
  & Flea Market
Old Bridge Rd.
(732) 446-9644
40 acres, indoor & outdoor
stalls. Sat & Sun.

Englishtown Antiques &
  Used Furniture
42 Main St.
(732) 446-3330
Gen line, antiq & usd furn,
vint clothing.

Fair Haven

Blue Stove Antiques
769 River Rd.
(732) 747-6777
Silv, porc & furn. Spec:
clocks & watches,1700-1998.

Farmingdale

Cobwebs Cottage
58 Main St. (Rts. 524 & 547)
(732) 938-2626
Multi-dealer co-op.

Freehold

County Seat Antique
  Center
28 W. Main St.
(732) 431-2644
Multi-dealer shop specializing in furniture, smalls,
crystal, cut glass and
Depression glass. Dealers
welcome!

Frantiques
33 W. Main St.
(732) 780-8872
Multi-dealer shop.

Freehold Antique Gallery
21 W. Main St.
(732) 462-7900
Multi-dealer co-op.

Freehold Furniture Exchange
2 Monmouth Ave.
(732) 462-1333
General line.

Laura's Doll Houses
  & Collectibles
103 Koster Dr.
(732) 294-7407
Cookie jars, S & P shakers,
teapots & advertising.

Highlands

Forever Antiques
120 Bay Ave.
(732) 872-6200
General line.

Holmdel

Raritan Bay Auction Services
26-A Van Brackle Rd.
(732) 264-6532
Call for auction dates& times.

Howell

Gemco Gold Buying Service
4335 Rt. 9
(732) 370-1959
Jewelry.

Gemini Antiques
In Collingswood Flea Market
Collingswood Auction
(732) 938-4441
Usd furn. & dec.

Howell Station Antique Mall
  & Flea Market
2301 Rt. 9 N
(732) 308-1105

Katarina's Antiques
In Collingswood Flea Market
Rt. 33
Farmingdale, NJ
(732) 938-4170

Keyport

Collector's Cottage
34 Main St.
(732) 264-2453
Gen line.

Grandma's Olde & New
34 W. Front St.
(732) 335-4190
Furn, lamps & clocks.

Keyport Antique Emporium
46-50 W. Front St.
(732) 888-2952
Jewlry, porc & Dep glass.

Keyport Consignment Shop
242 Broad St.
(732) 739-4626
Consignment shop.

North River Antiques
2 W Front St.
(732) 264-0580
Call for auction dates & times.

Patricia's Antiques
  & Collectibles
13 W. Front St.
(732) 335-0208
15 dealers. Vintage furniture, antiques & collect-
ables. Scientific instru-
ments. Depression glass.
Open Wed-Sun 11-5.

Ron's Lionel Trains
  & Accessories
At Patricia's Antiques
13 W. Front St.
(732) 308-9631-Home
(732) 335-0208-Shop
All gauges bought & sold.
From one piece to whole
collections.

Second Hand Lil
24 Broad St.
(732) 264-0777
General line.

Second Hand Prose
8 Main St.
(732) 335-9090
Usd. Books.

The Front Porch
36 W. Front St.
(732) 335-0826

The Keyport Antique
  Market
17-21 W. Front St.
(732) 203-1001
www.KeyportAntiqueMarket.com
25,000 sq. ft. Largest Indoor
market in New Jersey. 200
dealers. Open 7 days: Tues
10-3, Wed-Mon 10-5. Air
conditioned. 45 mins from
NYC. 15 mins from Red
Bank. Exit 117 Garden
State Parkway.

Twice is Nice
24 W. Front St.
(732) 888-9596
2,500 sq. ft. of antiques,
collectibles & quality pre-
owned furniture. Turn of
the century to present.
Known for maple: tables,
chairs, hutches & desks.
Sell full line of Howard
products.

Little Silver

Mill House Antiques
32 Willow Dr.
(732) 741-7411
Spec: Eng, Fr & Am furn.

Locust

Locust Antiques
487 Locust Point Rd.
(732) 291-4575
General line.

Long Branch

Antiques by John Gormley
269 Broadway
(732) 571-4849/244-7724
Furniture.

Stan Buck Restorations
& Antiques
553 Broadway
(908) 229-0522
Furn & dec.

Take A Gander
84 Brighton Ave.
(732) 229-7389

Manalapan

NJ Galleries
161 Pension Rd.
(732) 446-9490
Furniture & fine art.

Manasquan

Carriage House Center
140 Main St.
(732) 528-6772
Multi-dealer co-op.

Casey's Alley
79 Main St. &
South St. Plaza
(732) 223-0064
General line.

Eclectic Mix
73 Main St.
(732) 223-7170
Gen line, 1930's-60s.

Marlboro

Grandma's Treasures
35 N. Main St.
(732) 462-2381
General line.

Marlboro Country Antiques
233 Rt. 79
(732) 946-8794
General line.

Middletown

A Paradiso Garden
212 Rt. 35
(732) 758-1340
Country antiques.

Millstone

Mid Jersey Antiquarian
Book Center
480 Rt. 33
(732) 446-5656
Rare & OP book. Maps, prints, autographs, photos & ephemera.

Red Bank

Antiques Associates
205 W. Front St.
(732) 219-0377
Furn, mirrors, porc, china & glass.

Antique Corner
65 Broad St.
(732) 450-0054
Multi-dealer co-op.

Aunt E's Attic
30 Monmouth St.
(732) 842-3651
Vintage clothing.

British Cottage Antiques
126 Shrewsbury Ave.
(732) 530-0685
Euro pine furn. & custom pine repro.

Cool Carousel
28 Broad St.
(732) 758-1700
Repro, all periods & styles.

Classic Revival
16 Wallace St.
(732) 530-6707
Asian & Euro furn & dec.

Copper Kettle Antiques
15 Broad St.
(732) 741-8583

Double Dutch Antiques
18 Wallace St.
(732) 345-0845
Pine furn from Holland.
Repro from salvage.

Downtown Antiques
27 Monmouth St.
(732) 219-8955
Multi-dealer co-op.

Galleria Antiques
Bridge Ave. & W. Front St.
(732) 530-7300
Furn, mirrors, chandeliers,
period-coll. Appt. only.

Gaslight Antiques
212 W. Front St.
(732) 741-7323

Les Femmes des Roses
214 W. Front St.
(732) 758-9550
19th & 20th c. porc,
crystal, linens, sterling.

Mayfair House
60 Monmouth St.
(732) 219-8955
19th & 20th c. paintings,
period frames & restoration.

Monmouth Antique Shoppes
217 W. Front St.
(732) 842-7377
Multi-dealer co-op

Plum Cottage
Riverside Dr. & Allen Place
(732) 219-5044

**Riverbank Antiques
& Interiors
169 W. Front St.
(732) 842-5400
Offering: All styles of
furniture, iron & brass
beds, chandeliers, crystal,**

**china & silver, collectibles
& smalls, architecturals,
fine art & rugs.
Design services available.
Open 7 days 11-5.**

**The Antiques Center of Red
Bank in three buildings:**
"Not to be missed antique
center." Newark Star Ledger.
**100 shops in 3 bldgs.
The Antiques Center-
Building I
195B W. Front St
(732) 741-5331
The Antiques Center-
Building II
195 W. Front St.
(732) 842-3393
The Antiques Center-
Building III
226 W. Front St.**

**Red Bank, NJ
(732) 842-4336**

The Art & Attic
12 Broad St.
(732) 747-7007
Jewlry, silv, furn, quilts & art.

The Golden Cherub
161 Shrewsbury Ave.
(732) 933-9555

T Berry Square
20 Broad St.
(732) 576-1819
Chandeliers, furn & linens.

Tower Hill Antiques
147 Broad St.
(732) 842-5551
Furn & dec. Spec: lamps.

Two Broad Antiques
160 Monmouth St
(732) 224-0122
Formal country furn & clocks.

Used Furniture Center of Red Bank
197 Shrewsbury Ave.
(732) 842-1449
Usd & antiq furn.

Wild Flower Antiques
19 N. Bridge Ave. (Off W. Front)
(732) 933-7733

Rumson

Mary Jane Roosevelt
109 E. River Rd.
(732) 842-3159
Fr art glass, paintings, sterling,
porc, prints, pottery & jewelry.

Sea Girt

H.E.Y. Enterprises
2100 Rt. 35, #26A
(732) 974-8855
Smalls & coins.

Spring Lake

A Touch of the Past
410 Rt. 71
(732) 974-9200
Furn, china, glass, paintngs,
silver, jewelry & lighting.

Gallery III Antiques
1720 Rt. 71
(732) 449-7560
Jewelry, glass, art, china
& vint clothing.

Spring Lake Antiques
1201 3rd Ave.
(732) 449-3322

Vitale & Vitale
  Museum Gallery
315 Morris Ave.
(732) 449-3000

Wall

Pot O Gold Antiques
2383 Ramshorn Dr.
(Off Rt. 34)
(732) 528-6648
By appointment.

Wanamassa

About Time
1411 Wickapecko Dr.
(732) 775-4650
17th & 18th c. Fr clocks.

West Belmar

Belmar Trading Post
1735 Rt. 71
(732) 681-3207

West End

Antiques & Accents
55 Brighton Ave.
(732) 222-2274

Hy'Spot Antiques & Interiors
61 Brighton Ave.
(732) 222-7880
Spec: Fr & country furn.

MORRIS COUNTY

Boonton
Butler
Chester
Dover
Kenvil
Long Valley
Madison
Mansfield
Mendham
Myersville
Millington
Morristown
Newfoundland
Pine Brook
Pompton Plains
Riverdale
Rockaway
Stirling

MORRIS COUNTY NEW JERSEY

Boonton

Blue Shutters Antiques
& Lamps Hospital
321 Main St.
(973) 299-1344
Gen line. Spec: 20s-40s
bedrm & dining rm sets.

Boonton Antiques/
Buying Associates
521 Main St.
(973) 334-4416
General line, old to new.

Cameron & Coffin
819 Main St.
(973) 331-1300

Claire Ann's Antiques
815 Main St.
(973) 334-2421
General line.

Fox Hill Exchange
900 Main St.
(973) 263-2270

The Old Feed Mill
487 Division St.
(973) 334-0001
Call for auction dates and
times.

The Tyndale Collection
920 Main St.
(973) 334-3124
18th,19th & early 20th c.
fine art, furn & clocks.

Butler

CJ's Craft Cottage
7 High St.
(973) 492-0201
Gen line, turn of cent -1980s.

Chester

Aunt Pittypats Parlour
57 E. Main St.
Spec: refinished mahogany,
oak & walnut furn, Vic-1940.

Black River Trading
Company
15 Perry St.
(908) 879-6778
New furn from salvage.

Chester Antique Center
32 Grove St.
(908) 879-4331
Am furn & early lighting.

Chester Carousel
125 Main St.
(908) 879-7141

Doll Hospital
75 Main St.
(908) 879-4101
Dolls & doll hospital.

Great American Country
25'Main St.
(908) 879-7797
Antiq iron & brass beds.

Jantiques
10 Budd Ave.
(908) 879-9409
Gen line, antiq & repro.

Marita Daniels Antiques
127 E. Main St.
(908) 879-6488

Norma Jean Antiques
484 Main St.
(908) 879-8304
Silver, furn, Persian rugs,
linens, paintngs, glass, porc.

Pegasus Antiques
98 W. Main St.
(908) 879-4792
General line.

Robins Nest
125 Maple Ave.
(908) 879-5131

Spinning Wheel Antiques
76 E. Main St.
(908) 879-6080
General line. Spec:
Country & Vic furn.

The Beauty of Civilization
Perry St.
(908) 879-2044
Furn, vint clothing, jewlry.
china, crystal silver & dec.

The Chester Timepiece
58 Main St.
(908) 879-5421
Antiq & new clocks.

The Joy of Antiques
87 Main St.
(908) 879-4103

Dover

Berman Auction Gallery
33 W. Blackwell St.
(973) 361-3110
Call for auction dates & times.

Duckworth's
1 W. Blackwell St.
Dover, NJ
(973) 361-7579
General line.

Iron Carriage Antiques Center
1-5 Blackwell St.
(973) 366-1440
Multi-dealer co-op, 40 dlrs.

Peddler's Shop
71 W. Blackwell St.
(973) 361-0545

The Antique Jungle
12 W. Blackwell St.
(973) 537-0099
Genral line, 1850s-1950s.
Spec: Deco lamps.

Kenvil

Country Rooster
438 Rt. 46
(973) 584-2874
Auction service.

Long Valley

Cottage Treasures
10 East Mill Rd.
(908) 876-1737
Gen line 1850-1930s.
Spec: primitive furn.

German Valley Antiques
18 Schooley's Mountian Rd.
(908) 876-9202
General line.

Neitzer Tavern Antiques
5 W. Mill Rd.
(908) 876-5854
Multi-dealer shop.

Ed & Mike's Store
In Ye Olde Ballantine Village
20 Schooley's Mountain Rd.
(908) 876-4255
Multi-dealer co-op.

Wasserhaus Antiques & Design
10 B East Mill Rd.
(908) 876-1933
Gen line & architecturals,
mid 1800-1950s.

Madison

British Pine Emporium
91 Mains St.
(908) 443-0303
Importers: pine & country
furn.

Rose's Closet
4 Lincoln Place
(973) 377-7673
Gen line.

The Chatham Bookseller
8 Green Village Rd.
(973) 822-1361
Usd & old books.

Time After Time
81 Main St.
(973) 966-6877
Vintage clothing, 1890-1980s.

The Ivy Porch
250 Main St.
(973) 514-1776
Gen line.

Mansfield

Engelmann Antiques
1966 Rt. 57
(908) 979-3030
Country furn. Primi-
tives & Folk art.

Mendham

Antique Chair Shoppe
6 Hilltop Rd.
(973) 543-2164

Crockett Ridge
3 W. Main St.
(973) 543-0466

Diane Smith Consignments
1 Hilltop Rd.
(973) 543-6199
General line: new,
usd, antq & repro.

Grand Bazaar
13 E. Main St.
(973) 543-4115
Gen line, early 1800-present.

Moorman's Gallery
Main St. (Rt. 24)
(973) 543-2030
Fine art & glass
15th c.-present

Painted Pony Antiques
16 W. Main St.
(973) 543-6484

The Acorn Shop
6 Hilltop Rd.
(973) 543-5914

The Flitrock Room
6 Hilltop Rd.
(973) 543-1861

Meyersville

Archie's Resale Shop
596 Meyersville Rd.
(908) 647-1149
General line. 4 bldgs.

The Trading Post Antiquities
211 Hickory Tavern Rd.
(908) 647-1959

Millington

Lou Souders-A Country Store
1901 Long Hill Rd.
(908) 647-7429

Morristown

Antique Buying Addition
4 South St.
(973) 539-7840
Gen line. Spec: jewelry,
oriental rugs & paintngs.

Bayberry
1001 Rt. 202
(973) 425-0101

Coletree Antiques
166 South St.
(973) 993-3011

Fearless Fearick's
166 Ridgedale Ave.
(973) 984-3140

Jeffrey Eger
42 Blackberry Lane
(973) 455-1843
Books. Appt. & mail order.

Marion Jaye Antiques
990 Mt. Kemble Ave.
(973) 425-0441
Am pressed glass & Am country furn.

Morristown Antique Center
45 Market St. (Rt. 202)
(973) 734-0900
Multi-dealer shop.

Old Book Shop
4 John St.
(973) 538-1210
Books, postcards &
Ephemera.

Robert Fountain Antiques
1107 Mt. Kemble Ave.
(973) 425-8111
19th c. Fr & Eng furn & art.

Rose Trellis
Mt. Kemble Ave. (Rt. 202)
(973) 425-1192
General line.

Newfoundland

Red Wheel Antiques
2775 Rt. 23
(973) 697-6133

Pine Brook

Dutch Gables Antiques
58 Maple Ave.
(973) 227-2803

Pompton Plains

Wayside Antiques Shop
5 Jackson Ave.
(973) 839-8129

Riverdale

Colonial Farm Antiques
44 Post Rd.
(973) 835-5916
General line.

Post Mills
41 Post Rd.
(973) 831-9287
Country furn, primitves & dec.

Rockaway

Grandma's Attic Inc.
282 W. Main St.
(973) 625-1156
General line.

Stirling

The Restore
253 Main St.
(908) 647-0613

OCEAN COUNTY

Barnegat
Barnegat Light
Bay Head
Beach Haven
Beach Haven Crest
Beachwood
Brick
Cedar Run
Eagleswood Township
Forked River
Holland Park
Jackson
Lakehurst
Lavalette
Long Beach
Manahawkin
Mayetta
New Egypt
Point Pleasant
Point Pleasant Beach
Surf City
Toms River
Tuckerton
Waretown
West Creek

"A Multi-Dealer Antique Market Place"

West Bay Antiques

349 S. Main St. (Route 9)
Barnegat, NJ 08005
609-698-3020
Fax: 609-698-3059

Open 7 Days A Week

VISIT BARNEGAT NJ
Exit 67 Garden State Pkwy. South
AN UP & COMING ANTIQUE CENTER!

Barnegat

Barnegat Antique Country
684 E. Bay Ave.
(609) 698-8967

Barnegat Antiques & Uniques
323 Rt. 9
(609) 660-1464

Del's Antiques
307 S. Main St.
(609) 660-1688

First National
708 W. Bay Ave. &
Railroad Ave.
(609) 698-1413
Gen line. Spec:Vic furn.

Forget Me Not Shoppe
689 E. Bay Ave.
(609) 698-3107

Lindy's Military
Antiques
(Rt. 9)
(609) 698-2415
Military antiques: swords,
uniforms, helmets,
weapons, war posters, toy
soldiers, miniatures, &
beer steins.

Sneak Box Antiques
273 S. Main St.
(609) 698-8222

The Goldduster
695 E. Bay Ave.
(609) 698-2520
Jewelry, Dep glass & coll.

The Raintree Cottage
273 S. Main St.
(609) 660-0777

West Bay Antiques
Shoppers Corner
349 S. Main St. (Rt. 9)
(609) 698-3020
Exit 67 Garden State
Pkwy. South. A multi-
dealer antique market
place. The newest antique
destination. Open 7 days
a week

Barnegat Light

Americana by the Seashore
604 Broadway
(609) 494-0656
19th c. Oyster plates, tall
clocks & ancient coins.

Nichole's Antiques
410 Broadway
(609) 494-1557

Bay Head

Fables of Bay Head
410 Main Ave. (Rt. 35)
(732) 899-3633
Country Am furn (pine
& oak). Quilts & folk art.

Beach Haven

Pink Petunia
216 S. Bay Ave.
(609) 492-0023

Somewhere In Time
202 Centre Ave.
(609) 207-1221

Summerhouse
412 N. Bay Ave.
(609) 492-6420

Beach Haven Crest

Age of Antiquities
8013 Long Beach Blvd.
(609) 494-0735

House of Seven Wonders
7600 Long Beach Blvd.
(609) 494-9673
Gen line.

Wizard of Odds Antiques
7601 Long Beach Blvd.
(609) 494-5580.

Beachwood

All Antiques Appreciated
118 Atlantic City Blvd.
(732) 818-7719

OCEAN COUNTY, NJ

Brick

The Bargain Outlet
2104 Rt. 88
(732) 892-9007
Usd. furn.

Monique's
421 Rt. 73
(609) 753-8906
Spec: jewelry.

Pavilion Antiques
40 Brick Blvd.
(732) 864-1116
Multi-dealer co-op.

Cedar Run

Jo's Thrift Shop
Rt. 9 S.
(609) 597-1700

Eagleswood Township

Pine Barrens Antiques
476 Rt. 9S.
(609) 597-9300
Gen line. Spec: Am pottery.

Forked River

Victorian Charm
202 Rt. 9 (Main St.)
(609) 597-1122
Multi-dealer co-op.

Holland Park

Neil's Classic Novelty Emporium
179 Woodbridge Ave.
(732) 572-3286
General line.

Rutgers Gun Center
127 Raritan Ave.
(732) 545-4344
Guns & Swords.

Jackson

Unlock The Past
959 W. Veterans Hwy.
(732) 928-5600

Lakehurst

Good Old Times
3086 Rt. 571
(732) 657-4433
Multi-dealer co-op.

Treasure Chest
666 Rt. 70 W
(732) 657-2590

Lavalette

Clem's Antiques
1501 Rt. 35
(732) 793-2299
Gen line. Spec: Vic.

Curious Finds
1403 Rt. 35
(732) 793-5330
Furn & dec.

Long Beach

Ship Bottom Antiques
Central Ave. at 28th St.
(609) 361-0885

Manahawkin

Cornucopia
140 N. Main St.
(Old Rt. 9)
(609) 978-0099
Multi-dealer co-op.

The Shoppes
at Rosewood
182 N. Main St. (Rt. 9)
(609) 597-7331
Multi-dealer co-op.

Manor House Shops
160 N. Main St. (Rt. 9)
(609) 597-1122
Early 20th c. Mix of
primitives & Vic.

Mayetta

Country Charm Shoppes
775 S. Main St. (Rt. 9)
(609) 978-1737
Gen line.

New Egypt

New Egypt Auction
& Farmers Market
933 Rt. 537
(609) 758-2082
Auctions & flea market.

Red Barn Antiques
56 Maple Ave.
(609) 758-9152
Furn, glass & coll.

Step Back In Time
45 Main St.
(609) 758-9598

Point Pleasant

Concepts I Auction
1125 Arnold Ave.
(732) 892-6040

Pomegranate
707 Arnold Ave.
(732) 892-0200

Point Pleasant Beach

Avenue Antiques
638 Arnold Ave.
(732) 892-2770
General line.

Book Bin
725 Arnold Ave.
(732) 892-3456
Books only.

Classy Collectibles
633 Arnold Ave.
(732) 714-0957
Jewelry & collectibles.
Clock & Antique Shop
726A Arnold Ave.
(732) 899-6200
Clocks, watches & jewlry.

Fond Memories Antiques
625-R Arnold Ave.
(732) 892-4149
Gen line, late 1900-1960s.

Globetrotter
(Seasonal Location)
1809 Ocean Ave.
(732) 892-2001

Point Pavillion
608 Arnold Ave.
(732) 899-6330
Multi-dealer co-op.

**Point Pleasant
  Antique Emporium
Bay & Trenton Aves.
(732) 892-2222/800-322-8002
The Antique Emporium...
an exciting showcase of
antique furniture & col-
lectibles located down-
town in the famous resort
community of Point
Pleasant Beach. Over
125 dealers under one
roof buying & selling
quality antiques.**

**Shore Antique Center
300 Richmond Ave.
(Rt. 35 South)
(732) 295-5771
40 dealers. 10,000 sq. ft.
of: furn, nautical items,
early glass, souvenir
china, silver, pottery,
paintings, postcards,
records, modern design,
books, dec pieces & more.
Where the dealers shop.
Open daily, 11-5.**

The Company Store
628 Bay Ave.
(732) 892-5353
Multi-dealer co-op.

The Time Machine
516 Arnold Ave.
(732) 295-9695
Records, film/TV mem.
& coll.

Wally's Follies Antiques
718 Arnold Ave.
(732) 899-1840
Vint costume jewlry.

Willinger's Annex
626 Ocean Rd.
(732) 892-2217
Multi-dealer shop.

Surf City

Hill Galleries
1603 Long Beach Blvd.
(609) 361-8225

Toms River

Absolutely All Antiques
612 Helen St.
(732) 240-2429
Gen line, Warehse by appt.

Bulldog Glass Co.
10 W. Gateway
(732) 349-2742
Dep. glass & pottery.

Main Street Center
249-251 Main St.
(732) 349-5764
Multi-dealer co-op.

The Piggy Bank
2018 Rt. 37 (East)
(732) 506-6133
Antq & usd furn. 3 bldgs.

Tuckerton

Port of Entry
147 N. Main St. (Rt. 9)
(609) 294-1527
Gen line.

Used Furniture Outlet
1 Great Bay Blvd.
(609) 294-2606
Usd furn.

Waretown

Thrift Barn
Rt. 9
(609) 693-6306

West Creek

Helen's Antiques
662 Rt. 9
(609) 660-1230
General line.

PASSAIC COUNTY

Clifton
Passaic
Paterson
Pompton Lakes

PASSAIC COUNTY NEW JERSEY

Clifton

Antique Cottage
  Liquidators
35 Dermott Ave.
(973) 472-4251
Call for auction dates,
times & locations.

Granny's Attic
  Closeout Center
1080 Main St.
(973) 772-1929
Gen line: usd, antiq &
retro. Sat only.

Passaic

Jan, Jill & Jon
170 Main Ave.
(973) 777-4670

Our Favorite Things
90 Dayton Ave.
(973) 779-6997

Paterson

Lucky Thrifts
245 Crooks St.
(973) 684-4904

The Silk Mill
111 Marion St.
(201) 529-5516
Euro & Am furn & dec.
Sat & Sun or appt.

Pompton Lakes

Carroll's Antiques
326 Wanaque Ave.
(973) 831-6186

Charisma 7 Antiques
212 Wanaque Ave.
(973) 839-7779
Spec: Vint clothing &
jewlry.

Experienced Furniture
276 Wanaque Ave.
(973) 616-4720
Dec & hand painted furn.

M.T.H Gallery
322D Wanaque Ave.
(973) 831-4495

Miss Bailey's
229 Wanaque Ave.
(973) 248-1800
Furn & vintage toys.

Pickers Paradise
269 Wanaque Ave.
(973) 616-9500
Gen line: antiq, usd & new.

Sterling Antique Center
222 Wanaque Ave.
(973) 616-8986
Multi-dealer co-op.

SALEM COUNTY

Alloway
Elmer
Monroeville
Pennsville
Sharptown
Woodstown

SALEM COUNTY
NEW JERSEY

Alloway

Dorrell's Antiques
21 Lambert St.
(856) 935-4296

Seven Hearths Antiques
34 N.Greenwich St.
(856) 935-4976
Gen line. Spec: 18th
& 19th c. furn.

Elmer

George Hawriluk
Buck Rd.
(856) 358-7267

Monroeville

Elmer Auction Co.
260 Swedesboro Rd.
(856) 358-8433
Call for auction dates & times.

Pennsville

Country Peddlar
104 N. Hook Rd.
(856) 678-5509
General line.

Holly Tree Antiques
101 William Penn Ave.
(856) 678-7100
Spec: old glass & china.

Sharptown

Cow Town Flea Market
Rt. 40
(856) 769-3202
Indoor & outdoor flea market
every Tues & Sat.

Woodstown

Oakbarn Antiques
At Victorian Rose
Farm Bed & Breakfast
947 Rt. 40
(856) 769-4600
Multi-dealer co-op.

SOMERSET COUNTY

Bedminster

Bernardsville

Bound Brook

Blawenburg

Gladstone

GreenBrook

Kingston

Martinsville

North Branch

North Plainfield

Peapack

Pluckemin

Raritan

Somerville

Watchung

SOMERSET COUNTY NEW JERSEY

Bedminster

Baobab Books
1555 Lamington Rd.
(908) 234-9163
Books, by appoint.

Potters Shed Antiques
95 Sommerville Rd.
(908) 781-1935

Bernardsville

Bernardsville Antiques
111 Morristown Rd.
(908) 204-0868
Gen line. Spec: Paintings,
chandeliers & Oriental rugs.

Encore Consignments
123A Claremont Rd.
(908) 766-7760
Consignment shop.

Peter Sena
 Mine Brook Antiques
Rt. 202
(908) 766-3505
General line.

Bound Brook

DiBetti Antiques
16 Hamilton St.
(732) 356-3735
General line.

I Remember When
25 Hamilton St.
(732) 563-1012
Furn & collectibles.

Blawenburg

Decorators Consignment
 Gallery
Corner of Rts. 518 & 601
(609) 466-4400
Consignment shop.

Gladstone

Thompson's Antiques
279 Main St.
(908) 719-2424

Green Brook

Attic Treasures
319-323 Rt. 22
(732) 752-2442
Gen line.

Kingston

Quality Consignment
61 Main St.
(609) 924-3924

Martinsville

Martinsville Antique Center
1944 Washington Valley Rd.
(732) 302-1229
Multi-dealer co-op.

North Branch

Little House Antiques
3355 Rt. 22 (East)
(908) 526-6235
Refinished Vic furn.Spec:
iron & brass beds & lighting.

North Plainfield

Collector's Corner
326 Somerset St.
(908) 753-2650

Peapack

Ludlow & Ely Antiques
151 Main St.
(908) 781-6655
18th & 19th c. Eng & Am furn.
Sporting paintings & bronzes.

Pluckemin

Country Antiques
327 Rts. 202 & 206
(908) 658-3759
Multi-dealer. Spec: Country
furn, lighting & dec.

Raritan

Gold & Silver Antique Emporium
20 W. Somerset St.
(908) 725-9470
Spec: jewelry, 1830-1940.
Sterling, pottery & glass.

Village Antiques
44 W. Somerset St.
(908) 526-7920
Multi-dealer co-op.

Somerville

Antiques Emporium
70 W. Main St.
(908) 231-8850
Multi-dealer co-op.

County Seat Antiques
41 W. Main St.
(908) 595-9556
Multi-dealer co-op.

Incogneeto Neet-O-Rama
19 W. Main St.
(908) 231-1887
Toys, records, magazines,
TV, movie & rock'n roll mem.

P.M. Bookshop
59 W. Main St.
(908) 722-0055
Books.

Somerville Antique Center
17 Division St.
Somerville, NJ
(908) 526-3446
Multi-dealer co-op.

The Art Gallery Antiques
20 Division St.
(908) 429-0370
Mem, coll, toys, smalls
& books.

Torpedo's Art Glass
30 Division St.
(908) 595-9000
Glass: Venetian, Czech, Carnival, Perfumes, 50s/60s,
stained.

"Uptown" at Somerville
   Center Antiques
13 Division St.
Somerville, NJ
(908) 595-1294
Multi-dealer co-op.

Watchung

Valley Furniture Shop
20 Stirling Rd.
(908) 756-7623
Reproductions.

SUSSEX COUNTY

Andover
Branchville
Franklin
Hainesville
Lafayette
Montague
Newton
Sparta
Stillwater
Stockholm
Vernon

Andover

Andover Village Shops
125 Main Street
(973) 786-6494

Country and Stuff
127 Main St. (Rt. 206)
(973) 786-7086
Gen line. Spec: cameras,
trains, old & new dolls.

Great Andover Antique
   Company
124 Main St. (Rt. 206)
(973) 786-6384
Multi-dealer co-op. Spec:
Edison players w/ horns.

Long Ago Antiques
Main St.
(973) 786-5993

Oriental Rugs
Rt. 206
(973) 786-6004
New & old Oriental rugs.
Military, Civil War-WWII.

Red Parrot Antiques
118 Rt. 206
(973) 786-5007
Multi-dealer co-op.

Scranberry Coop
42 Main St. (Rt. 206)
(973) 786-6414
Multi-dealer co-op. 150+ dlrs.

Three Generations
1 Grist Mill Lane
(201) 786-7000

Branchville

Branchville Center
383 Rt. 206
Branchville, NJ
(973) 616-8986/948-0907
Multi-delaer co-op.

Franklin

Edison Antiques Inc.
49 Church St. (Rt. 631)
(973) 827-7136
Featuring Dining room
sets, china, silver, silver-
plate, jewelry, dolls,
framed prints, lace & vin-
tage clothing & much
more!! Easy to find!
Located between Rts. 23
& 94 on Rt. 631.
Open Fri-Sun, 11-5.

Munson Emporium
33 Munsonhurst Rd.
(973) 827-0409
Multi-dealer co-op.

Hainesville

Colophon Books
Ayers Rd.
(973) 948-5785
Books only.

Lafayette

Bogwater Jim Antiques
12 Morris Farm Rd.
(973) 383-6057/383-8170
Spec: pond boats.

Lafayette Mill Center
12 Morris Farm Rd.
(973) 383-0065
Multi-dealer co-op.

Lamplighters
156 Rt. 15
(973) 383-5513
Spec: lighting & oil
lamps.

Lockward Antiques
102 Rt.15
(973) 383-1434
Country antiques.

Mill Mercantile
11 Morris Farm Rd.
(973) 579-1588
Multi-dealer co-op.

Montague

Jean's Antiques
445 Rt. 206
(973) 293-7311
Gen line. Spec: Turn of
cent. furn.

Newton

Irene M. Pavese
7 Main St.
(973) 579-6469
Gen line. Spec: old, rare,
1st ed & OP books. Prints.

North East Stained Glass
55 Mill St.
(973) 383-0006
Sales & restoration of
stained glass.

Nostalgia Shop
139 Spring St.
(973) 383-7233
Spec: oak furn, costume
jewelry & postcards.

Pavese
7 Main St.
(973) 579-6469

Second Chance
37 Diller Ave.
(973) 579-2028
Used furn & coll.

EDISON ANTIQUES, INC.
49 Church Street • Franklin, New Jersey
973-827-7136
Friday - Sunday, 11:00 to 5:00

Featuring:

CHINA	DINING ROOM SETS	SILVER & SILVER PLATE	DOLLS
JEWELRY	LACE & VINTAGE CLOTHING & MUCH MORE!!		FRAMED PRINTS

LOCATED BETWEEN RTES. 23 & 94 ON RTE. 631
49 CHURCH STREET, FRANKLIN, NJ - EASY TO FIND
3/4 OF A MILE OFF RTE. 23
TURN AT LIGHT BY FRANKLIN DINER

Spring Street
103 Spring St.
(973) 3835950
Multi-dealer co-op.

Sparta

Sparta Antiques Center
24 Main St.
(973) 729-4545
18th & 19th c. Cont, Am &
Euro furn, jewelry & silver.

Stillwater

Antiques & Collectibles
923 Main St.
(973) 579-9933
Furn, primitives & coll.

The Wooden Skate
903 Main St.
(973) 383-3094
Primitives.

Stockholm

Snufftown Antiques
2760 Rt. 23
(973) 208-0135
Spec: the odd &
unusual.

Stockholm Antique Center
2841 Rt. 23 S.
(973) 697-9622
Multi-dealer co-op.

Second Time Around
2786 Rt. 23 N.
(973) 208-9006
Oak, primitive & country
furn.

Vernon

Antique Mania
399 Rt. 515
(973) 764-6981
Furn, art, silver, china.

UNION COUNTY

Cranford

Elizabeth

Garwood

Hillside

Linden

New Providence

Plainfield

Rahway

Roselle

Scotch Plains

Summit

Union

Westfield

UNION COUNTY NEW JERSEY

Cranford

Cobweb Collectibles
& Ephemera
9 Walnut Ave.
(908) 272-5777
Postcards, sheet music,
cameras & toys.

Dovetails
6 Eastman St.
(908) 709-1638
Artifacts & implements.

Nancy's Antiques
& 2nd Hand Furniture
7 Walnut Ave.
(908) 272-5056
General line.

Not Just Antiques
218 South Avenue E
(908) 276-3553
Furn, toys & dolls.

Shirley Green's Antiques
8 Eastman St.
(908) 709-0066
Spec: Fr ctry & formal. Antiq
& repro lighting & fixtures.

Elizabeth

G. Van Wolper Antiques
Elizabeth, NJ
(908) 354-8649
Fr art glass by mail order.

Lotus Books
544 Linden Ave.
(908) 354-7446
Rare, OP & 1st ed books.

Garwood

Antiques Nook
106 Center St.
(908) 233-2766
Gen line, turn of cent-1950s.

Classic Antiques
225 North Ave.
(908) 233-7667
18th, 19th & 20th c. furn &
dec.

Hillside

Turn of the Century
1538 Liberty Ave.
(973) 318-7100

Linden

Antiquities
523 N. Wood Ave.
(908) 925-1021

Just About Anything
911 W. St. George St.
(908) 935-3600
Antiqs & just about anything.

Time & Again Antiques
& Used Furniture
1080 Edward St.
(908) 352-6334
Gen line. Antiq & used.

New Providence

Dot's Wot Not Shop
1788 Springfield Ave.
(908) 464-3810
Consignment shop.

New Providence
Antique Center
1283 Springfield Ave.
(908) 464-9191
Gen. Line.

Plainfield

Antique Castle
900 Park Ave.
(908) 791-9700
Multi-dealer co-op,15 dlrs.

Kenny's Used Furniture
300 W. Front St.
(908) 753-4474
Usd & antiq furn.

Tierney's Antiques
515 Park Ave.
(908) 753-2417

Tony D's Used Furniture
414 Watchung Ave.
(908) 226-1025
Usd. & antiq furn.

Rahway

Ken's Antiques
1667 Irving St.
(732) 381-7306

Old Serendipity Shop
690 W. Grand Ave.
(732) 388-4393/388-1265

Tarnished Swan
74 E. Cherry St.
(732) 499-7111
Lighting, furn & jewelry.

Roselle

Haywood Antiques
316 Amsterdam Ave.
Roselle, NJ
(908) 241-9120
Used furn & objects of art.

Scotch Plains

Chem Clean Antiques,
  Furniture & Restorations
505 Terrill Rd. & E. 2nd St.
(908) 322-4433
Furn restorations, repairs
& sales.

Heinmeyer's Collectibles,
  Antiques & Records
1380 Terrill Rd.
(908) 322-1788
Spec: unique & unusual.

Seymour's Antiques &
  Collectibles
Scotch Plains, NJ
(908) 322-1300
General line.

Stage House Village
Park Ave. & Front St.
(908) 322-9090
Four shops:
1. Cottage Antiques
(908) 322-2553
2. Gallerie Ani-tiques
(908) 322-4600
Staffordshire dogs &
figurines, c. 1820-1890.
3. Stage House Center
(908) 322-2311
Furn, porc. & jewelry.
4. Parse House
(908) 322-9090
Multi dealer co-op.

Summit

Antiques & Art
  By The Conductor
88 Summit Ave.
(908) 273-6893
Furn, dec, paintings,
sterling & porc.

Charming Home
358 Springfield Ave.
(908) 598-1022
Vic porc. & transferware.

Consignment & Auction
  Galleries of Summit
83 Summit Ave.
(908) 273-5055
Call for auction dates & times.

Country House
361 Springfield Ave.
(908) 277-3400
Eng country furn.

Handmaids
37 Maple St.
(908) 273-0707
Dec, furn & painted furn,
linens, pottery & quilts.

Plumquin
12 Beechwood Rd.
(908) 273-3425
Antiq & new furn, linens
& small dec.

Summit Antiques Center
511 Morris Ave.
(908) 273-9373
Multi-dealer co-op.

Summit Showcase Gallery
83 Summit Ave.
(908) 608-1290
Multi-dealer co-op.

The Sampler
96 Summit Ave.
(908) 277-4747
Dec, furn, Vic jewlry,
architecturals & garden.

Second Hand Antiques
519 Morris Ave.
(908) 273-6021
Silver, coll, toys, china
glass & furn.

The Summit Exchange
29 Lafayette Ave.
(908) 273-2867

Union

Pastimes 'N Presents
1420 Burnet Ave.
(908) 688-6335

Union Galleries
1330 Stuyvesant Ave.
(908) 964-1440
Gen Line.

Westfield

Back Room Antiques
39 Elm St.
(908) 654-5777

Betty Gallagher Antiques
266 E. Broad St.
(908) 654-4222
Gen line. Spec: jewlry
& silver.

Linda Elmore Antiques
395 Cumberland St.
(908) 233-5443

MaryLou's Memorabilia
17 Elm St.
(908) 654-7277
Vint clothing, jewlry &
access.

The Attic
415 Westfield Ave.
(908) 233-1954
China, glass & small furn.

The Old Toy Shop
757 Central Ave.
(908) 232-8388
Toys, trains & dolls.

Westfield Antiques
510 Central Ave.
(908) 232-3668
19th & 20th c. furn, art
& dec.

**Westfield Circle Antique
  Gallery
540 South Ave. (Rt. 28)
(908) 928-0100
A beautiful new 12,000
sq. ft. antique mall.
Monthly auctions.
Booth, floor & showcase
space avail. for dealers of
quality antiques.
Open 7 days.
www.antiquesfind.com**

WARREN COUNTY

Belvidere

Buttzville

Columbia

Hackettstown

Harmony

Hope

New Village

Oxford

Phillipsburg

Port Murray

Stewartsville

Warren Glen

WARREN COUNTY NEW JERSEY

Belvidere

Major Hoops Emporium
13 Market St.
(908) 475-5031
Furn, china, glass, repros,
& collectibles.

The Painted Lady
16 Greenwich St.
(908) 475-1985
Vic furn, lighting, lamps,
silver,china & glass.

Buttzville

Buttzville Center
274 Rt. 46
(908) 453-2918

Columbia

Randi Roleson Antiques
468 Rt. 94
(908) 496-4610

Hackettstown

Family Attic Antiques
117 Main St.
(908) 852-1206
General line.

Furnishings By Adam
253 Main St.
(908) 852-4385
Porc, glass & pottery.

Gabriella's Garret
124 Main St.
(908) 852-9696
General line.

Grey Cat
112 Main St.
(908) 398-5131
Furn, porc, jewely & art.

Kathy's Kove
116 Main St. (Rt. 46)
(908) 684-8440
Multi-dealer shop.

Main Street Bazaar
128 Willow Grove St.
(908) 813-2966
Usd, classic & antiq furn.

Millie Flinks
212B Main St.
(908) 850-1904

The Antique Marketplace
156 Main St. (Rt. 46)
(908) 813-8384
Multi-dealer co-op.

The Mercantile
112B Main St.
(908) 684-0902
Furn, china, pottrey,
paintings & textiles.

Uptown Rose
122 Main St.
973-347-2529/852-2333
Multi-dealer co-op.

Harmony

Harmony Barn Antiques
2481 Belvidere Rd.
(Rt. 519 N.)
(908) 859-6159
Country furn, primitives
& early glass.

Hope

Wagon Wheel Antiques
420 Silver Lake Rd.
(908) 459-5392
Spec: oak furn.

New Village

New Village Antiques
2503 Rt. 57
(908) 213-0242
Gen line. Spec: stained glass
windows & lighting.

Oxford

Jack's Barn
Route 31
(908) 453-3665

Phillipsburg

Gracy's Manor
1400 Belvidere Rd.
(908) 859-0928

Michael J. Stasak Antiques
376 River Rd.
(908) 454-6136

The Trading Post
Still Valley Circle
(908) 454-6091

Port Murray

Rocking Horse Antiques
501 Rt. 57
(908) 689-2813
Antiq & new furn & dec.

Stewartsville

1764 House
509 Uniontown Rd.
(Rt. 519)
(908) 859-1414

Fieldstone Antiques
646 S. Main St.
(908) 454-7523
18th c. furn, paintings,
architecturals & pottery.

Stone House Farm Antiques
803 Rt. 57
(908) 213-1808
Country primitive oak &
pine. Glass & pottery.

Warren Glen

Gary's Antiques
638 Rt. 627
(908) 995-2750
Gen line: antiq, usd & repro.

DELAWARE

Kent County
New Castle County
Sussex County

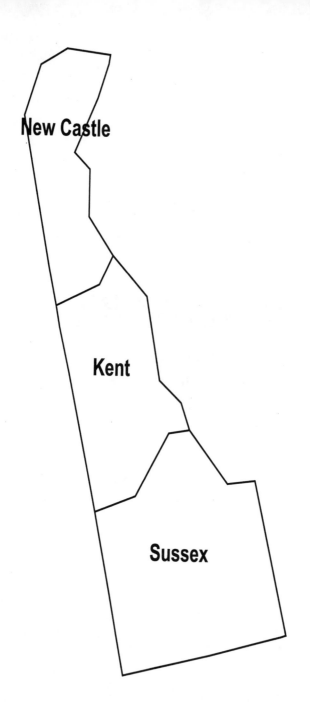

New Castle

Kent

Sussex

Delaware Counties

KENT COUNTY

Dover
Felton
Hartley
Leipsic
Smyrna

KENT COUNTY

Dover

Carol's Collectibles
N. Dupont Hwy. (Rt. 13)
No Phone
Gen line. Spec: kitchenware &
tools.

Dover Antique Mart
4621 Dupont Hwy. (Rt. 13)
(302) 734-7844
Multi-dealer mall. South-
bound Rt. 13, North
Dover, 1 mile North of Rt.
1, Exit 104. Pattern &
Depression glass, art pot-
tery, clocks, advertising
tins, & furnishings. Open
Mon-Sat 10-5. Sun 13-5.

Harmic's Antiques Gallery
Bishop's Corner & Rt. 13
(302) 736-1174
18th c. smalls, furn & dec. &
med and dental.

James M. Kilvington
103 N. Bradford
(302) 734-9124
By appointment.

Paul's Antiques & Furniture
4304 N. Dupont Hwy. (Rt.13)
(302) 734-2280
Spec: pine and oak country furn.

Robert's Antique Lamps
2035 S. Dupont Hwy. (Rt.13)
(302) 697-3414
Spec: Lamps & new & old
shades.

Spence's Auction, Farmer's &
Flea Market
550 S. New St.
(302) 734-3441
Call for flea & auction dates &
times.

Sweet Memories
5084 N. Dupont Hwy. (Rt. 13)
(302) 736-1311
Trunks, kitchenware & furn.

Then..Again...
28 W. Lockerman St.
(302) 734-1844
General line.

Felton

Canterbury Used Furniture &
Antiques
Intersect. Rts. 13 & 15
(302) 284-9567
Usd & antique home & office
furn.

Hartley

L.G. Antiques
1388 Hartley Rd.
(302) 492-8791
Spec: Flow blue, decoys &
hunt & fish related items.

Leipsic

Old Leipsic Antiques
Main St.
(302) 736-0595
By appt. Small dec access:
decoys, crocks, quilts.

Smyrna

A Bit of the Past Antiques
3511 S. Dupont Hwy. (Rt. 13)
(302) 653-9963
Spec: glass, porc, furn, art, china.

Attic Treasures
2119 S. Dupont Blvd.
(302) 653-6566/653-9520
Gen line.

C & J Antiques
5767 Dupont Hwy. (Rt. 13)
(302) 653-4903

Duck Creek Antiques
5756 N. DuPont Parkway
(Rt. 13)
302-653-8396
By. appt only. 18th c furn.,
paintngs, silv & china.

The Tin Sedan
12 N. Main St.
(302) 653-3535
Spec: toys and trains.

The What Nott Shop
5786 N. Dupont Hwy.
(302) 653-3855
Gen line Spec: hunt & fish
equip, radios & hardware.

NEW CASTLE COUNTY

Bellefonte

Centreville

Claymont

Delaware City

Elsmere

Greenville

Hollyoak

Middletown

New Castle

Newark

Newport

Stanton

Wilmington

Yorklyn

Bellefonte

Bellefonte Shoppe
901 Brandywine Blvd.
(302) 764-0637
Antiq & usd. furn. & smalls

Brandywine Resale Shop
900 Brandywine Blvd.
(302) 764-4544
Gen line Vic. to 1960's.

Brandywine Trading
804 Brandywine Blvd.
(302) 761-9175
Resale & thrift: furn. & dec.

The Annex
803 Brandywine Blvd.
(302) 761-9175
Resale & thrift: furn. & dec..

Centreville

Barbara's Antiques & Books
5900 Kennett Pike
(302) 655-3055
Gen line. Spec: smalls &
ephemera & Delawariana.

Centreville Antiques
5716 Kennett Pike
(302) 571-0771

Jackson-Mitchell Inc
5718 Kennett Pike
(302) 656-0110

**Ron Bauman Inc.
(Formerly David
Stockwell, Inc.)
5722 Kennett Pike (Rt. 52)
Centreville, DE
(302) 655-4466
18th & 19th c. American
furniture, tall case clocks
and related accessories.
One mile North of
Wintherthur.**

The Resettlers Galleries
5801 Kennet Pike
(302) 658-9097
Consignment shop.

Twice Nice Antiques &
Collectibles
Frederick's Country Center
5714 Kennett Pike
(302) 656-8881
Gen line: antique & repro.

**Windle's Antiques
Frederick Country
Center
Kennett Pike (Rt. 52)
Centreville, DE
(302) 994-2638
18th & 19th c. formal &
painted country furni-
ture. Quilts, accessories,
fine jewelry and early
iron.
Http://bmark.com/win-
dle.antiques**

Claymont

A A A Claymont Antiques
2811 Philadelphia Pike
(302) 798-1771
General line.

Lamb's Loft
16 Commonwealth Ave.
(302) 792-9620
Multi-dealer co-op.

Trescott Haines
2811 Philadelphia Pike
(302) 475-8398
By appointment only.

Delaware City

The Old Canal Shops
129 Clinton
(302) 834-5262

Elsmere

Merrill's Antiques
100 Northern Ave.
(302) 994-1765
Glass, china & crystal.

Greenville

Products of Great Import
Greenville Shopping Center
Rt. 52
(302) 654-5075
New & old oriental rugs.

The Furniture Exchange Ltd.
Greenville Crossing II
4001 Kennett Pike
(302) 658-1414
Consignment shop.

Hollyoak

Browse & Buy
1704 Philadelphia Pike
(302) 798-5866
Gen line. Spec: usd. furn.

Holly Oak Corner Store
1600 Philadelphia Pike
(302) 798-0255
Furn, toys & glass & china.

Middletown

Butler & Cook Antiques
13 E. Main St.
(302) 378-7022
Gen line of country antiq.
Spec: lighting-all periods

G.W. Thomas Antiques
2496 Dupont Pkwy. (Rt. 13)
(302) 378-2414
18th & early 19th c. furn. & dec.

MacDonough Antique Center
2501 Dupont Pkwy. (Rt.13)
(302) 378-0485
Gen line & stained glass repair.

New Castle

Cobblestones
406 Delaware St.
(302) 322-5088
60's & 70's china & vint
linens.

Lauren Lynch
1 East Second St.
(302) 328-5576
17th c. to 1960's smalls,
dec.arts & furn.

Opera House Antiques Center
308 Delaware St.
302-326-1211
Multi-dealer co-op, 17 dlrs.

The Raven's Nest
204 Delaware St.
(302) 325-2510
40's & 50s jewlry fine & costume. Dep. glass & furn.

Yesterday's Rose
204 Delaware St.
(302) 322-3001
General line.

Newark

Chapel Street Antiques
197 S. Chapel St.
(302) 366-0700
Spec: 17-20th c. glass &
ceramics. Period to present
furn.

Main Street Antiques
280 E. Main St.
(302) 733-7677
Multi-dealer co-op.

Old Tyme Antiques
294 E. Main St.
(302) 366-8411
Multi-dealer co-op, 35+ dlrs.

Newport

The Grey Parrot
13 W. Market St.
(302) 999-9609
General line.

Stanton

Impulse Antiques
216 E. Main St.
(302) 994-7737
Gen line. Spec: china, glass,
esp. Chintz & Shelley. &
Delaware collectibles.

Wilmington

Antique & Not So
24-A Trolley Square
(302) 656-3011

Brandywine Treasure Shop
1913 N. Market St.
(302) 656-4464

Catholic Thrift Center
1320 E. 23rd St.
(302) 764-2717
Thrift shop.

Catholic Thrift Center
4th & Union Sts.
302-655-9300
Thrift shop.

F. H. Herman Antiques
308 Philadelphia Pike
(302) 764-5333

Golden Eagle Shop
1905 N. Market St.
(302) 651-3460
Consignment shop.

Grandma's Treasures Inc.
1709 Philadelphia Pike
(302) 792-2820
Gen. line antiq. & usd furn &
dec.

Jung's Oriental Antiques &
Fine Arts
1314 W. 13 St.
(302) 658-1314
Oriental art & furn. Neolithic
to present.

Pine Classics
4117 Concorde Pike (Rt. 202)
Talleyville Shopping Center
302-475-7505
Importers: Euro antiq. and
repro furn.

Reeves Used Furniture
4821 Governor Printz Blvd.
(302) 764-5582

The Red Barn Shoppes
400 Silverside Rd.
(302) 792-0555
General line.

The Resettlers Annex
1005 West 27th St.
302-654-8255
Call for sale dates & times.

The Willow Tree
1605 E. Newport Pike
(Maryland Ave.)
(302) 998-9004
Multi-dealer co-op, 13 dlrs.

Warren's Antiques
1411 Philadelphia Pike
(302) 782-1612

Yorklyn

Charles Taylor & Sons
2870 Creek Rd.
302-234-4700
Wood from salvage.

SUSSEX COUNTY

Bethany Beach

Bridgeville

Clarksville

Coolspring

Dagsboro

Delmar

Ellendale

Fenwick Island

Georgetown

Greenwood

Gumboro

Harbeson

Laurel

Lewes

Milton

Millsboro

Millville

Ocean View

Rehoboth Beach

Seaford

Selbyville

SUSSEX COUNTY

Bethany Beach

Beach Plum Antiques
Fifth & Pennsylvania Ave.
(302) 539-6677
General line.

Bridgeville

Affordably Yours of
    Bridgeville
Rt. 404 (1/4 mi. W. of Rt. 13)
(302) 337-9747

**Art's Antique Alley
Rt 13 (Southbound)
(302) 337-3137
20,000 square feet of
antiques and furniture.
Heat, air conditioning,
wheel-chair accessibility,
restrooms, snacks, and
bus parking. Open every-
day 11 a.m. to 6 p.m.
50 Dealers.**

**None Such Farms
    Antiques
201 Main St.
(302) 337-3396
Located in the owners'
early 19th c. home.
Federal & primitive fur-
niture beautifully dis-
played w/ appropriate
companions. Affordably
priced. Proper tea is
served at 3:00 p.m. A
very special antiquing
experience.**

**Pioneer Antiques
111 Market St.
(302) 337-3665
Specializing in oak &
wicker furniture. Buy &**

sell antiques. 10:00 AM to
5 PM daily

The Bridgeville Emporium
105 Market St.
(302) 337-7663
General line.

Clarksville

Hudson's General Store
Corner Rt. 26 W & Rd. 348
(302) 539-8709
Furn, collectibles & folk art.

Coolspring

York's Homestead Antiques
Lewes-Georgetown Hwy. (Rt. 9)
(302) 684-3262
19th c. furn. & glassware.

Dagsboro

Red Rooster
503 Main St. (Rt. 26)
(302) 732-1088
Primitive furn. & collectibles.

Delmar

Joy's Antique Barn
610 N. 2nd St.
(302) 846-3671

The Trading Post
Rt. 13A
302-846-9863
Call for auction dates & times.

Ellendale

Collector's Exchange
Rt. 113 (northbound)
(302) 422-2255

Fenwick Island

Route 54 Antiques Complex
Rt. 54 (6 mi. East of Fenwick)
(302) 436-5189
Multi-dealer co-op.

Seaport Antique Village Inc.
Rt. 54 W (at the bridge)
(302) 436-8962
Multi-dealer co-op.

Seaside Country Store
Rt. 1 (southbound)
(302) 539-6110
Trunks, oyster plates, blue willow, golf clubs & recondi-
tioned cash registers.

Georgetown

Candlelight Antiques
406 N. Dupont Hwy.
(Rt. 113-northbound)
(302) 856-7880

Collectors Corner & Pawn
Shop
101 E. Market St.
(302) 856-7006
Jewelry, glass & furniture.

Generations Antiques
Rt. 9 (Westbound)
(3 miles East of Georgetown)
(302) 856-6750
Spec: furn., glass. & restorations.

Georgetown Antiques Market
105 E. Market St.
(One block East of the Circle)
(302) 856-7118
Multi-dealer co-op, 15+ dlrs.

Market Street Antiques &
    Collectibles
Rt. 9
(302) 856-9006
Multi-dealer co-op.

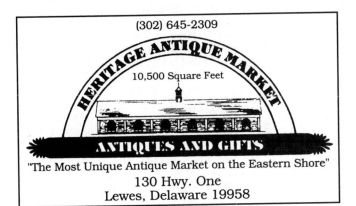

(302) 645-2309

HERITAGE ANTIQUE MARKET

10,500 Square Feet

ANTIQUES AND GIFTS

"The Most Unique Antique Market on the Eastern Shore"
130 Hwy. One
Lewes, Delaware 19958

Morgan's Antiques, Crafts &
Collectibles
134 East Market St. (Rt. 9-
Eastbound))
(302) 856-9147

Passwater's Antiques
1028 E. Market St. (Rt. 9 E)
(302) 856-6667
Gen line: "junk" to antiq.

Signs of the Past Antiques
Rt. 9 (westbound)
3-1/2 mi. East of Georgetown
circle
(302) 856-9189

Greenwood

Hilltop Station
Rt. 13 South & 16 West
(302) 349-9080

John O'Bier Antiques
Rt. 13 (N. of Greenwood)
(302) 349-4694
Spec: Vic. furn., lamps & china .

Ruth Mervine Antiques
Rt. 36 (approx. 1 mi. N. of Rt. 16)
(302) 349-4282
Glass, china & jewelry.

Gumboro

Cross Country Antiques
Intersection of Rts. 26 & 54
(302) 238-0129
Furn., china, silver & glass.

Memory Lane
Rt. 26 (westbound)
(302) 238-0100/ 238-7435

Harbeson

Brick Barn Antiques
Rt. 9 (Eastbound)
(302) 684-4442
(Open April-Dec.)

Pete's Antiques
Rt. 9
(302) 684-8188
General line: 1850-1950.

Laurel

Bargain Bill's Flea Market
Rts. 13 & 9 (S.E. corner)
(302) 875-9958/875-2478
Flea market-indoor and outdoor. Open Fri, Sat and Sun
year round.

Delaware Avenue Antique
Emporium
Delaware Ave.
302-875-1708
Multi-dealer co-op.

Delmarva Antiques
Rt. 13 (northbound)
(302) 875-2200
Gen line. Spec:Vic.& oak.

Oak Haven Antiques
S. Central Ave. (Extended)
Rt. 13A
(302) 875-3591
Furn.:walnut & mahogany. By
chance or appt.

O'Neal's Antiques
Rt. 13 & 466 (at light)
(302) 875-3391
Estate jewelry, furniture,
glassware, lamps, shades
and collectibles.
Appraiser. We buy!
Mon-Sat 10:00-5:00.

Reminisce/ Bargain Carnival
310 N. Central Ave.
(On alternate Rt. 13)
(302) 875-1662
Gen line & architecturals &
oddities.

Spring Garden Antiques
Delaware Ave. (Extended)
(302) 875-7015
Spec: Country primitives, Folk
art, architectural & garden ele-
ments.

The Golden Door
214 E. Market St.
(302) 875-5084

Wells Lamp Studio
Rt. 13 (northbound)
(302) 875-5611
Gen line. Spec: Lamps, mostly
oil era., shades & parts.

SUSSEX COUNTY, DE

Lewes

Antique Corner
142 Second St.
(302) 645-7233
Gen line. Spec:Vic. jewelry.

Antique Village (at Red Mill)
221 Rt. 1 (Northbound)
(302) 645-1940 (302) 644-0842
Multi-dealer co-op.

Auntie M's Emporium
116 West 3rd St.
(302) 644-1804
Repro Vic. garden accents.

Auntie M's Emporium
203 B Second St.
(302) 644-2242
2,000 used books, furn., pottery, glass.

Beaman's Old & Gnu Antiques
Rt. 1 (Northbound)
(302) 645-8080
Gen line pre-1930. Spec: blue willow.

Classic Country Antiques
3.5 miles West of Rt. 1 on Rt. 9 (Georgetown-Lewes Hwy.)
(302) 684-3285
Multi-dealer co-op, 24 dlrs.

Copper Penny Antiques
109 Market St.
(302) 645-2983
Copper, brass, silver, flow blue & lamps. Metal clean & polish service.

Feedmill Finds
831 Nassau Rd.
302-645-1640
Multi-dealer mall.

Garage Sale Antiques
1416 Rt. 1 (southbound)
(302) 645-1205
Gen line & architecturals.

Heritage Antique Market
130 Hwy. 1
(302) 645-2309
10,500 sq. ft. of: primitives, 19th c. furniture, oil paintings, Fostoria, toys
& dolls, Sterling silver, lamps & mirrors. Also offer Department 56 collectibles. Open daily 10-6 (closed Wed in Winter).

Jewell's Antiques & Jewelry
118 Second St.
(302) 645-1828
Gen line. Spec: Daulton & estate jewlry.

Josephine Kier, Ltd.
205 Second St.
(302) 645-9047
Oriental rugs,
fine art & antiques.
Http://www.lewes-beach.com/rugs.html
No retail sales tax in DE.

Lewes Mercantile Antique Gallery
109 Second St.
(302) 645-7900
Multi-dealer co-op 25 dlrs.

Practically Yours
Rt. 9
(302) 684-8936
Multi-dealer co-op.

Queen Anne's Antiques
King's Hwy.
(302) 644-1726

The Swan's Nest
107 Kings Hwy.
(302) 645-8403
Fine furn. Clocks-most pre-1850.

Then & Now Antiques
1552 Savannah Rd. (Eastbound Rt. 9)
(302) 645-9821

The Pack Rat
1165 Rt. 1 (northbound)
(302) 645-5277
Resale shop.

Thistles
203 Second St.
(302) 644-2323

Milton

Jail House Art, Antiques
& Unique Gifts
106 Union St.
(302) 684-8660
A wide variety of
antiques & collectibles:
china, glass, pottery and
linens. Primitives, furniture & gifts. Dealers welcome. Open daily 10-5.
Sun 11-4. Closed Wed.

The Riverwalk Shoppe
Milton Complex
105 Union St.
(302) 684-1500
Furn, Fostoria & Dep glass.

Vern's Used Furniture
128 Broad St.
(302) 684-4642
Gen line, antiq. & usd.

Millsboro

Antique Alley
225 Main St.
(302) 934-9841
Multi-dealer co-op, 40+ dlrs.

Antique Bouquet
201 N. Dupont Hwy.
(Rt. 113-northbound)
(302) 934-9175
Consignment.

Antique Mall of Millsboro
401 Dupont Hwy.
(Rt.113-norhtbound)
(302) 934-1915
Multi-dealer co-op.

Lynch's Antiques
320 Main St. (Eastbound)
(302) 934-7217

Millsboro Bazaar
238 Main St.
(302) 934-7413
800-917-4367
Vintage clothing. Sterling
& costume jewelry, furniture, lamps, china &

glass. 50's & 60's. Closed
Thursday.

Parson's Antiques
Rt. 24 (Eastbound)
(302) 934-6008
Furn., period glass & clocks.
Spec: oak.

The Consignery
201 Washington St. (Rt. 54)
(302) 934-8500
Gen line. Spec: dining &
bedrm sets.

Millville

Great Expectations
Rt. 26
(302) 537-6539
Gen line. Spec: costume jewlry
& Political mem.

Miller's Creek Antiques
Rt. 26 (westbound)
(302) 539-4513
Antiq, used & repro furn.

Reflections Antiques
Rt. 26 (westbound)
At the Old Blue Church
(302) 537-2308
Lighting & Am. stained glass,
dolls & toys.

Ocean View

Antique Prints Ltd.
Central Ave. (Southbound)
2 blocks N. of Rt. 26
(302) 539-6702
Prints.

Cinnamon Owl
Ocean View Center
Rt. 26 (westbound)
(302) 539-1336

Heirloom Trunks
Cedar Neck Rd. (Rt. 357)
(302) 539-8167
Steamer trunks restord and
original, 1850-1900.

Iron Age Antiques
Central Ave. (Southbound)
(302) 539-5344
Gen. Line. Spec:blacksmith
tools.

Kennedy's Classics
Rt. 26 (1.5 mi. West on Rt. 1)
(302) 537-5403
Art glass, 20th c. prints, Dep
glass, china & linens.

Sunny Lane Antiques
Rt. 26
302-539-9518

White House Antiques & Gifts
Rt. 26 (behind the Cinnamon
Owl)
(Open May -Labor Day)
Spec: vint. clothing, hats &
linens.

Rehoboth Beach

Affordable Antique Mall
4300 Rt. 1
(302) 227-5803
Multi-dealer co-op.

Early Attic
10 Sixth St.
(302) 227-0598
Spec: country primitives.

G.C. Vernon Fine Art
33B Baltimore Ave.
302-226-8850
Oils, oriental rugs, silver &
period furn.

Generations Antiques
237 Rehoboth Ave.
(302) 227-2443
Spec: furn, glass & restoration.

Just Looking
4147 Rt. 1
302-226-5088
Furn & dec., 50s, & consignment.

Stuart Kingston Incorporated
501 North Boardwalk (at
Grenoble Place)
(302) 227-2524
Furniture, paintings & jewelry.

The Collector
237 Rehoboth Ave.
(302) 227-1902
Gen line, formal to primitive.

The Glass Flamingo
216A Rehoboth Ave.
(302) 226-1366
50s and flamingos.

Blue Barn Thrift Shop
(302) 436-8451

Selbyville Antiques Emporium
Rt. 113 Southbound
(302) 436-4056
Multi-dealer mall.

Sidetracked Antiques
Church St. & Railroad Ave.
(302) 436-4488
General line.

Seaford

**Seaford Antique Emporium
218 High St.
(302) 628-9111
Over 3,000 sq. ft. Over 10
dealers. Military & Civil
War supplies, estate jew-
elry, furs, dolls & local
memorabilia.
Spec:today's collectibles:
Beanie babies, Limited
Treasures, Salvinos,
Bammers, Meanies,
Pocket Dragons & so
much more.
www.bambinos.web-
jump.com or
homepages.infoseek.com/
~Seafordemporium.**

Tea Tyme Antiques
Rt. 13 (north) and Tharpe Rd.
(302) 629-9313
Gen line. Spec: period, country
& painted furn.

Selbyville

Rt. 54 Antique Complex
Rt. 54 (eastbound)/4 miles E.
of Selbyville & 6 miles W. of
Fenwick
(302) 436-9948
Multi-dealer complex.

MARYLAND

Allegany County

Anne Arundel County

Baltimore City

Baltimore County

Calvert County

Caroline County

Carroll County

Cecil County

Charles County

Dorchester County

Frederick County

Garrett County

Harford County

Howard County

Kent County

Montgomery County

Prince Georges County

Queen Annes County

St. Mary's County

Somerset County

Talbot County

Washington County

Wicomico County

Worcester County

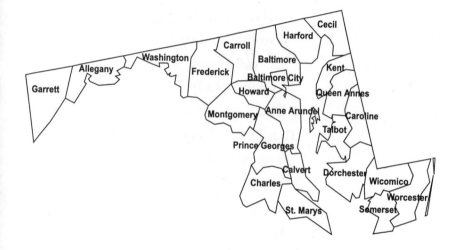

Maryland Counties

ANTIQUE MARYLAND

Antique Dealers Association of Maryland, Inc.

Maryland
With Pride

171 CONDUIT STREET • ANNAPOLIS, MD 21401

FREE DIRECTORY
410-269-1440

visit us at http://www.mdra.org

ALLEGANY COUNTY

Cumberland

ALLEGANY COUNTY

Cumberland

A to Z Antique Mall
405 Virginia Ave.
(301) 777-8333
Multi-dealer mall.

Antie's Antiques
328 Virginia Ave.
(301) 724-3729
General line.

Goodwood Old &
  Antique Furniture
329 Virginia Ave.
(301) 777-0422

Historic Cumberland
  Antiques Mall
55 Baltimore St.
(301) 777-2979
Multi-dealer mall.

L & M Timeless Treasures
203 Baltimore St.
(301) 724-0880

Queen City Collectibles
28 N. Centre St.
(301) 724-7392

Yesteryear
62 Baltimore St.
(301) 722-7531

ANNE ARUNDEL COUNTY

Annapolis

Arnold

Churchton

Crownsville

Galesville

Gambrills

Glen Burnie

Hanover

Harwood

Mayo

Millersville

Pasadena

Severna Park

ANNE ARUNDEL COUNTY

Annapolis

Absolutely Fabulous
14 Annapolis St.
(410) 268-8762
Furn.

Annapolis Antique Gallery
2009 West St.
(410) 266-0635
Multi-dealer co-op.

Annapolis Antique Shop
  & Consignment Mall
20 Riverview Ave.
(410) 266-5550
Multi-dealer co-op.

Baldwin & Claude Antiques
47 Maryland Ave.
(410) 268-1665
General line.

Bowerbird Antiques
25 Locust Ave.
(410) 269-1553

Clockmaker Shop
1935 Generals Hwy.
(410) 266-0770
Clocks.

Collector's Garden Limited
229 Prince George St.
(410) 268-0662

DHS Designs, Inc.
86 Maryland Ave.
(410) 280-3466
Architecturals, furn, paintngs,
& garden objects.

Featherstone Square
Rt. 5 & Whitehall Rd.
(410) 349-8317
Multi-dealer mall.

Gateway To Annapolis
67 West St.
(410) 263-8141
Vic furn, china, silver. & dec.

Joans' Gems
49 Maryland Ave.
(410) 267-7830
19th c. Vic furn & dec.

Joy Street Antiques
12 Annapolis St.
(410) 267-9355

Maryland Avenue Antiques
82 Maryland Ave.
(410) 268-5158
General line

Recapture The Past
69 Maryland Ave.
(410) 216-9067
General line.

Remember This, Inc.
50 Maryland Ave.
(410) 268-3486
Open salts, costume jewelry &
glassware.

Ron Synder Antique
  & Restorationss
1809 McGuckian St.
(410) 268-2405
Furn restoration &
cabinet making.

Ron Snyder Antiques
2011 West St.
(410) 266-5452
Am Federal furn.

Sixth Street Studio
422 6th St.
(410) 267-8233

Suhrprise Shop
3125 Portway Dr.
(410) 263-0368

Taylors House of Antiques
  & Auction House
103 Annapolis St.
West Annapolis
(410) 280-6770
Silver, jewlry, china, glass,
clocks & furn.

Third Millennium Design
57 Maryland Ave.
(410) 267-6428
Fine art & dec.

Walnut Leaf Antiques
62 Maryland Ave.
(410) 263-4885
Furn, Orientals. Prints,
paintings & sterling.

Arnold

Cathy Smith Quilts
520 Moorings Circle
(410) 647-3503

White Swan
1460 Ritchie Hwy.
(410) 349-8859

Churchton

Black Eyed Susan
5532 Shady Side Rd.
(410) 867-4322
China,glass, & coll.

Crownsville

Classic Designs
1205 Generals Hwy.
(410) 923-3766
Multi-dealer shop.

ANNE ARUNDEL COUNTY, MD

Galesville

Richard Rowland Antiques
970 Main St.
(410) 867-7858
Gen line. Spec: Decoys,
china & glass.

Gambrills

Days of Olde Antiques
710 Rt. 3 North
(410) 987-0397
Multi-dealer co-op.

Glen Burnie

Curiosity Unlimited Inc.
648 Balt-Annapolis Blvd.
(410) 768-8697
General line.

Fourth Crane Antiques
310 Crain Hwy. S.
(410) 760-9803
General line.

Neatest Little Shop
7462 Balt-Annap Blvd.
(410) 760-3610
Multi-dealer shop.

Rosie's Past & Present
7440 Balt-Annap Blvd.
(410) 760-5821
Gen line . Spec: glass.

Hanover

AAA Antiques Mall
2659 Annapolis Rd.
(410) 551-4101
Multi-dealer mall.

Harwood

Muddy Creek Antiques
4452 Solomons Island Rd.
410-867-2219/800 924-6150
Multi-dealer co-op &
auction house.

Mayo

Annapolis Auction & Antiques
1205 E. Central Ave.
(410) 798-6192
Gen line.

Millersville

Arundel Way Antiques
1004 Cecil Ave. S.
(410) 923-2977
Furn: mahog, walnut &
cherry. Glass & china.

Red Barn Antiques
241 Najoles Rd.
(410) 987-2267
General line.

Pasadena

Erika's Antiques
2531 Mountain Rd.
(410) 255-1275
General line.

Severna Park

Adair & Halligan
5 Riggs Ave.
(410) 647-0103
Fr & Eng country furn..
Persian & Russe rugs.

Antique Lovers
550 F Ritchie Hwy.
In Park Plaza Center
(410) 431-5211
Furn, jewelry, glass,
dolls & toys.

Antique Marketplace
4 Riggs Ave.
(410) 544-9644
Multi-dealer co-op.

Antiques In Severna Park
540 Balt-Annap Blvd.
(410) 544-5420
Furn & dec, jewelry, silv,
linens, glass rugs & garden.

Antiques In The Park
78 Point Somerset Ln.
(410) 544-2762

Browse & Buy Shoppe
Jones Station Rd.
& Balt-Annap Blvd.
(410) 544-3370
Consignment shop.

Hangers & Drawers
350 Ritchie Hwy.
(410) 518-9832
Antiq & usd furn.

Mary's Designer
Resale Boutique
554 Balt-Annap Blvd.
(410) 647-1142
Jewelry & vint fashions.

Taylors Antiques
555 Balt-Annap Blvd.
(410) 647-1701
Period furn, jewelry, porc,
silver,lamps, books.

BALTIMORE CITY

BALTIMORE CITY

Baltimore

A 1 Antiques
418 East 31st St.
(410) 235-7224
Spec: furniture.

Alex Cooper Auctioneers
908 York Rd.
410-828-4838/800 272-3145
Call for auction dates & times.

Along The Way
1719 Aliceanna St.
(410) 276-4461
General line.

Amos Judd & Son.
843 North Howard St.
(410) 462-2000
General line.

Angela R. Thrasher
833 N. Howard St.
(410) 523-0550

Another Period In Time
1708 Fleet St.
(410) 675-4776
Multi-dealer.

Antique Exchange
318 Wyndhurst Ave.
(410) 532-7000
Gen line. Spec: furn
& quilts.

Antique Man Ltd.
1806-1812 Fleet St.
(410) 732-0932
Gen line. Spec: the
unusual.

Antique Toy & Train World
3626 Falls Rd.
(410) 889-0040
Antiq toys & trains.

Antique Treasury
809 N. Howard St.
(410) 728-6363
Multi-dealer shop..

Antique Warehouse At 1300
1300 Jackson St.
(410) 659-0663
Mullti-dealer.

Antiques & Collectibles
1711 Aliceanna St.
(410) 563-9298
General line.

Bayshore Trading Company
7211 North Point Rd.
(410) 477-1804
Gen line.

Belle's Antiques
7399 Liberty Rd.
Liberty Crest Shoppng Cent
(410) 944-9686
General line.

Bowery Antiques
1709 Fleet St.
(410) 732-2778
General line.

Christies Auctioneers
100 West Rd. #310
(410) 832-7555

Collectiques
1806 Maryland Ave.
(410) 539-3474

Collector's Item
4903 Belair Rd.
(410) 483-2020
Toys, dolls & trains & doll hosp.

Connoisseur's Connections
869 N. Howard St.
(410) 383-2624
19th c. Fr & Am formal furn,
paintngs, porc. & textiles.

Consignment Galleries
6711 York Rd.
(410) 377-3067
Consignment shop.

Constance
1709 Aliceanna St.
(410) 563-6031

Craig Flinner Gallery
505 N. Charles St.
(410) 727-1863
Prints, maps & vint posters.

Cross Keys Antiques
801 N. Howard St.
(410) 728-0101
17th, 18th & 19th c. Euro.
& Am furn & dec.

Cuomo's Antiques
871 N. Howard St.
(410) 383-9195
Furn, china & glass, linens
& tabletop.

DJ's Antiques
2326 Belair Rd. #6
(410) 665-4344

Dubey's Antiques
807 N. Howard St.
(410) 383-2881
Am & Eng furn & dec,1750-
1840. Spec: Chi exprt porc.

E A Mack Antiques
839 N. Howard St.
(410) 728-1333
Late 18th & early19th c. Am
furn & dec.

Early Attic Furniture
415 E. 32nd St.
(410) 889-0122
Mahog, oak & marble top furn.
Lamps, clocks, china & glass.

Fat Elvis
833 W. 36th St.
(410) 467-6030
Gen line, 50s, 60s, 70s, coll,
furn, vint clothing & toys.

Fells Point Antique Mart
617 S. Broadway
(410) 675-1726
Multi-dealer co-op.

**French Accents Fine
Continental Antiques
3600 Roland Ave.
(410) 467-8957
E-mail:
accents@ix.netcom.com
On-line Gallery:
www.faccents.com
Baltimore's TOP purvey-
ors of 17th-early 20th
century European furni-
ture, lighting and acces-
sories.Professional an-
tique consulting, acquisi-
tions and design services
available. Showroom
hours: Tues-Sat 11:00 AM
- 4:00 PM or by appoint-
ment.**

Gaines Mc Hale Antiques
836 Leadenhall St.
(410) 625-1900
Spec: 18th & 19th c. Fr & Eng
furn & dec. Country & formal.

Greenbaum Radio Refinishing
1301 S. Baylis St. 4th Floor
(410) 276-4420

Gunpowder Galleries
12408 Eastern Ave.
(410) 335-7992

Hamilton House Antiques
865 N. Howard St.
(410) 462-5218
General line.

Harris Auction Galleries
875 N. Howard St.
(410) 728-7040
Call for auction dates & times.

Heirloom Jewels
5100 Falls Rd. #14
(410) 323-0100
Jewelry, early 19th c. to
present. Silver.

Heritage Antique
829 N. Howard St.
(410) 728-7033
Paintings, furn & sculpture.

Imperial Half Bushel
831 N. Howard St.
(410) 462-1192
Sterling silver. Spec:
Baltimore silver.

In The Groove
1734 Fleet St.
(410) 675-7174
Spec: Vic & Art Deco bedrm
& dining rm sets.

Janny's Antiques
3608 Falls Rd.
(410) 467-3818

John's Art & Antiques
1733 Eastern Ave.
(410) 675-4339
Gen line. Spec: oil paintings.

LA Herstein & Company
877 N. Howard St.
(410) 728-3856
New & antiq lamps &
chandeliers.

LT Antiques
1734 Thames St.
(410) 675-0450
Vintage movie posters & mem.

Max's Trading Co.
733 S. Broadway
(410) 675-6297
Cigar shop selling antiq
cigar related items & clocks.

Mel's Antiques
712 South Wolfe St.
(410) 675-7229
General line.

Michaels Rug Gallery
415 East 33rd St.
(410) 366-1515

Modest Rupert's Attic
919 S. Charles St.
(410) 727-4505

Mt. Vernon Antique
  Flea Market
226 W. Monument St.
(410) 523-6493

Nostalgia Too
7302 North Point Rd.
(410) 477-8440
Country furn, 1875-1930s.
Collectibles.

Olde Touch
2103 N. Charles St.
(410) 783-1493
Lalique. Euro furn & porc.
Paintings & bronzes.

Pieces of Olde
716 W. 36th St.
(410) 366-4949
Vint fabrics, 40s & 50s.
Posters & lithos 1890-1998.
Painted furn & architectrls.

Regency Antiques
895 N. Howard St.
(410) 225-3455
Euro repro & antiq. furn &
dec in Louis 14th & 15th
Eng Chipp style.

Reginald Fitzgerald
1704 Eastern Ave.
(410) 534-2942
General line.

Rocking Horse
111 Saint Helena Ave.
(410) 285-0280
Carousels, rocking horses
& Vic carrriages.

Saratoga Trunk
1740 Alicanna St.
(410) 327-6635
Gen line. Spec: fine art.

Silver Mine
1023 N. Charles St.
(410) 752-4141
Vint, new & antiq: silver.
Jewelry.Ivory carvings.

Sunporch
6072 Falls Rd.
(410) 377-2904
Gen line.

Thayne's Antiques
823 N. Howard St.
(410) 728-7109
General line.

The Rose Garden
1504 Light St.
(410) 659-5133
Small furn, linens & dec.

The Tin Angel Antiques
1448 Light St.
(410) 752-3466
Scenic painted furniture,
new paint on vint furn.

Time Bandit
1808 Maryland Ave.
(410) 576-2488

Treasures of Allegheny
17 Allegheny Ave.
(410) 296-2525
General line.

Turnover Shop Inc.
3855 Roland Ave.
(410) 235-9585
Furn, china & jewelry.

Turnover Shop Inc
3547 Chestnut Ave.
(410) 366-2988
Furn, china & jewelry.

Velveteen Rabbit
20 Allegheny Ave.
(410) 583-1685
Furn, antiq & repro.

Wintzer Galleries
853 N. Howard St.
(410) 462-3313

BALTIMORE COUNTY

Arbutus

Catonsville

Cockeysville

Essex

Fork

Hereford

Jacksonville

Monkton

Parkville

Phoenix

Reistertown

Sparks Glencoa

Timonium

Upper Falls

Upperco

White Hall

White Marsh

BALTIMORE COUNTY

Arbutus

Arbutus Emporium
  & Bargain Market
5305 East Dr.
(410) 242-4050
Multi-dealer mall.
Spec: guns & military.

Catonsville

A & M Jewelry
708 N. Rolling Rd.
(410) 788-7000
Estate jewelry.

Cockeysville

Abundant Treasures
10818 York Rd.
(410) 666-9797
Multi-dealer co-op.

Alley Shoppes
10856 York Rd.
(410) 683-0421
Multi-dealer co-op.

Anne M Fisher Antiques
10834 York Rd.
(410) 628-0530

Baltimore Estate
  Liquidators
10866 York Rd.
(410) 666-1034

Bentley's Antiques Show
10854 York Rd.
(410) 667-9184
Multi-dealer shop.

Brindley & Company Antiques
10828 York Rd.
(410) 666-7790
Multi-dealer shop.

Corner Cottage Antiques
11010 York Rd.
(410) 527-9535
Primitives & country
cupboards.

Cuomo's Interiors
10759 York Rd.
(410) 628-0422
Am. & Euro furn &
objets d'art.

Decorative Touch
11008 York Rd.
(410) 527-1075

Estate Liquidators of MD
10832 York Rd.
(410) 666-5066
Formal dining rooms. Ma-
hogany & Federal style furn.

Hunt Valley Antiques
10844 York Rd.
(410) 628-6869

Pack Rat Antiques
10834 York road
(410) 683-4812
2 floors of fine antiques
& reproduction furni-
ture, mirrors, fireplace
accessories, Kirk &
Steiff silver & oyster
plates. Quality antiques
purchased.

Sherwood Antiques
2 Sherwood Rd.
(410) 666-5433
18th & 19th c. Eng &
Fr furn. Am & Eng repro.

Essex

A Squirrel's Nest
400 Eastern Blvd.
(410) 391-3664
General line.

RAMM Antiques
811 Eastern Blvd.
(410) 687-5284
General line.

Thompson's Antiques
430 Eastern Blvd.
(410) 686-3107
General line. Spec: books
paper & mags & local hist.

Fork

Antiques
12548 Harford Rd.
(410) 592-5117
Oak furn, late 1800's-1920s.
Nippon china.

Hereford

Cook Limited
17006 York Rd.
(410) 357-8455
Gen line. Spec:
Majolica & Flow Blue.

Jacksonville

Kendall's Antique Shop
3417 Sweet Air Rd.
(410) 667-9235
China silver & glass. Spec:
oak, cherry, mahog furn.

Monkton

Monkton Mill Antiques
2029 Monkton Rd.
(410) 771-4302
Gen line. Spec: furn,
early 1800-1940s.

The Pack Rat
Antiques and Consignments
Fine Antique and Reproduction
Furniture • Mirrors • Fireplace
Accessories • Kirk and Stieff
Silver • Oyster Plates • Majolica

Quality Antiques Purchased

10834 York Road • Cockeysville, MD 21030
410-683-4812

Parkville

Dusty Attic
9411 Harford Rd.
(410) 668-2343
General line.

Jane's Flea
7118 Harford Rd.
(410) 254-3988
General line.

Charm City Treasures
7100 Harford Rd.
(410) 426-3099
Gen line, antiq &usd.
Spec: mahogany furn.

Dot's Pandoras Box
7010 Harford Rd.
(410) 426-0334
General line, new & old.

Wish Me Not Antiques
7012A Harford Rd.
(410) 444-5195
General line.

Phoenix

Manor Mischieve Antiques
14344 Jarrettsville Pike
(410) 666-1072
Multi-dealer shop.

Vintage House
13812 Jarretsville Pike
(410) 667-6311
General line.

Reiserstown

Curiozity Shoppes
17 Hanover Rd.
(410) 833-3434
General line.

Derby Antiques
230 Main St.
(410) 526-6678
Gen Line Spec: Art
pottery, Roseville.

New England
Carriage House
218 Main St.
(410) 833-4019

Now N' Then
208 Main St.
(410) 833-3665
Primitive furn, collectibles
& architecturals.

Relics of Olde
237-1/2 Main St.
(410) 833-3667
Spec: country & primitive
furn. Glass & china.

Star Hill Farm Antiques
Hanover Pike
(410) 526-2756

Things You Love
2234 Main St.
(410) 833-5019
General line.

Tina's Antiques & Jewelry
237 Main St.
(410) 833-9337
Furn, 1840-1920.
Spec: jewelry.

Sparks Glencoe

Glencoe Gardens
15900 York Rd.
(410) 472-2300
General line.

Timonium

Clearing House Ltd.
200 West Padonia Road
Timonium, MD 21093
(410) 561-4546
Consignment shop.

Cornerstone Antiques
2215 Greenspring Dr.
(410) 561-3767
Gen line. Spec: dark wood
& traditional styles.

BALTIMORE COUNTY, MD

Great Finds & Designs
1925 Greenspring Dr.
(410) 561-9413
Furn & dec.

Silk Purse
2330 York Rd.
(410) 561-4700
Primitives & country furn.

Upper Falls

Pete's Pickin's
7818 Bradshaw Rd.
(410) 592-6884
General line.

Upperco

Snoopery
3921 Mount Carmel Rd.
(410) 239-7454

White Hall

Dixon's Antiques
1348 Weisburg Rd.
(410) 357-5161
Victorian furniture.

White Marsh

Foley's Antiques
10807 Railroad Ave.
(410) 335-3313
General line.

CALVERT COUNTY

Chesapeake Beach
Dowell
Huntingtown
Lusby
North Beach
St. Leonard
Solomons

CALVERT COUNTY

Chesapeake Beach

A-1 Antiques
3726 Chesapeake
 Beach Rd.
(301) 855-4500
Gen line . Furn, 1800-1950s.
Spec: US coins & currency.

Blue Moose Traders
4510 Bayside Rd. (Rt. 261)
(410) 257-2721

J D Antiques
3723 Chesapeake
 Beach Rd.
(410) 257-6762
Gen line, new, used,
vint & antiq.

The What-Not
3725 E. Chesapeake
Beach Rd.
(410) 286-0240
General line.

Dowell

Grandmother's Store
13892 Dowell Rd.
(410) 326-3366
Multi-dealer shop.

Huntingtown

Bowen's Antique Center
Old Town Rd. (Rt. 254)
(410) 257-3105
Multi-dealer shop.

Cherub's Closet
3920 Old Town Rd.
(410) 414-5400
Furniture.

Southern Maryland
 Antique Center
Rt. 4
(410) 257-1677
Multi-dealer shop.

Lusby

Dodson's On Mill Creek
13690 Olivet Rd.
(410) 326-1369
Spec: Eng & nautical.

North Beach

Bay Avenue Antiques
9132 Bay Ave.
(410) 257-5020
Multi-dealer shop.

Chesapeake Antiques
4133 7th St.
(410) 257-3153
Multi-dealer shop.

Nice & Fleazy Antiques
91312 Bay Ave.
(410) 257-3044
Multi-dealer shop.

Willetta's Antiques
7th & Bay Ave.
North Beach, Md
(301) 855-3412
Formal & period furn.
Silver, porc, clocks & dec.

St. Leonard

**Chesapeake MarketPlace
5015 St. Leonard Rd.
410-586-3725/800-655-1081
80 dealer co-op in 6 bldgs.
offering a large & ever-
changing variety of
antiques, collectibles &
uniquities. Auctions held
every Friday, 6:00 PM.**

JAD Center
4865 St. Leonard Rd.
(Rt. 765)
(410) 486-2740
Multi-dealer co-op.

Solomons

Grandmother's Store
14538 Solomn's Island Rd.
In Harmon House
(410) 326-6848

Island Trader Antiques
225 Lore Rd.
(410) 326-3582
Gen line, Am. country furn.
Trunks, coll boxes & linens.

Lazy Moon Book Store
 & Barb's Attic
14510 Solomons Island Rd. S.
(410) 326-3720
30,000 usd, rare & OP books.
Country furn & collectibles.

CAROLINE COUNTY

Denton
Preston

CAROLINE COUNTY

Denton

Andrew A Curtis Auction
6939 American Corner Rd.
(410) 754-8826
Call for auction dates & times.

Attic Antiques
24241 Shore Hwy.
(410) 479-1889
Multi-dealer co-op.

Country Store
713 Market St.
(410) 479-2766
Gen line. Spec: glass & china.

Denton Antique Mall
24690 Meeting House Rd.
(410) 479-2200
Multi-dealer co-op.

White Swan Antiques
Rt. 404
(410) 479-4229
Painted furn, architecturals &
folk art.

Preston

Better Days
211 Main St.
(410) 822-2657

Country Treasures
208 Main St.
(410) 673-2603
18th & 19th c. country
painted furn.

Garden Basket
21084 Dover Brige Rd.
(410) 822-0575

CARROLL COUNTY

Eldersburg

Finksburg

Hampstead

Keymar

Manchester

Mt. Airy

Sykesville

Taneytown

Union Mills

Westminster

CARROLL COUNTY

Eldersburg

House of Past & Present
1337 Liberty Rd.
(410) 795-0135

Relish Lane Auctions
6000 Emerald Ln.
(410) 781-4623/800-617-6741
Call for auction dates & times.

Finksburg

Designs by Raphael Ltd.
2076 Brown Rd.
(410) 526-0134

Hampstead

King's Antiques
1133 S. Main St.
(410) 374-2079
Oak, mahogany, &
walnut furn. China.

Queen's Collectibles
1222 North Main St.
(410) 239-8988
Gen line. Spec: vint
clothing, turn of the cent.

Keymar

Looking Glass
950 Francis Scott Key Hwy.
(410) 775-2589
Pressed glass. By appt.

Memory Lane Postcards Inc
1217 Francis Scott Key Hwy.
(410) 775-0188
Over 1 million postcards,
national & international.

Manchester

Olde Times Antiques
4200 Hanover Pike
(410) 239-7982

R & M Treasures
4724 Hanover Pike
(410) 374-1273
Multi-dealer co-op.
Spec: Fenton glass.

Mount Airy

Ben Gue Antiques
6 S. Main St.
(301) 829-2112

Country House
309 S. Main St.
(301) 829-2528
Primitives: farm tables &
cupboards. Painted furn.

Natural Accents
3 S. Main St.
(301) 829-3609

Shops Of Yesteryear
102-104 Center &
Cross Sts.

Sykesville

Alexandra's Attic
7542 Main St.
(410) 549-3095
Gen line. Spec: any-
thing Victorian.

All Through The House
7540 Main St.
(410) 795-6577

Firehouse Antiques
7543 Main St.
(410) 549-4994
Country furn, primitves
& prints.Spec: lg. cupboards.

The Nostalgia Shop
7615 Main St.
(410) 552-0924
Primitives, tools & furn.

Sykesville Clocks
& Collectibles
7311 Springfiled Ave
(410) 549-1147
Over 350 clocks, furn, decoys
& E-shore style ships.

Yesterday Once More
6251 Sykesville Rd.
(410) 549-0212
Furn, glass & china.

Taneytown

Come Saturday Morning
8 Frederick St.
(410) 756-2805
Vic furn & lamps.

InnesFree Antiques
1241 Old Taneytown Rd.
(410) 751-6745
Spec: Am & Chinese furn.

Krogh's Nest
54 W. Baltimore St.
(410) 751-1529
Gen line. Spec: Bierdermeier
& Copehagen figs & china.

Taneytown Antique Shoppes
7 Frederick St.
(410) 756-4262
Gen line. Spec: books &
bottles.

Union Mills

Academy Antiques
3423 Littlestown Pike
(Rt. 97 N.)
(410) 857-4006
Multi-dealer shop.

Westminster

Academy Antiques
3423 Littlestown Pike
(410) 857-4006
General line.

Alton J Cabinets Inc.
3849 Littlestown Pike
(410) 346-7900

Deer Hill Antiques
2113 Sykesville Rd.
(410) 848-5015
Country furn, glass, porc,
china, toys & dolls.

Frizellburg Antique Store
1909 Old Taneytown Rd.
(410) 848-0664
Multi-dealer shop.

L. Kevin Wagman
153 E. Green St.
(410) 876-7421

Locust Wines & Antiques
10 East Main St.
(410) 876-8680
Gen line, formal &
country furn & dec.

Seven East Main Street
7 East Main St.
(410) 840-9123
General line.

Silver Image Antiques
299 East Main St.
(410) 848-0275

The Woodwards
3443 Uniontown Rd.
(410) 876-6554
Federal furn. Handmade
& custom reproductions.

Treasure Chest
236 E. Main St.
(410) 848-5019
Wicker, quilts, linens,
china & glass.

Westminster Antique Mall
433 Hahn Rd.
(410) 857-4044
Third largest antique
mall in Maryland. Over
165 dealers. 33,000
square feet of quality
antiques and collectibles.
Furniture, primitives,
glass, pottery, and paper.
Hours: 10-6 daily.

White's Emporium
10 West Main St.
(410) 848-3440
US & international coins,
currency & supplies.

CECIL COUNTY

Chesapeake City
Cecilton
Elkton
North East
Perryville
Rising Sun
Warwick

CECIL COUNTY

Chesapeake City

American Corner
3rd & Bohemia Av.
(410) 398-7640
Glass, jewelry, linens,
Blue & Pink Willow.

Antique Turtle
3rd & Bohemia Ave.
(610) 274-2450
19th & 20th c. furn & coll.

Black Swan Antiques
3rd Bohemia Ave.
(410) 275-8841
4 shops in one bldg.

Canal Lock
105 Bohemia Ave.
.(410) 885-2415
Glass & pottery.

Nostalgia Nook
3rd & Bohemia
(410) 392-5239
Glass, pottery, Am dinnerware,
linens & jewlry.

The Eagle's Perch
35 Peach Creek Rd.
(Off Rt. 213)
(410) 398-1045
Furn, lamps, silver, glass
& carved glass.

The Horn &The Hound
98 Bohemia Ave.
(410) 885-5770
Nautical, equest. & wildlife
art. Antq & repro furn & dec.

Cecilton

Calvert County Furniture
75 Armory Rd.
(410) 535-2389
Antiq & usd furn & arch-
itectural salvage.

Fish Whistle
Rt. 213
(410) 275-8627
General line.

Old Glory Days
109 W. Main St.
(410) 275-0045
Antiq & usd furn & coll.

Elkton

Fair Hill Antiques, Etc...
364 Fair Hill Dr.
9 mi. N. of Elkton
(Fairhill)
(410) 398-8426
Two level, multi-dealer
shop, over 2,800 sq. ft.
Open Thurs through Mon
10-5. Closed Tues & Wed.
One block S. Of 273 &
213 Intersection.

Flying Eagle
Landing Ln. & Mackall St.
(410) 392-0306
Multi-dealer shop.

Hunters Antiques Etc.
232 Fair Hill Dr.
(410) 398-8426

Iron Bridge Farm
2953 Appleton Rd.
(410) 398-0954
Furn & coll.
Spec: rush & cane.

North East

Booksellers Antiques
35 South Main St.
(410) 287-8652
Rare & OP books. Furn
& coll.

Day Basket Factory
714 W. Main St.
(410) 287-6100
Multi-dealer co-op.

Gary E Dennis Antiques
& The Annex
37 South Main St.
(410) 287-5711
Gen line. Prim to coll,
30s & 40s.

JB's Collectibles
32 S. Main St.
(410) 287-0400
General line.

Last Yankee Antiques
114 S. Main St.
(410) 287-2252
Early country furn, dec &
custom ligthing.

North Chesapeake
Antique Mall
2288 Pulaski Hwy. (Rt. 40)
(410) 287-3938
Multi-dealer co-op.

North East Galleries
Antiques & Flea Market
Rt. 40
(800) 233-4169
Every Sat & Sun.

Perryville

Furniture Doctors
300 Aiken Ave.
(410) 642-2285
Spec: furn

Rising Sun

Rising Sun Antiques
101 W. Main St.
(410) 658-7400
Gen line. Spec: oak furn,
country pine.

Warwick

Main Street Emporium
at Hidden Valley Farm
121 Church Rd.
(410) 755-6026

CHARLES COUNTY

Bryans Road

Hughesville

Indian Head

LaPlata

Newburg

Port Tobacco

Waldorf

White Plains

CHARLES COUNTY

Bryans Road

River Road Antiques
5910 River Rd.
(301) 375-7459
China, glass, pottery
& small furn.

Hughesville

Hughesville Bargain
  Barn #1 & #2
(Rt. 5) Leonardtown Rd.
(301) 274-3101
Multi-dealer co-op, 2 bldgs.

Memory Lane
8445 Leonardtown Rd.
(301) 274-3439
Gen line

Indian Head

Nostalgia Nook
36 Mattingly Ave.
(301) 753-6940
Eng & country furn & glass.

LaPlata

Highway 301 Antique Stop
Rt. 301 S. (At 3 mile marker.)
(301) 934-1950
Clocks, lamps & glass.
Spec: Carnival glass.

LaPlata Peddlers Paradise
Rt. 301 S.
(301) 870-4400
Flea market, Sat & Sun.

Newburg

Antique & Collectors Cove
US Hwy. 301 S.
(301) 259-2727
General line.

Port Tobacco

Stones Throw Antiques
6460 Rose Hill Rd.
(301) 934-8827
Gen line.

Waldorf

Heritage House
3131 Old Washington Rd.
(301) 932-7379
Multi-dealer co-op.

Lost Horizons
8377 Leonardtown Rd. (Rt. 5)
(301) 274-5931
Multi-dealer co-op.

Madatic's Atic
3141 Old Washington Rd.
(301) 645-6076

Mulberry Cottage Antiques
3145 Old Washington Rd.
(301) 645-0456
Multi-dealer co-op.

Southern Traditions
Rt. 5 (corner of Rt. 231)
(301) 274-5787
Multi-dealer co-op.

White Plains

**Antiques at the
Whistle Stop
Rt. 301
(301) 609-7322
Multi-dealer shop. Buy or
sell entire or partial
estates. Open Mon - Sat
10:30-6:00. Sun 12-6:00.**

Antique Center at White
Plains Crossing
4550 Crain Hwy. (Rt. 301 N)
(301) 932-6708
Multi-dealer co-op.

Jack's Antiques
Rt. 301 S.
Commerce Shopping Center
(301) 609-7751
General line.

DORCHESTER COUNTY

Cambridge

East New Market

Hurlock

Linkwood

Secretary

DORCHESTER COUNTY

Cambridge

Bay Country Antiques
415 Dorchester Ave.
(410) 228-5296
Furn, glass, china & lamps.

Donnies Antiques
411 Washington St.
(410) 228-1190
Advertising, decoys & furn.

Heirloom Antiques
419 Academy St.
(410) 228-8445
Gen line, repro & antiq
furn & glass, early 1900s.

Jones Antiques
520 High St.
(410) 228-1752
China, brass & silver.

Maloney's Antique Mall
2923 Ocean Gateway
(410) 221-1505
Multi-dealer co-op. 40 dlrs.

Mills Antiques
Rt. 50
(410) 228-9866
Books,china & glass.

Packing House Antique Mall
411A Dorchester Ave.
(410) 221-8544
Multi-dealer co-op.

East New Market

Country Peddler Antiques
5610 Hicksburg Rd.
(410) 943-4548
Spec: lamps.

Hurlock

The Country Pineapple
Rt. 16 at Cabin Creek
(410) 943-4970
18th & 19th c. country
painted furn & primitives.

Linkwood

J B's Collectibles
3843 Ocean Gateway
(410) 901-1051

Secretary

Jean's Jewelry
152 Main St.
(410) 943-1338
Costume jewelry,
antiq & vint.

FREDERICK COUNTY

Brunswick
Emmitsburg
Frederick
Knoxville
Libertytown
Middletown
New Market
Prince Frederick
Thurmont

FREDERICK COUNTY

Brunswick

Antiques N' Ole Stuff
6 W. Potomac St.
(301) 834-6795
Gen line,1900-1940.

Jimmy Jakes's Antique Center
24 West Potomac St.
(301) 834-6814
Multi-dealer, 2 bldgs.

Emmittsburg

Emmitsburg Antique Mall
1 Chesapeake Ave.
(301) 447-6471
Multi-dealer, 100 dlrs.

Frederick

American Auction Gallery
Rt. 144 East
(301) 662-3530

Antique Cellar
15 E. Patrick St.
(301) 620-0591
Mission & country furn, lamps
& prints. Empire & Vic.

Antique Galleries
3 E. Patrick St.
(301) 631-0922
Antq & repro furn. & dec.

Antique Imports
125 East St.
(301) 662-6200
Eng furn & dec, 1750-1950

Antique Station
194 Thomas Johnson Dr.
(301) 695-0888

Antiques at the Icehouse
221 East St.
(301) 663-8995
Multi-dealer co-op.

Braddock Mountian
1301 West Patrick St.
(301) 371-5591
Gen line.

Braddock Station Antiques
4802 Old National Pike
(301) 371-8820
Prims, furn, vint jewlry &
glass.

Brainstorm Comics
177 Thomas Johnson Dr. B
(301) 663-3039
Old & new comic books.

Brass & Copper Shop
13 South Carroll St.
(301) 663-4240

Cannon Hill Place
111 South Carroll St.
(301) 695-9304

Carroll Creek Antiques
14 E. Patrick St.
(301) 663-8574
Repro & antiq furn & dec.

Craftworks Antiques
55 East Patrick St.
(301) 662-3111
Multi-dealer co-op.

Creekside Antiques
112 East Patrick St.
(301) 662-7099
Multi-dealer co-op.

Donaldson Antiques Ltd.
222 East Patrick St.
(301) 698-1130

Family's Choice Antiques
Rt. 15 & Biggs Ford Rd.
(301) 898-5547
Gen line. Spec: mahog
20s-40s & complete sets.

Frederick's Best
East & 2nd St.
(301) 662-1597
Multi-dealer.

Gaslight Restoration
118 East Church St.
(301) 663-3717
Restorer: paintings, frames,
Japanese armor & statuary.

Heritage
400 North Market St.
(301) 694-4948

Homeward Bound
313 East Church St.
(301) 631-9094
Primitives & folk art.

Lady On Skates
823 N. Market St.
(301) 663-4594

Look To Die For
28 Victoria Square
(301) 696-9474

Off The Deep End
712 East St.
(301) 698-9006
1940-50s furn & housewares.
20,000 usd books.

Old Glory Market Place
5862 Urbana Pike
(301) 662-9173
Multi-dealer co-op.

Old Town Antiques
9809 Liberty Rd.
(301) 898-8100
Furn.

Ro Duk Hee Oriental
    Antiques
301 N. Market St.
(301) 662-9476

Venus On The Half Shell
152 N. Market St.
Frederick, MD 21701
(301) 662-6213
Vint clothing, costume
jewelry & access.

Victoria's Antiques
5801B Buckeystown Pk.
(301) 865-1522
Furn from reclaimed wood,
custom design & staining.
Stained glass, Vic -1940s.

Warehouse Antiques
47 E. All Saints St.
(301) 663-4778
Multi-dealer shop.

Warner's Antique Market
28 E. Patrick St.
(301) 682-3663
Furn & lighting.

Knoxville

Garretts Mill Antiques
1331 Weverton Rd.
(301) 834-8581

Schoolhouse Antiques
847 Jefferson Pike
(301) 620-7470

Libertytown

Duke's Woods Antiques
Liberty Rd.
(301) 898-1461
General line.

Libertytown Mercantile
12102 Liberty Rd.
(301) 898-1461
Multi-dealer shop.

Middletown

Middletown Antique
100 N. Church St.
(301) 371-7380
Multi-dealer co-op.

New Market

1812 House
48 W. Main St.
(301) 865-3040
Early porc. Country
& formal furn.

Acorn
75 W. Main St.
(301) 865-3217

Arlene's Antiques
41 W. Main St.
(301) 865-5554
Furn, clocks, china &
glass, 1700-1930s.

Before Our Time
1 W. Main St.
(301) 831-9203
Formal & country furn & dec.

Bob's Antiques
52 Main St.
(301) 815-4222
Gen line. Mahog & oak furn.

Browsery Antiques
55 Main St.
(301) 831-9644
Handcrafted furn.

Comus Antiques
1 N. Federal St.
(301) 831-6464
Country furn, dec & coll.

Country Squire Antiques
4 W. Main St.
(301) 865-3217

Fleshman's Antiques
2 W. Main St.
(301) 775-0153
Am oak & walnut furn.

Fromers Antiques
52 W. Main St.
(301) 831-6712

**Grange Hall Antiques
#1 Eighth Alley
(301) 865-5651
Closed Mondays.
WEB: www.newmarket-
md.com/grange.htm
Steiff Animals, Bears,**

Graniteware & Mini-
atures.
**GREAT VARIETY OF
COLLECTIBLES.**

John L Due Antiques
13 W. Main St.
(301) 831-9412
Eng & Cont 18th & 19th c.
furn & dec. Chin exprt porc.

Main St. Antiques
47 W. Main St.
(301) 865-3710
Spec: country store & ad-
vertising items, pre-1940.

Mimi's Antiques
3 Strawberry Alley
(301) 865-1644

Moore & Moore
45 W. Main St.
(301) 865-3710

R P Brady Antiques
3 E. Main St.
(301) 865-3666
Furn & paintings.

Thirsty Knight Antiques
9 E. Main St.
(301) 831-9889
Am furn & coll.
Spec: beer steins.

Tomorrow's Antiques
50 W. Main St.
(301) 831-3590
Gen line, mid 1800s-
mid 1900's.

Victorian Manor Jewelry
33 Main St.
(301) 865-3083
Jewelry, Deco, Vic, Art
Nouveau. Posters & paintings.

Village Antique Shop
79 W. Main St.
(301) 865-3450

Prince Frederick

Calvert County Furniture
75 Armory Rd.
(410) 535-2389/800-675-2389

Thurmont

Flea Factory
230 N. Church St.
(301) 271-3779

Forever Beautiful
106 Frederick Rd.
(301) 271-5362

Gates Antiques
13141 Creagerstown Rd.
(301) 271-7370

GARRETT COUNTY

Grantsville

McHenry

Oakland

Swanton

GARRETT COUNTY

Grantsville

Grantsville Antique Center
Main St. (Off Rt. 68)
(301) 895-5737
General line.

Mc Henry

Cobwebs
139 Gleanings Dr.
(301) 387-4611

Reminisce Antique Mall
25297 Garrett Hwy.
(301) 387-8275

Oakland

Book Mark'et
111 South 2nd St.
(301) 334-8778

Mt. Panax Antiques
27 Norris Welch Rd.
(301) 334-9249

Swanton

Swanton Antiques
3501 Swanton Rd.
(301) 387-2259

HARFORD COUNTY

Bel Air

Churchville

Darlington

Edgewood

Forest Hill

Havre De Grace

Street

HARFORD COUNTY

Bel Air

Back Door Antiques
106 N. Main St.
(410) 836-8608
Gen line. Spec: oak furn,
glass & china.

Bel Air Antiques Etc.
122 N. Main St.
(410) 838-3515
Multi-dealer co-op.

Bel Air Auction Galleries
13 E. Ellendale St.
410- 838-3000/800 451-2437

Chez Mole Studio
   & Oak Spring Antiques
311 St. John St.
(410) 575-6200
1800's oak & walnut furn,
vint clothing & dec.

Country Schoolhouse
1805 E. Churchville Rd.
(410) 836-9225

Oak Spring Antiuqes
1321 Prospect Mill Rd.
(410) 879-0942

Churchville

Country Scene
2819 Churchville Road
(410) 836-9071

Crossroads Antiques
2853 Churchville Rd.
(410) 734-4343
Am primitives,antiq
wicker & glassware.

Grassy Creek Antiques
3023 Churchville Rd.
(Rt. 22)
(410) 734-4556
Multi-dealer shop.

Ye Olde Curiosity Shop
3100 Aldino Rd.
(410) 734-6228
Gen line. Spec:Advertis-
ing, toys & military.

Darlington

Head Of The Bay
623 & Rt. 1 S.
(410) 457-4345
General line.

Edgewood

Victorian Lady Antiques
710 Edgewood Rd. (755)
(410) 676-4661
Furn, glass, linens &
Jewelry.

Forest Hill

Spenceola Antique Market
217 Bynum Rd.
(410) 803-0011
Multi-dealer co-op.

Havre De Grace

Bahoukas Collectibles
465 Franklin St.
(410) 939-4146
Coll, toys & sports mem.

Bank of Memories
319 Saint John St.
(410) 939-4343
Victorian furn.

Candlelight Antiques
3628 Level Village Rd.
(410) 734-6194

Eclections
101 N. Washington St.
(410) 939-4917

Franklin Street Antiques
464 Franklin St.
(410) 939-4220
Decoys, cookie jars, furn
& collectibles.

George's Place
141 N. Washington St.
(410) 939-6398
Porc, glass & china.

Golden Vein
408 N. Union Ave.
(410) 939-9595
Multi-dealer co-op.

**Havre de Grace
   Antique Center
408 N. Union St.
(410) 939-4882
A quality 40 dealer
Antique Mall offering a
collection of Formal to
Country furniture,
Glassware, Pottery, Rugs,
Jewelry, hardware sup-
plies, and The Trunk
Refinishing How-To Book
& Hardware.**

Investment Antiques
123 S. Main St.
(410) 939-1312
Furn, architecturals &
costume jewelry.

Mustard Seed Antiques
327 Saint John St.
(410) 939-0176

P.J. & Co.
457 Franklin St.
(410) 939-5019
General line.

Splendor In Brass
123 Market St.
(410) 939-1312
New, usd & antiq furn.
Architecturals.

Stephanie & Stephan's
  Clocks Ltd.
429 St. John St.
(410) 939-3334
Gen line. Spec: clocks.

Susquehanna Trading Co.
322 N. Union Ave.
(410) 939-4252
New & antiq Chesapeake
Bay decoys.

Washington Street
  Books & Antiques
131 N. Washington St.
(410) 939-6215
Rare & OP books, jewlry,
military, crystals & fossils.

Weber's Antiques
Chapel Rd.
(410) 939-8566

Street

Whiskey's Run
3501 Ady Rd.
(Rts. 543 & 646)
(410) 452-0433
Multi-dealer co-op.

HOWARD COUNTY

Columbia
Ellicott City
Savage

Columbia

The Mall in Columbia
    Antique Market
at The Mall in Columbia
(410) 679-2288
Sundays, April-Oct.

Ellicott City

American Military
8398 Cour t Ave.
(410) 465-6827

Antique Depot
3720 Maryland Ave.
(410) 750-2674
Multi-dealer co-op.

Antique Row
at the Historic Oella Mill
840 Oella Ave.
(410) 465-8708
Multi-dealer co-op.

Caplan's Antiques
8125 Main St.
(410) 750-7678
Furn, repro & antiq. Stained
glass & jewlry.

ANTIQUE MALL
OVER 80 DEALERS

Three Large Floors of Quality
Antiques & Collectibles

✦ Furniture   ✦ Toys
✦ Pottery   ✦ Books
✦ Linens   ✦ Jewelry
✦ Cameras   ✦ Paper
✦ Primitives   ✦ Maps
✦ Tools   ✦ Dried Flowers

**8307 Main Street in
Historic Ellicott City Maryland**
410-461-8700

Mon.-Sat. 10-5, Sun. 12-5
★ ATM ON PREMISES ★

Caplan's Ellicott City
    Auction
840 Oella Ave.
(410) 750-7676
Call for auction dates & times.

Casey's Antiques
9905 Whitworth Way
(410) 461-1141

Catonsville Village Antiques
787 Oella Ave.
(410) 461-1535
Primitives, cast iron, tools,
& collectibles.

Cottage Antiques
8181 Main St.
(410) 465-1412
Furn. Eng china & porc.
Early sports mem.

Dundalk Antiques Inc.
8307 Main Street
(410) 461-8744

Dusty Treasures
8307 Main St.
(410) 566-4013

Generations Inc.
8307 Main St.
(410) 203-1914

Historic Framing
    & Collectibles
8344 Main St.
(410) 465-0549
Military antiqs & conservation framing.

Maxines Antiques
8116 Main St.
(410) 461-5910
Jewelry, glass & china.

Oella Flea Market
787 Oella Ave.
(410) 461-1535

The Shops At Ellicott Mills
8307 Main St.
(410) 461-8700
Over 80 dealers. Three large well lighted floors of quality antiques and collectibles. ATM on premises. Hours: Monday-Saturday 10-5, Sunday 12-5.

Taylor's Antique Mall
8197 Main St.
(410) 465-4444
Multi-dealer co-op.

Wagon Wheel Antiques
8061 Tiber Alley
(410) 465-7910
Spec: furn.

Westwood Antiques
13554 Triadelphia Rd.
(410) 531-4831
Am furn & importers of Euro antiqs.

Visit Three Unique Antique Centers with over 225 dealers, and E.J. Grants with exquisite & exciting antiques. The biggest mall on the East Coast. Hours: M-W 10am-6pm, Th-Sat 10am-9 pm, Sun 11am-6pm. Directions: 95 N. to Rt. 32 E. Then take Rt. 1 Laurel South. Right on Howard St. then follow signs to Savage Mill.

E J Grant Antiques
8600 Foundry St.
In the Red Barn
(301) 953-9292
18th & 19th c. Euro formal/country Furn & ojets d'art.

Savage

Historic Savage Mill
8600 Foundry St.
(800) 788-MILL
www.savagemill.com

KENT COUNTY

Chestertown
Galena
Kennedyville
Lynch
Rock Hall

KENT COUNTY

Chestertown

Alexander Antiques
315 High St. #102
(410) 778-9277

Amaryllis Vintage Company
118 S. Lynchburg St.
(410) 556-6407
Furn, stained glass,rugs,
mirrors, lamps & art.

Blue Heron Antiques
215 High St.
(410) 778-8118

Chestertown Antiques
6612 Church Hill Rd.
(410) 778-5777

Crosspatch
107 South Cross St.
(410) 778-3253
Furn, stained glass,
lamps, art & china

Hey Jude Antiques
111 N.Main St.
(410) 648-6761

Sassafras River Antiques
111 N. Main St.
(410) 648-5997
Spec: stained glass,
architecturals & garden.

Second Chance
22532 Tolchester Beach Rd.
(410) 778-2493

Seed House Antiques
860 High St. Extended
(410) 810-1513
2,000 sq. ft. of furniture,
iron, folk art, books,
linens, stained glass &
clothing. Period to retro.
Way cool stuff!

Galena

Auntie Q
Main St.
(410) 648-5808

Cross Street Station
Antiques & Collectables
105 W. Cross St.
P.O. Box 57
(410) 648-5776
15+ dlrs. in 4,000 sq. ft.
Selling: smalls to fine per-
iod furniture to reproduc-
tions. Buy one item or en-
tire estate. Open 7 days a
week 10-5. Dlr. space
available. Close to
historic Chestertown.

Firehouse Antiques Center
102 N. Main St.
(410) 648-5639
Multi-dealer co-op.

Galena Antiques Center
108 N. Main St.
(410) 648-5781
Multi-dealer co-op.

Kennedyville

Betty's Florist & Antiques
29475 Old Locust Grove Rd.
(410) 778-5011

Lynch

Company Store
11551 Lynch Rd.
(410) 348-2104
Furn, paintings, silver
& garden furn.

Rock Hall

Fishbone Antiques
21326 Sharp St.
(410) 639-7655

MONTGOMERY COUNTY

Barnesville

Bethseda

Boyds

Brookeville

Burtonsville

Chevy Chase

Clarksburg

Damascus

Gaithersburg

Kensington

Laytonsville

Olney

Potomac

Rockville

Sandy Spring

Takoma Park

MONTGOMERY COUNTY

Barnesville

B & T Antiques
Rt. 109
(301) 972-8714
19th c. Furn. Glass, china,
linens & jewelry.

Bethesda

Carole A. Berke, Ltd.
4918 Fairmont Ave.
(301) 656-0355
Gen line. Spec: 20th c.
dec arts, glass, china.

Grapevine of Bethesda
7806 Old Georgetown Rd.
(301) 654-8690
Consignment shop.

Limon's-Gems & Jewels
7909 Norfolk Ave.
(301) 657-8585
Jewelry.

Second Story Book
   Warehouse
4836 Bethesda Ave.
(301) 656-0170
Books & Prints

The Cordell Collection
4911 Cordell Avenue
(301) 907-3324
Consignment shop.

Versaille Oriental Rugs
7101 Wisconsin Ave.
(301) 657-3646
New & antiq oriental rugs.

Washington Antiques Center
6708 Wisconsin Ave.
(301) 654-3798
Multi-dealer co-op.

Boyds

Boyds Station Antiques
15114 Barnesville Rd.
(301) 972-1474
Gen line. Spec:
Depression glass.

Brookeville

Pleasant Valley Antiques
2100 Georiga Ave. (Rt. 97)
(301) 924-2293

Burtonsville

**Country School Antiques
3411 Spencerville Rd.
(Rt. 198)
(301) 421-9871
Quality antiques and fine
vintage furniture, decor-
ative accessories, archi-
tectural pieces & col-
lectibles. Knowledgeable
dealers always available
to assist you.
Open: Friday, Saturday
& Sunday 11-6.**

**J & K Jewelers
at Country School Antiques
3411 Spencerville Rd.
(Rt. 198)
(301) 384-4274
Fine antique & estate
jewelry at exceptional
prices. Platinum &
Victorian pieces a
specialty. Jewelry repair,
watch repair, engraving
& appraisal services.
Open Friday, Saturday &
Sunday 11-6.**

Chevy Chase

Antiques Inc.
6826 Winsconsin Ave.
(301) 656-1911

Boone & Sons Inc.
5550 The Hills Plaza
(301) 657-2144
Spec: antiq & new jewlry.

Gaylord Lamps & Shades
4620 Leland St.
(301) 986-9680
Spec: Jpns & Chinse mid-
late 1800s lamps.

Heller Jewelers
5454 Wisconsin Ave.
(301) 654-0218
Jewelry & sterling.

Clarksburg

Ashley's Antiques
23346 Frederick Rd.
(301) 972-5593
Period furn, glass & paintings,
pre 1900.

The Homefront
   & The Vintage Bride
23330 Frederick Rd (Rt. 355)
(301) 540-3540
Gen line consignment. Spec:
vint bridal.

Damascus

Antiques By Wallace
Rt. 27
(301) 253-6881
Smalls/tabletop. Bronzes,
jewlry, dolls & transfrwre.

Appleby's Antiques Inc.
24219 Ridge Rd.
(301) 253-6980
Gen line. Spec: period furn,
glass & lamps.

Bea's Antiques
24140 Ridge Rd.
(301) 253-6030
Am & Euro furn, silver,
jewelry & porc.

Gaithersburg

Art of Fire
& Sunporch Antiques
7901 Hawkins Creamery Rd.
(301) 253-6642
Restorer of glass & porc.
Spec: primitives, porc,
glass, stoneware & tools.

Americana Resources
7518 Rickenbacher
(301) 926-8663
Smalls, paper & political mem.
By appt.

Craft Antiques
405 S. Frederick Ave.
(301) 926-3000
Gen line. Spec:18th &19th c.
furn, porc & glass.

Emporium of Olde Towne
223 E. Diamond Ave.
(301) 926-9148
Multi-dealer shop.

Gaithersburg Antiques
5 N. Summit Ave.
(301) 670-5870
Gen line. Spec: tea
accessories.

Grace's Antiques
434 East Diamond Ave.
(301) 963-6522

Julia's Room
9001 Warfield Rd.
(301) 869-1410
19th c. Belg, Fr & Eng
furn & Eng china.

Olde Soldier Books
18779B N. Frederick Ave.
(301) 963-2929
OP books, letters, photos,
medals, currncy & military.

Olde Town Antiques
223 E. Diamond Ave.
(301) 926-9490
Multi-dealer co-op.

Peking Arts Inc.
7410 Lindbergh Dr.
(301) 258-8117
Chns lamps. Porc & pottery.

Kensington

Accent On Antiques
3758 Howard Ave.
(301) 946-4242

Antique & Art Galleries
3760 Howard Ave.
(301) 946-2152
Spec: mahog dining rm furn
& oil paintings.

Antique Emporium
3786 Howard Ave.
(301) 942-0137

Antique Market I
3762 Howard Ave.
(301) 949-2318
Multi-dealer co-op.

Antique Market II
3750 Howard Ave.
(301) 933-4618
Multi-dealer co-op.

Antique Scientific
Instruments
3760 Howard Ave.
(301) 942-0636

Antique Village
3762 Howard Ave.
(301) 949-5333
Multi-dealer co-op.

Antiques & Uniques
3762 Howard Ave.
(301) 942-3324

Aunt Betty's
3734 Howard Ave.
(301) 946-9646

Chelsea & Company
4218 Howard Ave.
(301) 897-8886

Diane's Antiques
3748 Howard Ave.
(301) 946-4242
General line.

European Antiques
4080 Howard Ave. #A
(301) 530-4407

Feng's Antiques
3786 Howard Ave.
(310) 942-0137

Furniture Mill
4233 Howard Ave. #B
(301) 530-1383

Great British Pine Mine
4144 Howard Avenue
(301) 493-2565
Importers, Eng pine furn.

International Parade
10414 Montgomery Ave.
(301) 933-1770

James of Kensington
3706 Howard Ave.
(301) 933-8843

Jantiques
10429 Fawcett St.
(301) 942-0936

Jill & Company
3744 Howard Ave.
(301) 946-7464
Painted furn, folk art,
quilts & architecturals.

Kensington Antique Market
3760 Howard Ave.
(301) 942-4440
Multi-dealer shop.

Kensington Station
3730 Howard Ave.
(301) 942-4535

Lionel Buy & Sell
3610 University Blvd. W.
(301) 949-5656

Maria's Place
3758 Howard Ave.
(301) 949-2378

Moon Beam & Company
4080 Howard Ave. #A
(301) 564-9464

Nina's Antiques
10419 Fawcett St.
(301) 942-7711

Onslow Square Antiques
4131 Howard Ave.
(301) 530-9393
Am & Euro furn.

Oriental Antiques
3740 Howard Ave.
(301) 946-4609

Paris-Kensington
4128 Howard Ave. #A
(301) 897-4963

Phyllis Van Auken
10425 Fawcett St.
(301) 933-3772

Prevention of Blindness
3716 Howard Ave.
(301) 942-4707
General line.

Pritchard's
3748 Howard Ave.
(301) 942-1661
Furn, art glass, stained glass &
Art Deco chandlrs.

Sally Shaffer Interiors
3742 Howard Ave.
(301) 933-3750
Furn, architecturals &
garden accents.

Sparrows
4115 Howard Ave.
(301) 530-0175
Fr. Furn & dec, late
18th c.-Art Deco.

Thomas-Matthews
4218 Howard Ave.
(301) 564-4971

Timeless Reflections
3776 Howard Ave.
(301) 933-4070

Laytonsville

Griffith House
21415 Laytonsville Rd.
(Rt. 108)
(301) 926-4155
Spec: books. Furn from salvge
& antiq furn.

New to You Shoppe
6920 Sundowne Rd.
(301) 977-7691
Thrift shop.

The Red Barn Shops
6860 Laytonsville Rd.
(301) 926-3053/840-8577
Multi-dealer co-op.

Olney

Briars Antiques
4121 Briars Rd.
(301) 774-3596
Gen line Spec: Vic
jewelry.

Cahoots
5410 Olney-Layonsville Rd.
(Rt. 108)
(301) 977-6840
China & glass.

Hyatt House Antiques
16644 Georgia Ave.
(301) 774-1932

Olney Antique Village
16650 Georgia Ave. (Rt. 97)
(301) 774-4263
Multi-dealer complex.

Potomac

Potomac Antiques
12211 River Rd.
(301) 983-0140
Gen line.

Rockville

Don's Antiques
16800 Baederwood Ln.
(301) 840-8417

Second Story Book
  Warehouse
121260 Parklawn Dr.
(301) 770-0477
Books & prints.

Sloan's Auctions
4920 Wyaconda Rd.
301-468-4911/800-649-5066
Call for auction dates & times.

Global Gallery
20 Baltimore Rd.
(301) 424-5737

Secondhand Rose
730 East Gude Dr.
(301) 424-5524

Young's Gallery
706 Rockville Pk. #A
(301) 309-0226
Repro wholesaler.

Sandy Spring

Yesterday's Treasures
809 Olney-Sandy Spring Rd.
(301) 774-4333
Gen line.

Takoma Park

Blue Moon Antiques
7000 C Carroll Ave.
(301) 270-6659
Period furn, pottery, coll &
vint jewlry.

Takoma Underground
7000B Carroll Ave.
(301) 270-6380
Gen line, Vic-50s.

Tallulah's Antiques
6915 Laurel Ave.
(301) 270-2333
Gen line. Spec: Deco furn
& Euro armoires,1900-40.

PRINCE GEORGES COUNTY

Bowie

Brandywine

Hyattsville

Laurel

Riverdale

PRINCE GEORGES COUNTY

Bowie

Antique Depot
13014 9th St.
(301) 809-6988
Multi-dealer co-op.

Bets Antiques
8519 Chestnut Ave.
(301) 464-1122
Am. Country furn, quilts,
crocks, lighting.

Draley's Antiques
13031A 11th St.
(301) 262-8647
Gen line. Spec: Heisey
& clocks.

Fabian House
8519 Chestnut Ave.
(301) 464-6777
Gen line. Country/prim
furn, quilts, glass & china.

Fireside Antiques
13010 9th St.
(301) 262-2878
Spec: furn, pine, walnut,
& mahogany.

House of Hegedus
8521 Chestnut Ave.
(301) 262-4131
General line.

Keller's Antiques
13031 9th St.
(301) 805-9593
Gen line. Spec: furn.

Old Bowie Antique
  Clockshop
13031 11th St.
(301) 805-6799
Antq & new clocks & repair.

Welcome House Antiques
8604 Chestnut Ave.
(301) 262-9844
Multi-dealer co-op.

Brandywine

Bev's Antiques
13700 Old Brandywine Rd.
(301) 782-7728
General line.

Scoshie's
14134 Brandywine Rd.
(301) 645-7734
General line.

Hyattsville

Antique Jewelry Specialists
4212 Gallatin St.
(301) 779-3696
Estate jewelry. By appt. only.

Ellington's
1401 University Blvd. E.
(301) 445-1879

Jean's Antique Shop
5924 Riggs Rd.
(301) 853-1531
General line.

Laurel

Anna's Antiques & Bits
304 Compton Ave.
(301) 604-8868
Furn, cut crystal, sterling,
china, glass, art & lamps.

Antique Alley
99 Main St.
(301) 490-6500
General line.

Antique Center
515 Main St.
(301) 725-9174
General line.

Antique Market
9770 Washington Blvd. N.
(301) 953-2674

Cherry Lane Antiques
8687 Cherry Lane
(301) 953-1815
Furniture.

David's Antiques
353 Main St. #A
(301) 776-5636

Foxfire Gallery
4414 Main St.
(301) 317-6747
Collectibles & art.

Geary's Antiques
508 Main St.
(301) 725-7733

Main Street Corner Shoppe
401 Main St.
(301) 725-3099
Multi-dealer.

North Laurel Park
  Antique Center
9902 Washington Blvd. N.
(301) 776-5125

Riverdale

Taylor Wells Interiors
6220 Rhode Island Ave.
(301) 864-9457

QUEEN ANNES COUNTY

Centreville
Chester
Church Hill
Crumpton
Grasonville
Queenstown
Stevensville
Sudlersville

QUEEN ANNES COUNTY

Centreville

Gary Young Antiques
128 S. Commerce St.
(410) 758-2132
18th c. Eng & Irish furn,
& dec.

Unique Antiques
102 N. Commerce St.
(410) 758-8575
Furn, lamps & picture
frames.

Chester

Does It Matter Antiques
1626 Postal Rd.
(410) 643-2553
Furn, coll & refinishing.

Church Hill

Amarylis Vintage Co.
3401 Church Hill Road
(rt. 213 at Clabber Hill Rd.)
(410) 556-6407
Furn, lighting, rugs & stained
glass,1840-1940.

Price's Station
  General Store
1107 Price Station Rd.
(410) 556-6172
Spec: advertising, tools.

Crumpton

Dixon's Furniture Auction
2017 Dudley's crn. Rd.
(410) 928-3006
Call for auction dates & times.

Grasonville

Dutch Barn Antiques
3712 Main St.
(410) 827-8656
Prim-formal: furn, rugs,
paintings, mirrors.

Eastern Bay Trading
4917 Main St.
(410) 827-9286
Gen line. Spec: Architurals,
custom farm tables

Going Home
337 Saddler Road
(410) 827-8556
Knife rests, glass, furn
& collectibles.

Queenstown

Chesapeake Antique Center
Routes 301 & 56
(410) 827-6640
Multi-dealer co-op.

DHS Designs
6521 Friel Rd.
(410) 827-8167
Architecturals, artifacts,
furn, paintings & garden .

Stevensville

Stevensville Antiques
105 Market Court #16
(410) 643-8130
Multi-dealer co-op.

Schoolhouse Antiques
201 Love Point Rd.
(410) 604-1545
Furn, nautical, toys,
china & glass.

Lowery & Turner Antiques
307 State St.
(410) 643-6250
Furn, glass, linens & cast
iron .

Ye Olde Church House
426 Love Point Rd.
(410) 643-6227
Spec: 18th c. Crafts.

Sudlersville

Les' Antiques
105 Leager Rd.
(410) 438-4938
Am cut & art glass.

SAINT MARY'S COUNTY

California
Great Mills
Hollywood
Leonardtown
Loveville
Mechanicsville
Ridge

SAINT MARY'S COUNTY

California

St. Mary's Antiques
22958 Three Notch Rd.
(301) 863-0187
Furn. Books, late
1800s-1930s.

Great Mills

Cecil's Country Store
Indian Bridge Rd.
(301) 994-9622
Late 1800s-1930s furn.

Hollywood

Joyces Antiques
Rts 235 & 245
(301) 373-8974
Furn, primitive & painted.
Country coll.

Leonardtown

Antiques On The Square
22725 Washington St.
(301) 475-5826
Multi-dealer shop.

Maryland Antiques Center
26005 Point Lookout Rd.
(Rt. 5)
(301) 475-1960
Multi-dealer shop.

Loveville

Loveville's Antique
   & Collectible Shop
28345 Point Lookout Rd.
(Rt. 5)
(301) 475-2211
Unique antiques & collectibles.

Traditons of Loveville
28420 Point Lookout Rd.
(Rt. 5)
(301) 475-8280
18th & 19th c. furn. Repro.
Pottery & jewelry.

Mechanicsville

Apple Basket Antiques
847 Mt. Zion Church Rd.
(301) 884-8118
Furn, advertising, jewelry,
china & glass.

Village Antiques & More
28155 Old Village Rd.
(301) 884-7524
Last of the curiousity shops.

Ridge

Seasons
13450 Point Lookout Rd.
(Rt. 5)
(301) 872-4471
Art, furn & coll.

SOMERSET COUNTY

Crisfield

Princess Anne

Westover

SOMERSET COUNTY

Crisfield

Country Quest Antiques
Rt. 413 & Lawsonia
Barnes Rd.
(410) 968-2708
General line.

Princess Anne

Aileen Minor Antiques
30550 Washington St.
(410) 651-0075

King's Creek
   Antique Center
30723 Perry Rd.
(410) 651-2776

Westover

East Antiques
8815 Lisa Lane
(410) 651-1533

Olson's Antiques
31648 Curtis Chapel Rd.
(410) 957-1650

TALBOT COUNTY

Bellevue

Cordova

Easton

Oxford

Royal Oak

Sherwood

St. Michaels

Tilghman Island

Trappe

TALBOT COUNTY

Bellevue

Bellevue Store & Antiques
5592 Poplar Lane.
(410) 745-5282
Multi-dealer co-op.

Cordova

The Chicken Coop
31010 Skipton-Cordova Rd.
(410) 364-5897
Furn & collectibles.

Easton

American Pennyroyal
5 N. Harrison St.
410- 822-5030/800 400-8403
Gen line.

Antiques Centre of Easton
7813 Ocean Gateway
(410) 820-5209
Multi-dealer mall.

Camelot Antiques Ltd.
7871 Ocean Gateway
(410) 820-4396
Multi-dealer shop.

Chesapeake Antique
Center-The Gallery
29 S. Harrison St.
(410) 822-5000
Furn, art, vint garden
furn & architecturals.

Delmarva Jewelers
210 Marlboro Ave.
(4100 822-5398

Easton Maritime
Antiques
27 S. Harrison St.
(410) 763-8853
All things naitucal,
1400-present.

Foxwell's Antiques
7793 Ocean Gateway
(410) 820-9705
Multi-dealer co-op.

Home Beautiful/Picket
Fence Antiques
218 N. Washington St.
(410) 822-3010
Nauticals, furn, jewelry,
OR rugs & dec.

Janet Fanto Antiques
& Rare Books
13 N. Harrison St.
(410) 763-9030
Gen line. Spec: rare books.

Kathe & Company
20 S. Harrison St.
(410) 820-9153

Lanham-Merida
218 N. Washington St.
(410) 763-8500
18th & 19th Am furn, art,
silver, porc & crystal.

Lesnoff Antiques
8659 Commerce Dr.#1
(410) 820-8771
Imported Fr furn & dec.

Little Creek Antiques
7827 Ocean Gateway
(410) 770-5710
Glass, decoys & nauticals.

N. Nicklby Antiques
21 N. Harrison St.
(410) 820-0587
Early Am 18th c. furn.
Art & porc.

North Bend Galleries
28220 St. Michaels Rd.
(410) 820-6085
General line.

Oxford Antiques
& Art Gallery
21 N. Harrison St.
(410) 820-0587
18th & 19th c. furn. 19th
& 20th c. oils. Chns porc.

Pauline's Place
717 Goldsborough St.
(410) 763-7162

**Smith-Callaghan Antiques
& Decorative Accessories
29 S. Harrison St.
(410) 770-8280
Fax: (410) 819-3628
Interesting mix of furn-
iture, lamps & paintings.
Spec: textiles. Open Wed
thru Sat, 10-4. Sun. Mon
& Tues by chance or
appt.**

Stock Exchange Antique Mall
8370 Ocean Gateway
(410) 820-0014
Multi-dealer mall.

Sullivan's Antique
Warehouse
28272 St. Michaels Rd.
(410) 822-4723
Usd furn & dec. Spec:
Asian furn & dec.

Tharpe House Antiques
28 S. Washington St.
(410) 820-7525
Furn, silver, china, & linens.

The Flo-Mir
23 E. Dover St.
(410) 822-2857
China & paintings.

Wings of Easton
7 N. Harrison St.
(410) 822-2334
Eng & primitive furn & dec.

Oxford

Americana Antiques
111 S. Morris St.
(410) 226-5677

Anchorage House
5600 Oxford Rd.
(410) 822-8978

Oxford Salvage Company
301 Tilghman St.
(410) 226-5971

Royal Oak

Collection Box
Rt. 329
(410) 745-9064
General line.

Oak Creek Sales
25939 Royal Oak Rd.
(410) 745-3193
Furn, glass & china.

Sherwood

Sherwood Antiques
Off Rt. 33
(410) 886-2562
18th & 19th c. furn,
transferware & crystal.

St. Michaels

Back Street Antiques
102 Fremont St.
(410) 745-5399
Multi-dealer co-op.

Canton Row Antiques
216 Talbot St.
(410) 745-2440
Multi-dealer co-op.

Corner Antiques
116 N Talbot St.
(410) 745-5589
Multi-dealer shop.

Freedom House Antique
415 S. Talbot St.
(410) 745-6143
Gen line.

Kasias Treasures Inc.
406 S. Talbot St.
(410) 745-6643

Pennywhistle Antiques
408 S. Talbot St.
(410) 745-9771
Gen line. Spec: decoys.

Saltbox Antiques
310 S. Talbot
(410) 745-3569

Sentimental Journey
402 Talbot St.
(410) 745-9556
Furn, jewlry, trunks, glass.
Spec:Oyster plates.

Silver Chalice Antiques
400 S. Talbot St.
(410) 745-9501
Depression era glass.

Swan Cove Flowers
& Antiques
953 S.Talbot St.
(410) 745-3135
Furn, china, glass & silver.

Tilghman Island

Nothing New In Tilghman
Rt. 33
(410) 886-2173
Dep glass, china & Euro porc.

Trappe

Defender Collection
29375 Maple Ave.
(410) 822-0994
Multi-dealer shop.

Defender Collection
Maple Ave. & Main St.
(410) 476-9923
Multi-dealer shop.

Queen Mary Antiques
1601 Marina Dr.
(410) 476-4679
Multi-dealer co-op.

WASHINGTON COUNTY

Boonsboro

Brownsville

Funkstown

Hagerstown

Hancock

Sharpsburg

WASHINGTON COUNTY

Boonsboro

Fitz's Place Antiques
7 N. Main St.
(301) 432-2919
Gen line. Spec:
Dep glass.

The Olde Times Shop
27 S. Main St.
(301) 416-2494
General line.

Brownsville

D & J's Antiques
2450 Boteler Rd.
(301) 432-2952
General line.

Funkstown

Hudson House Galleries
100 E. Baltimore St.
(301) 733-1632
Furn, & coll. & repros.
Spec: glass.

RoosterVane Gardens
2 South High St.
(301) 739-2439
Gen line. Spec: archi-
tecturals & garden.

Hagerstown

A & J
20154 National Pike (Rt. 40)
(301) 745-4757
Gen line. Spec: Advertising
& country store.

Antique Crossroads
20150 National Pike
(301) 739-0858
Multi-dealer co-op.

Back Door Antiques
49 E. Franklin St. Rear
(301) 739-1406
Glass, silver, occ Japan,
jewelry & books.

Beaver Creek Antique Market
20202 National Pike
(301) 739-8075
Multi-dealer co-op.

Beaver Creek Country Store
9722 Country Store Lane
(301) 733-3847
Primitives & coll.

Brass Note
835 S. Potomac St.
(301) 739-4940
Spec: antq & vint metals.

Copper Kettle
158-1/2 S. Potomac St.
(301) 791-4555
Vint, old, usd. & antq. metals.
Spec: lighting, 1910-1930s.

Country Village
of Beaver Creek
20136 National Pike
(301) 790-0006
Spec: country & prim
painted furn. Folk art.

Halfway Antiques Collectibles
11000 Bower Ave.
(301) 582-4971
Multi-dealer mall & vintage
record shop.

Memory Lane
1350 Dual Hwy.
(301) 733-7491
Multi-dealer co-op.

Ravenswood Antique Center
216 W. Franklin St.
(301) 739-0145
General line.

Hancock

Hancock Antique Mall
266 N. Pennsylvania Ave.
(301) 678-5959
Multi-dealer mall.

Sharpsburg

Gale Antiques
At Sharpsburg
109 W. Main St.
(301) 432-4065
Country prims & folk art.

J & B Antiques
104 W. Church St.
(301) 432-8413

WICOMICO COUNTY

Mardela Springs
Salisbury

WICOMICO COUNTY

Mardela Springs

C U Antiques
2600 Oceangate Way (Rt. 50)
(410) 749-0373
General line.

Charlene Upham Antiques
25542 Ocean Gateway
(410) 742-1392
18th & 19th c. furn & dec.

Salisbury

All Manor of Things
700 N. Division St.
(410) 219-9022
Handpainted furn. Refin-
ished furn, vint clothng &
glass.

Happy Hollow Antiques
1415 S. Salisbury Blvd.
(410) 341-6155
Dep glass, advertising,
pottery & local coll.

Henrietta's Attic
205 Maryland Ave.
(410) 546-3700
Glass, pottery (Roseville),
toys & coll.

Holly Ridge Antiques
1411 S. Salisbury Blvd.
(410) 742-4392
18th & 19th c. furn & dec.

Market Street Antiques
150 W. Market St.
(410) 749-4111
Multi-dealer co-op.

Parker Place
234 W. Main St.
(410) 860-1263
Multi-dealer co-op.

Springhill Antiques
& Reproductions
2704 Merritt Mill Rd.
(410) 546-0675
Repro furn,late 1800s-
early 1900s.

WORCESTER COUNTY

Berlin
Girdletree
Ocean City
Snow Hill

WORCESTER COUNTY

Berlin

Antiques Marketplace
Old Ocean City Blvd.
(410) 629-1600

Findings
104 Pitts St.
(410) 641-2666
Prims,architecturals, stained glass. Furn from salvg.

Once Upon A Rose
1 N. Main St.
(410) 641-0979

Sassafrass Station
111 N. Main St.
(410) 641-0979

Something Different
2 S. Main St.
(410) 641-1152

Town Center Antiques
1 N. Main St.
(410) 629-1895
Multi-dealer co-op.

Girdletree

Rusty Nail
2801 Snow Hill Rd.
(410) 632-1902
Furn & primitive smalls.

Ocean City

Bookshelf Etc.
8006 Coastal Hwy.
(410) 524-2949

Brass Cannon
204 S. St. Louis Ave.
(410) 289-3440

Edgemoor Antiques
10009 Silver Point Ln.
(410) 213-2900
Gen line. Spec: oak furn.

G G's Antiques
9 Somerset St.
(410) 289-2345

Snow Hill

The Cannery
5305 Snow Hill Rd.
(410) 632-1722
Multi-dealer co-op.

Goodman's Antique Mall
110 W. Green St.
(410) 632-2686
Multi-dealer co-op.

Opera House, Act II
20 N. Washington St.
(410) 632-1860
Multi-dealer shop.

WASHINGTON, DC

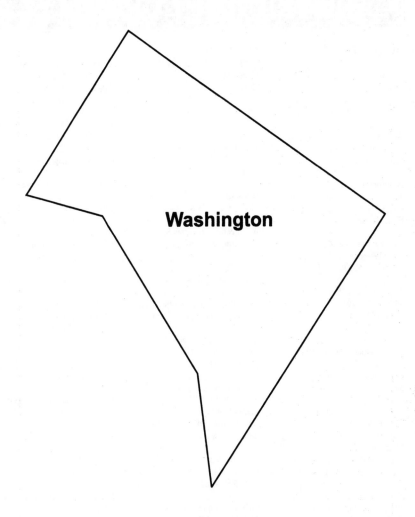

Washington

Washington D.C.

WASHINGTON, DISTRICT OF COLUMBIA

Washington D.C.

Adam A Weschler & Son
909 East St. NW
(202) 628-1281/800-331-1430
Call for auction dates & times.

Adams Davidson Galleries, Inc.
2727 29th St. NW
(202) 965-3800

Alcoforado Gallery
1673 Wisconsin Ave. NW
(202) 338-6417
Furn. & rugs.

Andrew Leddy & Co.
1639 Wisconsin Ave.
(202) 638-5394

Antique Textile Resource
1730 K St. NW
(202) 293-1731

Antiques Anonymous
2627 Connecticut Ave NW
(202) 332-5555
Costume & fine Jewlry;Vic-
50s.

Antiques of Georgetown
3210 O St. NW
Georgetown
(202) 965-1165
Spec: lighting, fireplace
access, Eng. & Am furn.

Antiques-On-The-Hill
701 N. Carolina Ave. SE
(202) 543-1819
Gen line, Pre-Columbian-
Deco. Spec: paintings.

Arise Gallery of Asian Arts
6925 Willow St. NW
(202) 291-0770
Asian Furn, textiles & dec.

Asian Art Center
2709 Woodley Place NW
(202) 234-3333

Blair House Antiques
1663 Wisconsin Ave. NW
Georgetown
(202) 338-5349
China, glass, dolls,
small furn & jewlry.

Bombe Chest
2629 Connecticut Ave. NW
(202)387-7293
Thrift shop.

Brass Knob
2311 18th St. NW
(202)332-3370
Architectural antiques.Spec:
in lighting & hardware.

Brass Knob's Warehouse
2329 Champlain St. NW
(202) 265-0587
Lg. salvage items: doors, tubs,
radiators, fencing & columns.

Calvert Gallery At Shorham
2500 Calvert St. NW
(202) 387-5177

Chenonceau Antiques
2314 18th St. NW
(202) 667-1651
1800s-early 1900s art, pottery,
furn, rugs & linens.

Cherishables
1608 20th St. NW
(202) 785-4087

Cherub Antiques Gallery
2918 M St. NW
(202) 337-2224
Spec: signed Art Nouveau, Art
Deco and Arts & Crafts pieces.

Chevy Chase Antique Center
5215 Wisconsin Ave. NW
(202) 364-4600
Multi-dealer, 70+ dlrs.

China Gallery
2200 Wisconsin Ave. NW
(202) 342-1899
Spec: Asian arts:porc, glass,
textiles, furn & art.

Christ Child Opportunity Shop
1427 Wisconsin Ave. NW
(202) 333-6635
Thrift & consignment.

Christie's Fine Art Auctioneer
1228 31st St. NW
(202) 333-7459
Call for auction dates & times.

Consignment Galleries
3226 Wisconsin Ave. NW
(202) 364-8995
Pre-owned art, china & furn.

Dalton Brody Limited
3412 Idaho Ave. NW
(202) 244-7197
China, crystal & silver.

David Bell Antiques
1655 Wisconsin Ave. NW
(202) 965-2355
Gen line. Spec:Am. & Cont.
garden architecturals.

Dunnan's Antiques Inc.
3209 O St. NW
(202) 965-1614
Furn & smalls.

Frank Milwee Antiques
2912 M St. NW
(202) 333-4811
Sterling silver, corkscrews,
paintings, crystal & china.

Galerie L'Enfant
2601 Connecticut Ave. NW
(202) 265-4096
18th, 19th & early 20th c.
Cont. & Am. furn, porc. & art.

Geoffrey Diner Gallery
1730 21st St. NW
Dupont Circle Area
(202) 483-5005
Late 19th c. & early 20th c.
Eng & Am. Arts & Crafts furn
& dec art.

Glorious Revivals
1749 Connecticut Ave.NW
(202) 232-5416
Glass, china, vintage costume
jewlry and clothing 20s-60s.

Golden Days Antiques
1520 U St. NW
(202) 387-7057

Good Wood, Inc.
1428 U St. NW
(202) 986-3640
Antique & vintage furn.

Hastening Antiques Ltd.
1651 Wisconsin Ave. NW
Georgetown
(202) 333-7662
French furn, pottery & dec.

Janis Aldridge Inc.
2900 M St. NW
(202) 338-7710
17th-20th c. furn, engravings
and dec.

Julie Walters Antiques
1657 Wisconsin Ave. NW
(202) 625-6727
Cont. furn, lighting & garden
antiques.

Justine Mehlman Antiques
2824 Pennsylvania Ave. NW
Georgetown
(202) 337-0613
Jewelry, decorative art & art
prints.

Kelsey's Kupboard
30003 P St. NW
Georgetown
(202) 298-8237
Gen. line antiq, repro & vintage furn. & smalls.

Litwin Furniture
637 Indiana Ave. NW
(202) 628-7030
Antiq. and vintage furn.

Liz Jean's Thrift Shop
1543 New Jersey Ave. NW
(202) 483-1099
Thrift shop

Logans Antiques
3118 Mt. Pleasant St. NW
(202) 483-2428
Gen line

Marston Luce
1314 21st St. NW
(202) 775-9460
18th & 19th c. French furn,
dec & garden.

Michael Getz Antiques
2918 M St. NW
Georgetown
(202) 338-3811
Spec:18th-20th c. Eng., Am. &
Cont. silver. Fireplace access.

Millennium Decorative Arts
1528 U Street NW
(202) 483-1218
Spec: gen line of mid-20th c.
modern.

Miller & Arney Antiques Inc.
1737 Wisconsin Ave. NW
(202) 338-2369
18th & 19th c. Eng, Am. &
Euro. furn & dec.

Mom & Pop Antiques
3534 Georgia Ave. NW
(202) 722-0719
20th c. furn, smalls & unusuals.

Mood Indigo
1214 U St. NW
(202) 265-6366
Vintage clothing,1920's-80s.

New, Used & Unabused
1320 9th St. NW
(202) 387-3347

New, Used & Unabused
2612 28th St. NW
(202) 526-0262

Old Print Gallery Inc.
1220 31st St. NW
(202) 965-1818
Prints: maps, hist prints,
botanicals, architecturals.

Rooms With A View Antiques
1661 Wisconsin Ave. NW
(202) 625-0610
Early Am. painted furn & folk
art. 19th c. textiles. Architecturals.

Ruff & Ready Furnishings
1908 14th St. NW
(202) 667-7833
Antiqs, collectibles to oddities,
early 1900s-1950s.

Second Story Books &
Antiques
2000 P St. NW
(202) 659-8884
Usd & antiq: books, ephemera,
maps, prints and posters.

Sotheby's Fine Art Auctioneers
2201 Wisconsin Ave. NW # 390
(202) 457-1910

Susan Calloway Prints
1657 Wisconsin Ave. NW
(202) 965-4601
17th & 18th c. prints; garden,
views & architectural subjs.

Susquehanna Antique Company
3216 O Street NW
Georgetown
(202) 333-1511
Spec: 18th & Early 19th c. Am.,
Eng. & cont. furn & fine art.

Tiny Jewel Box Inc
1147 Connecticut Ave. NW
Downtown area
(202) 393-2747
Estate jewelry.

Two Lions Antiques
621 Pennsylvania Ave. SE
(202) 546-5466
Late 19th c. furn, mirrors,
lamps, china, crystal & silver.

VIP Antiques
1665 Wisconsin Ave. NW
Georgetown
(202) 965-0700
1900-1950 smalls. Spec:
jewlry costume & fine.

Washington Doll's House
  & Toy Museum
5236 44th St. NW
Chevy Chase, DC
(202) 244-0024
Museum & Consign shop of
dolls, houses, toys & games.

Attention Dealers & Collectors!

Contact us regarding: new shops, shop location changes, new hotspots, favorite shops or general comments and suggestions.

Call: (610) 722-0919
Fax: (610) 722-0440
E-mail: Seabrooksantique@Juno.com

Or send: Seabrook's Antique Shop Guide
1512 West Chester Pike, #174
West Chester, PA 19382

Please provide the following information:

Name or Shop Name: _____

Address: _____

City: _____

State: _____

Zip: _____

Phone: _____

E-mail: _____

Shop Description or Specialty: _____

Comments: _____

_____

_____

_____

_____